A HISTORY
OF THE MISHNAIC LAW
OF HOLY THINGS

PART FIVE

STUDIES IN JUDAISM IN LATE ANTIQUITY

EDITED BY

JACOB NEUSNER

VOLUME THIRTY

A HISTORY
OF THE MISHNAIC LAW
OF HOLY THINGS

PART FIVE

A HISTORY OF THE MISHNAIC LAW OF HOLY THINGS

BY

JACOB NEUSNER
University Professor
Professor of Religious Studies
and
The Ungerleider Distinguished Scholar of Judaic Studies
Brown University

PART FIVE

KERITOT, MEILAH, TAMID, MIDDOT, QINNIM
TRANSLATION AND EXPLANATION

Wipf and Stock Publishers
199 W 8th Ave, Suite 3
Eugene, OR 97401

A History of the Mishnaic Law of Holy Things, Part 5
Keritot, Meilah, Tamid, Middot, Qinnim: Translation and Explanation
By Neusner, Jacob

ISBN 13: 978-1-55635-353-6
ISBN 10: 1-55635-353-7
Publication date 3/20/2007
Previously published by E. J. Brill, 1980

For

Jack Nathan Lightstone

TABLE OF CONTENTS

Preface IX
Abbreviations and Bibliography XI
Transliterations XVII

KERITOT

I. Introduction to Keritot 3
II. Keritot Chapter One 7
III. Keritot Chapter Two 19
VI. Keritot Chapter Three 28
V. Keritot Chapter Four 39
VI. Keritot Chapter Five 49
VII. Keritot Chapter Six 62

MEILAH

VIII. Introduction to Meilah 79
IX. Meilah Chapter One 85
X. Meilah Chapter Two 99
XI. Meilah Chapter Three 104
XII. Meilah Chapter Four 119
XIII. Meilah Chapter Five 125
XVI. Meilah Chapter Six 134

TAMID

XV. Introduction to Tamid. Tamid Chapters One through Seven 147

MIDDOT

XVI. Introduction to Middot. Middot Chapters One through Five 169

QINNIM

XVII. Introduction to Qinnim. Qinnim Chapters One through Three 191
. . . . 217

ILLUSTRATIONS

Fig. 1. Ground plan of the Sanctuary (Temple and Courts), according to Maimonides 170
Fig. 2. The Temple of Herod, inside the Temple Mount . . 171

Source: *The Code of Maimonides. Book Eight. The Book of the Temple Service.* Translated from the Hebrew by Mendell Lewittes. Yale University Press, New Haven.

PREFACE

The five tractates of the present volume are joined only for convenience's sake. But Keritot and Meilah treat Lev. 5:17-19 and 5:14-16, respectively. Tamid, Middot, and Qinnim bear no special relationship to one another, as do, e.g., Arakhin and Temurah, Zebahim and Menahot or Keritot and Meilah. All make their sizable contributions to the Mishnaic law of Holy Things, of course, and the translation and explanation of each are necessary. Our purpose is fulfilled, however, solely in the historical studies to come in Part VI. The exegesis of the law is accomplished only so far as it is required for the ultimate intention of the work as a whole. It is kept brief and pays attention solely to those issues which clearly inhere in the law's earliest historical stratum of meaning.

My purpose is to uncover the history of the formation of earlier Rabbinic Judaism, down to the redaction of Mishnah in ca A.D. 200. The sole reliable route is through the analysis of the earliest sources, beginning with Mishnah, from the perspectives required, in particular, for a history of the law and of its religio-legal conceptions; What do the sources mean in their original circumstance? What ideas are taken for granted in them? What are the literary and intellectual traits exhibited by them? When these questions have been thoroughly dealt with, we proceed to the next stage in the work. Our sole purpose in this part, therefore, is the exegesis of the sources. When the analytical work is accomplished, we turn to the synthetic procedures of historical restoration and the reconstruction of the history and structures of the kind of Judaism revealed in Mishnah and associated, to begin with, with the names of its authorities. The exegesis is accomplished in two stages, first, through form-analytical translation, second, through an explanation of what has been translated. In all I aim at a severe economy of intellect, dealing, as is clear, only with questions important for the larger venture.

My colleague, Professor Richard S. Sarason, kindly took time out of his own scholarly work to criticize mine. His work on Tamid is particularly important and detailed. I am especially grateful.

This work carries forward the sequence of dedications to my students, each advancing the work of teaching and scholarly research begun in my seminar at Brown University.

Providence, Rhode Island
4 December 1977
24 Kislev 5738

J.N.

ABBREVIATIONS AND BIBLIOGRAPHY

AE	=	*Tosafot* R. ʿAqiba Egger. From Mishnah, ed. Romm.
Ah.	=	ʾAhilot
Albeck	=	Ḥanokh Albeck, *Shishah sidré mishnah. Seder Qodoshim.* (Tel Aviv, 1959).
Allony	=	See GF
Altschuler	=	Ezra Altschuler, *Taqqanat ʿEzraʾ ... ʿal masekhet Meʿilah* (Piotrkov, 1931).
AN	=	Abraham Mesokhtschub. *Hagahot abné nezer.* In QMH.
Ar.	=	ʿArakhin
A.Z.	=	ʿAbodah Zarah
B.	=	Babylonian Talmud
B.B.	=	Babaʾ Batraʾ
B.M.	=	Babaʾ Meṣiʿa
B.Q.	=	Babaʾ Qammaʾ
Ber.	=	Berakhot
Berger	=	Isaiah Berger, ed., *Analytical Index to The Jewish Quarterly Review.* 1889-1908 (N.Y., 1966).
Berlin, 1968	=	Charles Berlin, *Harvard University Library. Catalogue of Hebrew Books* (Cambridge, 1968) I-VI.
Berlin, 1972	=	*Supplement* (Cambridge, 1972) I-III.
Berlin, 1971	=	*Widener Library Shelflist, 39. Judaica* (Cambridge, 1971).
Bert.	=	Obadiah of Bertinoro. From Mishnah, ed. Romm.
Bes.	=	Beṣah
Bik.	=	Bikkurim
Blackman	=	Philip Blackman, *Mishnayoth.* Volume V. *Order Qodashim. Pointed Hebrew Text, Introductions, Translation, Notes, Appendix, Supplement Indexes* (London, 1954).
Büchler	=	Adolph Abraham Büchler, *Hakkohanim veʿabodatam* (Jerusalem, 1966). Trans. into Hebrew by N. Ginton. English title page: *The Priests and their Cult in the Last Decade of the Temple in Jerusalem.*
C	=	H. Loewe, *The Mishnah of the Palestinian Talmud* (*Hammishnah ʿal pi ketav-yad Cambridge*) (Jerusalem, 1967).
Cashdan, *Menahoth*	=	Eli Cashdan, *Menahoth. Translated into English with Notes, Glossary and Indices* (London, 1948).
Cashdan, *Hullin*	=	Eli Cashdan, *Hullin. Translated into English. With Notes, Glossary, and Indices* (London, 1948).
Cohn	=	John Cohn, *Ordnung Kadaschim, übersetzt und erklärt* (Third ed., Basel, 1968).
Danby	=	Herbert Danby, *The Mishnah* (London, 1933).
Danby, *Offerings*	=	Herbert Danby, trans., *The Code of Maimonides. Book Nine. The Book of Offerings.* (New Haven, 1950).
Dem.	=	Demaʾi
Deut.	=	Deuteronomy
Ed.	=	ʿEduyyot
EG	=	*Hiddushé Eliyyahu MiGreiditz.* From Mishnah, ed. Romm (Vilna, 1887).

EK = Yeshoshuᶜa Yosef Hakkohen, *ᶜEzrat kohanim ... ᶜal mishnayyot masekhet Middot* (Warsaw, 1873) I-III.

Epstein, *Nusaḥ* = Y. N. H. Epstein, *Mabo lenusaḥ hammishnah* (Tel Aviv, 1954).

Epstein, *Tan.* = Y. N. H. Epstein, *Meboᵓot lesifrut hattanaᵓim. Mishnah, tosefta, ummidrashê halakhah.* Ed. E. Ṣ. Melammed (Tel Aviv, 1957).

Erub. = ᶜErubin

Freedman = H. Freedman, *Zebahim. Translated into English with Notes, Glossary, and Indices* (London, 1948).

GF = *Geniza Fragments of Rabbinic Literature.* Ed. Nehemya Alloni (Jerusalem, 1973).

GRA = Elijah ben Solomon Zalman ("Elijah Gaon" or "Vilna Gaon"), 1720-1797. For Tosefta: Babli, ed. Romm (Vilna, 1887), Vol. XVII.

Gelbstein = Hillel Moshe Mishil Gelbstein, *Sefer mishkenot leᵓabir Yaᶜaqob. Ḥiddushim ubbeᵓurim bemasekhet Tamid* (Repr. Jerusalem, 1972).

Ginzberg, *Tamid* = Louis Ginzberg, "The Mishnah Tamid," *Journal of Jewish Lore and Philosophy*, 1, 1919, pp. 33-44, 197-209, 265-295.

Git. = Giṭṭin

Gray = George Buchanan Gray, *Sacrifice in the Old Testament. Its Theory and Practice* (1925. Repr.: N.Y., 1971).

HA = Emanuel Hai Riqi. *Hon ᵓashir.* In QMH.

Hag. = Ḥagigah

Hakkohen = Alexandry Hakkohen, *Sefer haᵓagudah leseder qodoshim veseder ṭohorot* (Jerusalem, 1975).

Hakkohen-Zaks = Israᵓel Meᵓir Hakkohen, *Sefer liqutê halakhot.* Ed. Menaḥem Mendel Yosef Zaks (Jerusalem, 1971). I. *Zebaḥim, Menaḥot, Tamid, Temurah, Meᶜilah.* II. *Bekhorot, Keritot, ᶜArakhin, Nazir, Soṭah, Niddah.*

Hal. = Ḥallah

Ḥayyot = Yiṣḥaq Ḥayyot, *Zeraᶜ yiṣḥaq.* Ed. H. Y. L. Deutsch (N.Y., 1960).

HD = *Hasdê David.* David Pardo, *Hasdê David.* IV. *Tosefet Qedushah* (Repr., Jerusalem, 1970).

Hildesheimer = ᶜAzriᵓel Hildesheimer, *Middot bet hammiqdash shel hordos bemasekhet Middot ubekitbê Yosef b. Matityahu* (Jerusalem, 1974). [Compare "The Herodian Temple according to the Treatise Middoth and Flavius Josephus," *Palestine Exploration Fund Quarterly Statement*, 1886, pp. 92-113, and Israel Hildesheimer, *Gesammelte Aufsätze* (Frankfurt a/M, 1923)].

Holtzmann, *Middot* = Oscar Holtzmann, *Middot (Von den Massen des Tempels). Text, Übersetzung, and Erklärung. Nebst einem textkritischen Anhang* (Giessen, 1913).

Holtzmann, *Tamid* = Oscar Holtzmann, *Tamid (Vom täglichen Gemeindeopfer). Text, Übersetzung, und Erklärung. Nebst einem textkritischen Anhang* (Giessen, 1928).

Holtzmann, *Qinnim* = Oscar Holtzmann, *Qinnim (Von den Vogelopfern). Text, Übersetzung, und Erklärung. Nebst einem textkritischen Anhang* (Giessen, 1931).

Hor. = Horayot

Hubert & Mauss	= Henri Hubert and Marcel Mauss, *Sacrifice: Its Nature and Function.* (Chicago, 1964). Translated from the French, "Essai sur la nature et la fonction du sacrifice," *L'Année sociologique*, 1898, by W. D. Halls.
Hul.	= Ḥullin
HY	= *Tosefta Ḥazon Yeḥezqel* by Yeḥezqel Abramsky (Jerusalem, 1954).
ID	= Nathan Lebam, *Imré da^cat.* In QMH.
Jastrow	= Marcus Jastrow, *A Dictionary of the Targumim, the Talmud Babli, and Yerushalmi, and the Midrashic Literature* (1904, Repr., N.Y., 1950) I-II.
Jung, *Arakin*	= Leo Jung, *ᶜArakin. Translated into English. With Notes, Glossary, and Indices* (London, 1948).
K	= Georg Beer, *Faksimile-Ausgabe des Mishnacodex Kaufmann A 50* (Reprint: Jerusalem, 1968).
Katsh	= Abraham I. Katsh, *Ginzé Mishna. One Hundred and Fifty-Nine Fragments from the Cairo Geniza in the Saltykov-Shchedrin Library in Leningrad Appearing for the First Time with an Introduction, Notes and Variants* (Jerusalem, 1970).
Kel.	= Kelim
Ker.	= Keritot
Kil.	= Kilaᵓyim
Klien	= *The Code of Maimonides. Book Six. The Book of Asseverations.* Translated from the Hebrew by B. D. Klien (New Haven and London, 1962).
KM	= *Kesef Mishneh.* Joseph Karo. Commentary to Maimonides, *Mishneh Torah.* Published in Venice, 1574-5. Text used: Standard version of Maimonides, *Mishneh Torah.*
Krupp	= Michael Krupp. *ᶜArakin (Schätzungen). Text, Übersetzung, und Erklärung. Nebst einem textkritischen Anhang* (Berlin & N.Y., 1971).
Lehrman	= S. M. Lehrman, *Ḳinnim. Translated into English. With notes, Glossary, and Indices* (London, 1948).
Levin and Boyden	= S. I. Levin and Edward A. Boyden, *The Kosher Code of the Orthodox Jew* (Minneapolis, 1940. Repr. N.Y., 1975).
Levine, 1971	= Baruch A. Levine, "Prolegomenon." in *Sacrifice in the Old Testament. In Theory and Practice.* By George Buchanan Gray (Repr. N.Y., 1971), pp. vii-xliv.
Levy, *Wörterbuch*	= Jacob Levy, *Wörterbuch über die Talmudim und Midrashim* (1924. Repr., Darmstadt, 1963) I-IV.
Lewittes	= Mendell Lewittes, trans. *The Code of Maimonides. Book Eight. The Book of the Temple Service* (New Haven, 1957).
M	= *Babylonian Talmud Codex Munich* (95) (Repr., Jerusalem, 1971).
M.	= Mishnah
Ma.	= Maᶜaserot
Maimonides, *Comm.*	= Moses b. Maimon, *Mishnah. Seder Qodoshim.* Trans. by Yosef Kappaḥ (Jerusalem, 1967).
Maimonides, *Valuations*	= See Klien.
Mak.	= Makkot
Makh.	= Makhshirin

Me.	= Me^cilah
Meg.	= Megillah
Meiri	= Menaḥem Shelomoh lebet Meir, *Bet habbeḥirah ᶜal masekhet Ḥallah, Sheqalim, Tamid, veMiddot* (Jerusalem, 1977). Ed. by Abraham Sofer.
Meiri, *Hul.*	= Menaḥem Shelomoh lebet Meir, *Bet habbeḥirah ᶜal masekhet Ḥullin* (Jerusalem, 1974). Ed. by Abraham Liss.
Melammed, *Midrash*	= E. Ṣ. Melammed, *Hayyaḥas sheben midrashé halakhah lammishnah velattosefta* (Jerusalem, 1967).
Melammed, *Talmud*	= E. Ṣ. Melammed, *Pirqé mabo lesifrut hattalmud* (Jerusalem, 1973).
Men.	= Menaḥot
Miller and Simon	= L. Miller and Maurice Simon, *Bekoroth. Translated into English. With Notes, Glossary, and Indices* (London, 1948).
Miller, *Temurah*	= L. Miller, *Temurah. Translated into English. With Notes, Glossary, and Indices* (London, 1948).
Miq.	= Miqvaᵓot
ML	= *Mishnah Lammelekh.* Commentary to Maimonides, *Mishneh Torah.* Judah Rosannes 1657-1727. For source see KM.
M.Q.	= Moᶜed Qaṭan
MS	= *Meleᵓkhet Shelomo.* Shelomo bar Joshua Adeni, 1567-1625. From Mishnah, ed. Romm.
N	= *Mishnah ᶜim perush HaRambam. Defus rishoᵓn Napoli* 5252 [1492] (Jerusalem, 1970).
Naz.	= Nazir
Netibot haqqodesh	= *Netibot haqqodesh ... Zebaḥim.* By A. I. M. Salman (Jerusalem, 1956).
Ned.	= Nedarim
Neg.	= Negaᶜim
Nezer	= *Nezer haqqodesh ᶜal masekhet Zebaḥim.* By Moses Rosen (N.Y., 1953).
Nid.	= Niddah
Num.	= Numbers
Noah	= Aminoaḥ Noaḥ, *The Redaction of the Tractate Qiddushin in the Babylonian Talmud.* In Hebrew (Tel Aviv, 1977).
NS	= Ṣevi Gutmacher, *Naḥalat ṣevi.* In QMH.
Oh.	= ᵓOhalot
Or.	= ᶜOrlah
Oṣar shiṭṭot	= *Oṣar shiṭṭot. ᶜArakhin* (Jerusalem, 1972). *Bekhorot* (Jerusalem, 1973). *Keritot* (Jerusalem, 1973). *Temurah* (Jerusalem, 1973).
P	= *Shishah sidré mishnah. Ketab yad Parma DeRossi* 138 (Reprint: Jerusalem, 1970).
Pa	= *Mishnah ketab yad Paris, Paris* 328-329 (Reprint: Jerusalem, 1973).
Par.	= Parah
PB	= *Mishnah Codex Parma "B" DeRossi 497. Seder Tehoroth.* Introduction by M. Bar Asher (Reprint: Jerusalem, 1971).
Pes.	= Pesaḥim
Porusch, *Kerithoth*	= I. Porusch, *Kerithoth. Translated into English. With Notes, Glossary, and Indices* (London, 1948).
Porusch, *Meilah*	= I. Porusch, *Meᶜilah. Translated into English. With Notes, Glossary, and Indices* (London, 1948).

Prov.	= Proverbs
Purities	= Jacob Neusner, *A History of the Mishnaic Law of Purities* (Leiden, 1974-1977) I-XXII.
QA	= *Qorban Aharon.* Aaron Ibn Ḥayyim (d. 1632), *Qorban Aharon, Perush LaSefer Sifra* (Dessau, 1749).
Qahaty	= Pinhas Qahaty, *Seder Qodoshim* (Jerusalem, 1976) I-II.
QH	= Moshe Zakhuta, *Qol haramaz.* In QMH.
QMH	= *Qebuṣat meforshê hammishnah* (Jerusalem, 1962).
QS	= Ḥayyim Sofer, *Qol Sofer.* In QMH.
Rabad	= Supercommentary to Maimonides, *Code.*
Rabad, Sifra	= R. Abraham ben David, Commentary to Sifra. From Sifra, ed. Weiss.
Rabinowitz	= *The Code of Maimonides. Book Five. The Book of Holiness.* Translated from the Hebrew by Louis I. Rabinowitz and Philip Grossman (New Haven and London, 1965).
Ralbag	= Yiṣḥaq Ralbag, *Ma^{c}ayanné hattalmud ... ^{c}al masekhet Keritot* (Jerusalem, 1971).
Rappaport	= Ṣevi Hirsch Hakohen Rappaport, *Torat Kohanim*, with the commentaries *^{c}Ezrat Kohanim* and *Tosefet Ha^{c}Ezrah* (Jerusalem, 1972).
Ray	= Benjamin Ray, "Sacred Space and Royal Shrines in Buganda," *History of Religions* 16, 4, 1977, pp. 363, 373.
R.H.	= Rosh Hashshanah
Rosen, *Bekhorot*	= Moshe Rosen, *Sefer nezer haqqodesh ^{c}al masekhet Bekhorot* (Newark, 1945).
Rosen, *Temurah*	= Moshe Rosen, *Sefer nezer haqqodesh ^{c}al masekhet Temurah* (Newark, 1936).
San.	= Sanhedrin
Sens	= Ya^{c}aqob David Ilan, *Tosafot Shenṣ* (Bené Beraq, 1973).
Shab.	= Shabbat
Shabu.	= Shabu^{c}ot
Sheb.	= Shebi^{c}it
Sheq.	= Sheqalim
SifraFink.	= *Sifra or Torat Kohanim. According to Codex Assemani LXVI.* With a Hebrew Introduction by Louis Finkelstein (N.Y., 1956).
SifraHillel	= *Sifra,* With the Commentary of *Hillel b. R. Eliaqim.* Ed. by Shachne Koleditzky (Jerusalem, 1961).
Sifra ed. Weiss	= *Sifra,* ed. Isaac Hirsch Weiss (Repr. N.Y., 1947).
SifHillel	= *Sifre ... ^{c}im Perush ... Rabbenu Hillel bar Eliaqim.* Ed. Shachne Koleditzky (Jerusalem, 1958).
SifHorovitz	= *Siphre d'Be Rab. Fasciculus primus: Siphre ad Numeros adjecto Siphre Zutta.* Ed. H. S. Horovitz (Leipzig, 1917).
SifIshShalom	= *Sifré debe Rab. ^{c}Im Tosafot Meir ^{c}Ayin.* Ed. Meir IshShalom (Friedman). (Vienna, 1864).
SifLieberman	= *Siphre Zutta* (*The Midrash of Lydda*). II. *The Talmud of Caesarea* (N.Y., 1968).
SifNeṣiv	= *Sifré ... ^{c}Emeq HaNeṣiv.* Naftali Ṣevi Yehudah Berlin (Jerusalem, 1960).
SifPardo	= *Sefer Sifré debe Rab.* David Pardo (Salonika, 1799. Reprint Jerusalem, 1970).
SifVolk	= *Sifré ... ^{c}im Hagahot ... HaGRA ve^{c}im perush Keter Kehunah.* Ṣevi Hirsch Hakkohen Volk. Ed. Ya^{c}aqob Hakkohen Volk (Jerusalem, 1954).

SifYasq = *Sifré Zuṭṭa leSeder Bamidbar ... ʾAmbuhaʾ deSifré.* Yaʿaqov Zeʾev Yaskobitz (Lodz, 1929. Reprint Bené Beraq, 1967) I-II.

Simon, *Tamid* = Maurice Simon, *Tamid. Translated into English. With Notes, Glossary, and Indices* (London, 1948).

Simon, *Middoth* = Maurice Simon, *Middoth. Translated into English. With Notes, Glossary, and Indices* (London, 1948).

SM = *Shiṭṭah mequbeṣet ʿal masekhet ʿArakhin* (Bené Beraq 1976). Ed. Yaʿaqob David Elan. *Bekhorot* (Bené Beraq, 1975). *Temurah* (Bené Beraq, 1975).

Sot. = Soṭah

Suk. = Sukkah

T. = Tosefta

T = *Sidré Mishnah. Neziqin, Qodoshim, Ṭohorot. Ketab yad Yerushalayim, 1336. Ketab Yad beniqud lefi massoret Teman.* (Reprint Jerusalem, 1970). Introduction by S. Morag.

Ta. = Taʿanit

Tem. = Temurah

Ter. = Terumot

Toh. = Ṭohorot

TR = Saul Lieberman, *Tosefet Rishonim.* II. *Seder Nashim, Neziqin, Qodoshim* (Jerusalem, 1938).

T.Y. = Ṭebul Yom

TYB = Tifeʾret Yisraʾel Boʿaz. See TYY.

TYT = *Tosafot Yom Ṭob.* Yom Tob Lipmann Heller, 1579-1654. From reprint of Mishnah, ed. Romm.

TYY = *Tifeʾret Yisraʾel, Yakhin.* Israel ben Gedaliah Lipschütz, 1782-1860. (With supercommentary of Baruch Isaac Lipschütz = TYB.) From reprint of Mishnah, ed. Romm.

Uqs. = ʿUqṣin

V = *Talmud Babli. Nidpas ʿal yedé Daniel Bomberg bishenat 5282* [= 1522]. *Venezia.* (Venice, 1522. Reprint Jerusalem, 1971). *Nazir, Sotah, Qodoshim.*

V* = *Talmud Babli* ... [as above]. *Zebaḥim.*

Vat118 = *Manuscripts of the Babylonian Talmud from the Collection of the Vatican Library* (Jerusalem, 1974). IV. *Vat. Ebr. 118. Zevachim, Menahot.*

Vat119 = As above. V. *Zevachim, Temura, Arechim, Bechorot, Meilah, Keritut.*

Y. = Yerushalmi. Palestinian Talmud.

Y.T. = Yom Ṭob

Yad. = Yadayim

Yeivin = Israel Yeivin, *A Collection of Mishnaic Geniza Fragments with Babylonian Vocalization. With Description of the Manuscripts and Indices* (Jerusalem, 1974).

Yeb. = Yebamot

Z = M. S. Zuckermandel, *Tosephta. Based on Erfurt and Vienna Codices* (Repr., Jerusalem, 1963).

Zab. = Zabim

Zeb. = Zebaḥim

ZY = *Zeraʿ yiṣḥaq.* By Yiṣḥaq Ḥayyot (Brooklyn, 1960).

TRANSLITERATIONS

א	=	ʾ
ב	=	B
ג	=	G
ד	=	D
ה	=	H
ו	=	W
ז	=	Z
ח	=	Ḥ
ט	=	Ṭ
י	=	Y
ך כ	=	K
ל	=	L
ם מ	=	M
ן נ	=	N
ס	=	S
ע	=	ʿ
ף פ	=	P
ץ צ	=	Ṣ
ק	=	Q
ר	=	R
שׁ	=	Š
שׂ	=	Ś
ת	=	T

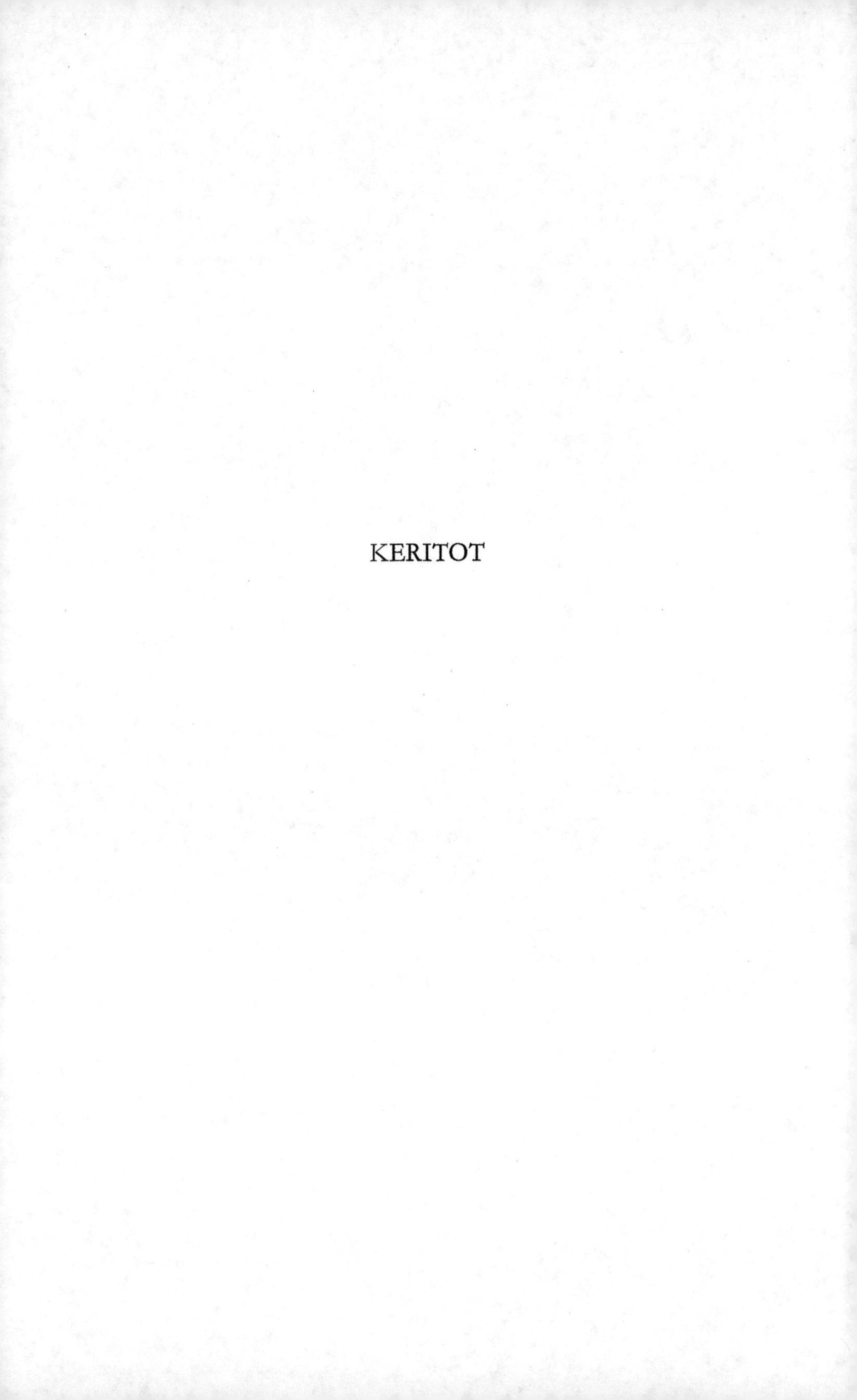

KERITOT

CHAPTER ONE

INTRODUCTION TO KERITOT

Our tractate is devoted to the definition of occasions on which one is obligated to bring a sin-offering and a suspensive guilt-offering. It begins with attention to those sins, for the commission of which one is punishable by either extirpation, in the case of deliberate commission, or the bringing of a sin-offering, in the case of an inadvertent act, or the bringing of a suspensive guilt-offering, in the case of doubt as to whether or not a sin has been committed at all. It is on account of its opening pericope that the tractate bears the name Keritot—sins punishable by extirpation—even though, belonging as it does in our order, its principal interest is not in extirpation but various kinds of animal-offerings which expiate sin. In point of fact, a title such as "Sin-Offerings and [Suspensive] Guilt-Offerings" would have proved more accurate, since the principal units of the tractate are devoted to these matters. At the foundation is Lev. 5:17-19: *If any one sins, doing any of the things which the Lord has commanded not to be done, though he does not know it, yet he is guilty and shall bear his iniquity. He shall bring to the priest a ram without blemish out of the flock, valued by you at the price for a guilt offering, and the priest shall make atonement for him for the error which he committed unwittingly, and he shall be forgiven. It is a guilt offering; he is guilty before the Lord.* It is in three principal units:

I. *The sin-offering.* 1:1-2:2

- 1:1-2 Thirty-six transgressions subject to extirpation are in the Torah. For those sins are people liable: for deliberately doing them, to the punishment of extirpation; for accidentally doing them, to the bringing of a sin-offering; and for not being certain of whether or not one has done them, to a suspensive guilt-offering.
- 1:3-5 There are women who bring an offering (= sin-offering) after childbirth and it is eaten, who bring an offering and it is not eaten, and there are women who do not bring an offering at all.
- 1:6 She who produces an abortion on the night of the eighty-first day—liability to a sin-offering.
- 1:7 The woman who is subject to doubt concerning the appearance of five fluxes brings a single offering.

2:1-2 There are four whose atonement is not complete until they bring an offering, and four bring an offering for a transgression done deliberately as for one done inadvertently.

2:3-6 [1] Five bring a single offering for many transgressions. And five bring a sliding-scale-offering.

II. *A single sin-offering and multiple sins.* 2:3-3:10

3:1 If they said to him, You have eaten forbidden fat, he brings a sin-offering. If one witness says, "He ate," and one says, "He did not eat," he brings a suspensive guilt-offering.

3:2-3 If he ate forbidden fat and did so again in a single spell of inadvertence, he is liable for a single sin-offering. If he ate forbidden fat, blood, remnant, refuse, in a single spell of in-inadvertence, he is liable for each and every one of them.

3:4-6 There is he who carries out a single act of eating and is liable on its account for four sin-offerings and one guilt offering. There is he who carries out a single act of sexual intercourse and becomes liable on its account for six sin-offerings.

3:7-10 ᶜAqiba: I asked Gamaliel and Joshua: He who has sexual relations with his sister and his father's sister and his mother's sister in one spell of inadvertence—what is the rule? A limb which is dangling from a beast—what is the rule? He who slaughters five animal-sacrifices outside the courtyard in a single act of inadvertence—what is the law?

ᶜAqiba: I asked Eliezer: He who performs many acts of prohibited labor on many Sabbaths but of a single sort of prohibited labor in a single spell of inadvertence—what is the law? [How many sin-offerings?]

III. *The suspensive guilt-offering.* 4:1-6:8

4:1 It is a matter of doubt whether or not one has eaten forbidden fat, etc.—he brings a suspensive guilt-offering.

4:2-3 Just as if he ate forbidden fat and again ate forbidden fat in a single spell of inadvertence, he is liable for only a single sin-offering [M. 3:2], so if he is uncertain about such things, he is liable to bring only a single guilt-offering. Just as if he ate forbidden fat and blood and remnant and refuse in a single spell of inadvertence, he is liable for each and every one, [M. 3:2], so in connection with a situation of uncertainty, he brings a suspensive guilt-offering for each and every one.

---

[1] "On formal grounds these pericopae belong with M. 2:1-2. The unit is articulated with a numerical mnemonic, 4, 4:5, 5. M. 3:1, 2-3 are joined with each other on the basis of a common case, eating forbidden fat, though not a common problem. The issue of a single sin-offering for multiple sins begins at M. 3:2-3. The pericopae, M. 2:3-6, may be said thematically to form a transition to that unit (although M. 3:1 interrupts the theme), and the ultimate redactor has nicely juxtaposed the two units, but it remains the case that Chapters Two and Three are articulated as separate units".—Richard S. Sarason.

5:1-3 ᶜAqiba: One is liable to a suspensive guilt-offering in the case of a matter of doubt, in the case of a sin, the certain commission of which imposes the liability to a guilt-offering [not only a sin-offering, as at M. 1:2]—specifically, in the case of sacrilege. Sages hold that a suspensive guilt-offering is required only in a case in which, if one surely has inadvertently committed a transgression, he brings a sin-offering (= M. 1:2).

5:4-8 Five-part formal construction involving (1) ᶜAqiba's and sages' dispute on bringing a suspensive guilt-offering in a case in which, if a sin certainly has been committed, one does not bring a sin-offering; and (2) Yosé's and Simeon's disagreement on whether or not two people bring a single guilt-offering or a single sin-offering.

6:1-2 How do we dispose of a suspensive guilt-offering when it is discovered that the person in fact has not committed a sin at all.

6:3 Eliezer: A sin-offering not needed for one sin can be offered for one other than the one for which it was originally designated (restatement of his subordinated position of M. 4:2-3).

6:4-5 The disposition of sin-offerings and guilt-offerings owed by people and not brought before the Day of Atonement. Suspensive guilt-offerings not brought before the Day are not required thereafter.

6:6-7 If one set aside a sin-offering and died, his heir cannot offer the sin-offering for some other purpose. M. 6:6 serves as a prologue to this item: the rules of sacrilege pertinent to one who has set aside two *selas* for a guilt-offering, then purchased animals for some other purpose. [M. 6:6-7 also link our tractate to the following one.]

6:8 If one set aside funds for the purchase of a sacrifice for a particular sin, he may use them for the purchase of a different sort of animal for that same particular sin.

6:9 Concluding homily, irrelevant to the tractate.)

The tractate treats, first of all, the sin-offering, second, the occasions on which it is offered, third, the suspensive guilt-offering (subject to the rules of the second unit). Obviously, it cannot have treated the latter, then the former. The sin-offering is treated from two perspectives. First, at unit I, we define those who are obligated to bring a sin-offering. Then we raise the quite separate question of how many sin-offerings are required for multiple violations of a given rule, unit II. Then, at unit III, we turn to the suspensive guilt-offering, which for its part is thoroughly analyzed. As I pointed out, a number of sizable pericopae seem to have taken shape before being inserted whole into our tractate, of which M. 3:7-10 is the most important example. The whole of Chapters Four and Five is constructed with remarkable care.

Chapter Six, for its part, has some miscellanies, though one can explain why its several units have been included. Over all, the tractate is a delight as a formal and redactional exercise. It is rich in large and elegant constructions, and these are so arranged that the redaction, as much as what is redacted, contributes to the making of some of the tractate's most important points. I must regard the work as exemplary of Mishnah at its formal and redactional pinnacle.

CHAPTER TWO

KERITOT CHAPTER ONE

The catalogue of offerings required for various transgressions and other penalties incurred on their account begins with a list of thirty-six sorts of sins for which the penalty of extirpation is incurred, M. 1:1 + 2. M. 1:1 + 2 adds that extirpation is incurred specifically when said transgression is done deliberately. If it is done inadvertently, a sin-offering is required. If one is not sure whether or not the transgression has been done, a sliding-scale-offering is brought. The second and final unit of the chapter is another well disciplined formal construction, M. 1:3-5, with two supplements, M. 1:6,7. The construction lists women who bring an offering which is eaten, that is, women who certainly are liable for the offering in consequence of childbirth, Lev. 12:1-6; then, those who bring an offering which is not eaten, since we are not certain that the woman is required to bring the offering; and, finally, those who bring no offering at all, since the woman surely does not owe an offering for having given birth. The first supplementary problem is at M. 1:6, a Houses' dispute on whether the woman who has an abortion on the night preceding the eighty-first day after the birth of a female child is obligated to bring an offering. The details of the problem are spelled out in due course. The second supplementary problem, M. 1:7, deals with a woman who is subject to doubt as to the appearance of five fluxes. Have these occurred on *Zibah*-days, in which case she is a confirmed *Zabah* and owes five offerings in due course? Or is she in doubt as to the status of five abortions (M. 1:4)? In either instance she is liable to bring only one offering. The problem is developed further, but its purpose, to enrich M. 1:3-5, is self-evident. The two-part chapter thus is tightly formulated, both in its parts and as a whole.

1:1

A. Thirty-six transgressions subject to extirpation are in the Torah:

B. He who has sexual relations with (1) his mother, and (2) with his father's wife, and (3) with his daughter-in-law;

C. he who has sexual relations (4) with a male, and (5) with a beast; and (6) the woman who has sexual relations with a beast;

D. he who has sexual relations (7) with a woman and with her daughter, and (8) with a married woman;

E. he who has sexual relations (9) with his sister, and (10) with his father's sister, and (11) with his mother's sister, and (12) with his wife's sister, and (13) with his brother's wife, and (14) with his father's brother's wife, and (15) with a menstruating woman (Lev. 18:6ff.):

F. (16) he who blasphemes (Num. 15:30), and (17) he who performs an act of blasphemous worship (Num. 15:31), and (18) he who gives his seed to Molekh (Lev. 18:21), and (19) one who has a familiar spirit (Lev. 20:6);

G. (20) he who profanes the Sabbath-day (Ex. 31:14);

H. and (21) an unclean person who ate a Holy Thing (Lev. 22:3), and (22) he who comes to the sanctuary when unclean (Num. 19:20);

I. he who eats (23) forbidden fat (Lev. 7:25), and (24) blood (Lev. 17:14), and (25) remnant (Lev. 19:6-8), and (26) refuse (Lev. 19:7-8);

J. he who (27) slaughters and who (28) offers up [a sacrifice] outside [the Temple court] (Lev. 17:9);

K. (29) he who eats leaven on Passover (Ex. 12:19); and he who (30) eats and he who (31) works on the Day of Atonement (Lev. 23:29-30);

L. he who (32) compounds anointing oil [like that made in the Temple (Ex. 30:23-33)], and he who (33) compounds incense [like that made in the Temple], and he who (34) anoints himself with anointing oil (Ex. 30-32);

M. [he who transgresses the laws of] (35) Passover (Num. 9:13) and (36) circumcision (Gen. 17:14), among the positive commandments.

M. 1:1

A. For those [transgressions] are people liable, for deliberately doing them, to the punishment of extirpation,

B. and for accidentally doing them, to the bringing of a sin-offering,

C. and for not being certain of whether or not one has done them, to a suspensive guilt-offering [Lev. 5:17]—

D. "except for the one who imparts uncleanness to the sanctuary and its Holy Things,

E. "because he is subject to bringing a sliding-scale offering (Lev. 5:6-7, 11)," the words of R. Meir.

F. And sages say, "Also: [except for] the one who blasphemes, as it is said, *You shall have one law for him that does anything unwittingly* (Num. 15:29)—excluding the blasphemer, who does no concrete deed."

M. 1:2

The list announced and carried through at M. 1:1 is then tied to M. 1:2A-C. But only M. 1:2A is relevant to the foregoing, since M.

1:2B and C refer not to extirpation but to animal-offerings. [1] Scripture refers, M. claims, to thirty-six sorts of transgressions subject to the penalty of extirpation. If one deliberately does any of these transgressions, he is liable to extirpation. M. 1:2B-C add that if he does them inadvertently, he brings a sin-offering, and if he is not sure whether or not he has done them, he brings a suspensive guilt-offering, as noted above. I am inclined to see M. 1:1A as somewhat misleading, because of M. 1:2A-C, all of which are served by the same list. But this is a quibble. [2] M. 1:2 lists exceptions to M. 1:2B-C, and D-E and F. Meir refers to M. 1:1K (22), though he does not explicitly refer to its language. If a person is in doubt about whether or not he has accidentally entered the Temple while in a state of uncleanness, or whether or not he has eaten Holy Things in a state of uncleanness, he brings a sliding-scale-offering (Lev. 5:2). It follows that in this case we do not invoke M. 1:2C. And it further follows that what serves Meir is not the superscription, M. 1:1A, but the subscription, M. 1:2A-C. Sages, M. 1:2F, refer to the language of M. 1:1F(16); this one does not do an actual deed but only says things he should not say, so is excluded. But they too refer not to M. 1:1A, 1:2A, but to M. 1:2B, C: such a one does not bring a sin-offering if he is certain he has done the deed or a suspensive guilt-offering if he is not certain. [3]

A. *He who blasphemes* [M. Ker. 1:1F]—

B. R. Judah [alt.: ᶜAqiba] declares [him] liable to an offering, since extirpation is stated in his regard [*vs.* sages, M. 1:2F].

C. And it is said, *That man shall bear his sin* (Num. 9:13).

D. *He who anoints* [*himself*] *with the oil of anointing* [like] that which Moses made in the wilderness, lo, this one is liable to extirpation [M. Ker. 1:1L/34].

E. *Passover and circumcision*, even though [people] are liable for

---

1 "M. 1:2A-C form an integral unit (A is phrased so as to lead automatically to B, C) which refers back to the foregoing. If anything, M. 1:2A-C expand the superscription of 1:1A in a typically "Mishnaic" fashion, noting all of the categories relevant to the previously-listed items (a standard piece of Mishnaic *Listenwissenschaft*)."—Richard S. Sarason.

2 "It is not M. 1:1A that is misleading, but the title of the tractate, which has been lifted from M. 1:1A. 1:1A, as I indicated, is expanded and clarified by 1:2A-C, which *do* articulate the theme of the tractate as a whole. This (*post facto*) confusion could have been avoided if M. 1:2A-C formed the superscription at 1.1A, instead of a subscript. But it would be imprudent to try to second-guess the redactor's rationale here."—R.S.S.

3 "The articulation of Meir's and sages' opinions makes clear that they respond to M. 1:1B-C, to which they syntactically are connected. Once again, the logic of the chapter flows from M. 1:2A-C, not 1:1A."—R.S.S.

deliberate transgression thereof to extirpation [M. Ker. 1:1P], are not subject to an offering,

F. because they are [commandments] which require concrete action ["they are subject to, 'Arise and do' "].

T. 1:1 Z p. 560, ls. 36-38

A. *An unclean person who ate a Holy Thing, and he who comes to the sanctuary while unclean* [M. Ker. 1:1H],

B. even though they are liable, for deliberately doing so, to extirpation, and, for accidentally doing so, to a sin-offering,

C. are not subject to a suspensive guilt-offering,

D. because they are subject to a sliding-scale-offering [= Meir, M. 1:2E].

T. 1:2 Z p. 560, ls. 38-9, p. 561, l. 1

A. He who curses his father and his mother, and he who says to his fellow, "Go and perform an act of idolatrous worship," and he who incites, and he who leads astray, and false prophets, and conspiring witnesses,

B. even though they are liable to be put to death at the hands of a court,

C. are not subject to bringing an offering,

D. because their [transgressions] do not contain a concrete deed.

T. 1:3 Z p. 561, ls. 1-3

A. He who hits his father and his mother, and he who kidnaps an Israelite, and an elder who rebels against a court ruling, and a wicked and incorrigible son, and a murderer,

B. even though [their transgressions] involve a deed, and even though they are subject to be put to death by a court,

C. are not subject to an offering,

D. because they are punished by extirpation.

T. 1:4 Z p. 561, ls. 3-5

A. These are those [transgressions] punishable by death:

B. (1) He who eats untithed food, and (2) a non-priest who ate clean heave-offering, and (3) an unclean priest who ate clean heave-offering—

C. and (4) a non-priest, (5) one who had immersed that self-same day, (6) one who lacked proper garments, (7) one who lacked proper completion of rites of purification, (8) one with unkempt hair, (9) one who was drunk, [any one of whom] served [at the altar]—

D. all of them are subject to the death penalty.

E. But the uncircumcised [priest], and the priest in mourning, and the priest who was sitting down, lo, these are subject to warning.

F. "A blemished priest [who served at the altar] is subject to the death-penalty," the words of Rabbi.

G. And sages say, "[He is subject to the penalty for having transgressed] a negative commandment [= T. Zeb. 12:17]."

T. 1:5 Z p. 561, ls. 5-9

A. He who deliberately commits sacrilege—
B. Rabbi says, "[He is subject to] the death penalty."
C. And sages say, "[He is subject to the penalty for having transgressed] a negative commandment [= T. Zeb. 12:17]."
D. This is the general principle: [For violation of] any negative commandment containing within itself a concrete deed do [violators] receive the penalty of forty stripes.
E. And for the violation of any which does not contain within itself a concrete deed they do not receive the penalty of forty stripes.
F. And as to all other negative commandments in the Torah, lo, these are subject to warning.
G. He who transgresses them violates the decree of the King.

T. 1:6 Z p. 561, ls. 9-12

T. 1:1 sets Judah in opposition to M. [4] Its other glosses of M. are clear as stated. T. 1:2 glosses M. 1:1H by qualifying the application to that item of M. 1:2A-C. [5] T. 1:3 expands the application of the theory of M. 1:2F. The next item complements M., T. 1:4 having its own items for the list of those subject to the penalty of extirpation. T. 1:5-6 are autonomous of M.

1:3-5

A. (1) There are women who bring a [sin-] offering [after childbirth], and it is eaten [by the priests], (2) and there are women who bring an offering, and it is not eaten, (3) and there are women who do not bring [an offering].
I B. These [women after childbirth] bring an offering, and it is eaten:
C. (1) "She who aborts something which is like a beast or a wild animal or a bird," the words of R. Meir.
And sages say, "[She does not bring an offering] unless it bears human appearance."
D. She who aborts (1) a sandal or (2) an afterbirth or (3) a fully-fashioned foetus or (4) an offspring which is cut up [during delivery].
E. And so a bondwoman who gives birth brings an offering, and it is eaten.

M. 1:3

II A. These bring [an offering], but it is not eaten:
B. (1) She who aborts, and it is not known what it is that she has aborted;
C. and so: two women who aborted, one [producing] something

---

[4] "T. 1:1 sets Judah in opposition to sages at M. 1:2F. Thus Judah agrees with M. 1:1-2A-C."—R.S.S.

[5] "T. 1:2D agrees with Meir at M. 1:2E."—R.S.S.

which is exempt [from the requirement of bringing an offering], and one [producing] something which is liable [to an offering].

D. Said R. Yosé, "Under what circumstances? When this one went east and that one west. But if the two of them are standing together, they [together] bring [one] offering, and it is eaten."

M. 1:4

III A. These are those who do not bring [an offering at all]:

B. She who aborts a foetus (1) filled with water, (2) filled with blood, (3) filled with variegated matter;

C. she who aborts something shaped like (1) fish, (2) locusts, (3) abominable things, or (4) creeping things;

D. she who aborts on the fortieth day.

E. And [she who produces] that which comes forth from the side.

F. R. Simeon declares liable in the case of [producing] that which comes forth from the side.

M. 1:5

This sizable standard construction poses no major formal or exegetical problems. M. 1:3B-D illustrate M. 1:3A1, M. 1:4, M. 1:3A2, and M. 1:5, M. 1:3A3. There is no clear effort internally to match the several collections of illustrative materials against one another. M. 1:3C is a dispute unto itself and hardly belongs here. [6] D is satisfactory, and E, an appendage. M. 1:4, by contrast, bears illustrations at B and C-D [7] M. 1:5 is probably the best example, having a fine set of materials at B, C and D, (adding up to nine if we include E). E-F are distinct from the foregoing. [8] Women bring a sin-offering (Lev. 12:6) which is eaten in the case of any normal or viable birth. The issue of the dispute at M. 1:3C is clear because of sages' opinion. D's items all are viable, or deemed part of a viable birth (M. Nid. 3:5). (E's point of course is entirely separate; it stresses that the Canaanite bond-woman is liable to carry out the Israelite commandments). M. 1:4's items leave a doubt as to whether or not a woman is liable to bring an offering, or whether or not, if she does, the offering is her own. At M. 1:4B we do not know what the woman has produced; it may fall under the items of M. 1:3B-D or of M. 1:5. At M. 1:4C, we do not know to which woman the offering belongs. Yosé qualifies the rule. If both women are before the priest, then they between themselves bring one

---

6 "M. 1:3C indeed belongs here. Meir's lemma substantively parallels D."—R.S.S.

7 "D glosses and exemplifies C."—R.S.S.

8 "M. 1:5 is the cleanest member, bearing no internal glosses, but a dispute at E-F, which ends the set. We must include E in our count of items. It is no less integral to the construction than any other item. E-F are not distinct from the foregoing. E depends on A and is congruent with B-D."—R.S.S.

offering as partners, with the condition that the offering belongs to the one who actually is liable to bring it. M. 1:5's first list, B, includes things which are in no way viable. M. 1:5C falls under the conception of sages, M. 1:3C. What is aborted on the fortieth day of conception is deemed nothing but liquid. The dispute, E-F, is whether the child born through Caesarean section subjects the mother to the law of Lev. 12:1-6. Simeon maintains that it does. M. Nid. 3:2-4, 7, and 5:1 go over the ground of this pericope.

A. She who aborts after the completion of the days of purifying,
B. and she who aborts an eight-month-old foetus, alive or dead, or a child past term [*TR* II, p. 293]—
C. and a proselyte who converted while circumcized,
D. and a deaf-mute, an imbecile, and a minor who lacked the completion of atonement rites
E. bring an offering, and it is eaten.

T. 1:7 Z p. 561, ls. 12-14

A. [If] a woman is subject to doubt whether or not she gave birth to any thing at all,
B. or [if] she is in doubt that it is viable or not viable,
C. of [if] she is in doubt that [the foetus] does or does not bear human appearance,
D. she brings an offering, but it is not eaten.

T. 1:8 Z p. 561, ls. 14-16

T. 1:7 adds to M. 1:3, and T. 1:8 to M. 1:4. T. 1:8's formulation is superior to M.'s.

1:6

A. She who produces an abortion on the night [prior to the dawn] of the eighty-first day—
B. The House of Shammai declare [her] exempt from bringing an offering.
C. The House of Hillel declare [her] liable.
D. Said the House of Hillel to the House of Shammai, "What is the difference between the night [prior to the dawn] of the eighty-first day from the eighty-first day itself [when she certainly would be liable]?"
E. "If it [the night] is equivalent to it [the day] in respect to uncleanness, should it not be equivalent to it in respect to an offering?"
F. Said to them the House of Shammai, "No. If you have said so [that a woman is liable] in the case of the woman who aborts on the eighty-first *day*, at which point it [the abortion] went forth at a time at which it is fitting to bring an offering, will you say so of the one who aborts on the *night* of the eighty-first day, at which point it [the abortion] did not go forth at a time at which it is fitting to bring an offering?"

G. Said to them the House of Hillel, "And lo, she who produces an abortion on the eighty-first day which coincides with the Sabbath will prove [our case].

H. "For it did not go forth at a time at which it is fitting to bring an offering. Yet she is liable to bring an offering."

I. Said to them the House of Shammai, "No. If you have said so in the case of her who aborts on the eighty-first day which coincides with the Sabbath, at which time, even though it is not fitting to bring an individual's offering, it is fitting to bring the community's offering, will you say so in the case of her who aborts on the night of the eighty-first day, for the night is not a time fitting for bringing either an individual's offering or the community's offering.

J. "Her blood [uncleanness] does not prove the matter.

K. "For she who produces an abortion during the days of purifying, her blood is unclean. And she is free of the obligation to bring an offering."

M. 1:6

The formal traits of this classic pericope are flawless, except for the somewhat unsatisfying conclusion to the debate, I, J-K. We should have had, after the balanced dispute, A-C, three opinions, the House of Hillel, the House of Shammai, then the House of Hillel. The additional opinion of the House of Shammai, I, followed by yet another argument, curiously undeveloped, J-K, which also leaves the Shammaites in the winning corner, is strange. The woman who produces a female child is unclean as a menstruant for two weeks, then sits out sixty-six days of purifying (Lev. 12:5-6). On the eighty-first day she is to bring a burnt-offering and a sin-offering. If, then, she produces an abortion on the night prior to the eighty-first day, what is her status? Had the abortion appeared during the days of purifying, she would have counted afresh from the date of the abortion. After the completion of the days of purifying for the abortion, she would have brought a single sin-offering for both births (K). But now she has aborted after the eighty days of purifying, but before she has brought the offering. The House of Shammai say she does not have to bring an offering for the second one. The House of Hillel require that she bring an offering for the second birth. The opening argument, D-E, is clear as stated. All agree that the abortion produced on the eighty-first day (inclusive of the antecedent night) imparts the status of uncleanness. Why? Because it comes after the days of purifying. Since the night is no time for a sacrifice, it is deemed part of the (antecedent) days of purifying (D). The Shammaites, F, distinguish the night from the day, and the rest of the argument devolves upon the datum of the difference. J-K revert to E. The issue of the status of the blood—it is unclean when produced on the eighty-first day, after the days of purifying have come to an end—is likewise irrelevant. For there is a substantial difference between the woman's status if she produces an abortion on the days of purifying in which case the blood is unclean, but no obligation to bring a sacrifice is incurred—and her status if she produces an abortion on the night of the eighty-first day. That is, to be sure, begging the question, since what is to be proved is adduced in proof.

A. She who aborts during the days of purifying is exempt from all [offerings].

B. The House of Shammai and the House of Hillel concur in the case of one who sees a drop of blood on the night of the eighty-first day, that the blood is unclean.

C. And she who aborts on the eighty-first day should be liable for an offering [M. 1:6A, C].

D. Said the House of Hillel to the House of Shammai, "Do you not agree in the case of the woman who sees a drop of blood on the night of the eighty-first day, that her blood is unclean? [M. Ker. 1:6J-K].

E. "Then she who aborts on the eighty-first day should be liable to an offering.

F. "For what difference does it make to me whether it is day or night [M. Ker. 1:6D], or whether it is blood or a birth?"

G. Said to them the House of Shammai, "No. If you have stated the rule in regard to the day, which is fitting for the bringing of an offering, will you state it in regard to the night, which is not fitting for bringing an offering [M. Ker. 1:6F]?

H. "As to blood to which you referred: distinguish between blood and birth.

I. "For she who sees blood during the days of purifying— her blood is [*TR* II, p. 293:] clean.

J. "And she who aborts during the days of purifying—her blood is unclean.

K. "She who aborts during the days of purifying is free of all [offering]."

L. *Said to them the House of Hillel, "Now lo, she who aborts on the eighty-first day which coincides with the Sabbath will prove the matter. For it did not go forth at a time which is fitting, to bring an offering* [M. Ker. 1:6G-H].

M. "And this will prove [that] she who aborts on the night of the eighty-first, any day of the year,

N. "for thus did it go forth at a time that is fitting to bring an offering, is liable for an offering."

O. Said to them the House of Shammai, "No. If you have so stated in connection with her who aborts on the eighty-first day at any day of the year, which is joined together with the day which follows it,

P. "so that, even though it is not fitting for an offering of an individual, it is fitting for an offering of the community,

R. "will you say so in the case of her who aborts on the night of the eighty-first day of any day of the year, for the night is not fitting either for the offering of an individual or for the offering of the community [M. Ker. 1:6I]?"

S. Said to them the House of Hillel, "Lo, you have yourselves said that the night joins together with the day which follows it.

T. "So just as she is liable for what happens on the day of the eighty-first, so should she be liable for what happens on the night of the eighty-first.

U. "And let not the day of the eighty-second prove anything, for at that point it [the abortion] has gone forth at a time at which it is fitting to bring an offering."

T. 1:9 Z p. 561, ls. 16-32

T. fills M.'s gap by taking up the allusion of M. 1:6J-K and spelling out the argument contained therein. It then restates M.'s materials without major changes.

1:7

A. The woman who is subject to a doubt concerning [the appearance of] five fluxes,

B. or the one who is subject to a doubt concerning five miscarriages

C. brings a single offering.

D. And she [then is deemed clean so that she] eats animal-sacrifices.

E. And the remainder [of the offerings, A, B] are not an obligation for her.

F. [If she is subject to] five confirmed miscarriages,

G. or five confirmed fluxes,

H. she brings a single offering.

I. And she eats animal-sacrifices.

J. But the rest [of the offerings, the other four] remain as an obligation for her [to bring at some later time].

K. MᶜŠH Š: A pair of birds in Jerusalem went up in price to a golden *denar*.

L. Said Rabban Simeon b. Gamaliel, "By this sanctuary! I shall not rest tonight until they shall be at [silver] *denars*."

M. He entered the court and taught [the following law]:

N. "The woman who is subject to five confirmed miscarriages [or] five confirmed fluxes brings a single offering.

O. "And she eats animal-sacrifices.

P. "And the rest [of the offerings] do *not* remain as an obligation for her."

Q. And pairs of birds stood on that very day at a quarter-*denar* each [one one-hundredth of the former price].

M. 1:7

This is another fine construction, because the perfectly balanced legal ruling, A-E, F-K, is cited in the *maᶜaśeh*, O-Q=F=K, except for the italicized word. The *maᶜaśeh*, itself is clear as stated, and to the *maᶜaśeh* O-Q are absolutely essential, though, of course, not necessarily in the given formulation. The woman in A has produced blood for five consecutive months on three days running. But she does not know whether these five incidents occured when she was in her cycle of menstrual days or when she was in her cycle of *zibah*-days. If in the latter, then she is confirmed as a *Zabah*. B has a woman who has five times produced some sort of an abortion but is not sure of its character (M. 1:4). One burnt-offering and one sin-offering suffice. The woman then is deemed clean so as to eat Holy Things. The offerings for the other four appearances of flux or miscarriages are null. The contrast in the other case—five confirmed fluxes, meaning, three consecutive days of flux during the *zibah*-days—leaves the woman definitively unclean and owing the five sacrifices, all of which are to be brought. But after bringing only one of them she is clean for the purposes of eating Holy Things (J).

A. A woman who is subject to the offering for giving birth and for yet another offering for giving birth,

for an offering for flux and for yet another offering for flux,

B. brings a single offering.

C. [If she is subject to an offering for] giving birth and [for an offering for suffering] flux,

D. she brings two offerings.

E. [If she is subject to an offering for] possibly having given birth and [to an offering for] certainly having given birth,

F. [to an offering for] possibly suffering a flux and [to an offering for] certainly having suffered a flux,

G. she brings an offering [for each obligation to which she is] certainly subject among them [and] has fulfilled her obligation.

H. [If she was subject to] a confirmed birth and a birth which is subject to doubt,

I. a confirmed flux and a flux which is subject to doubt,

J. "she brings one offering and she says, 'If it was confirmed, this is for it. If not, lo, this is for the one which was confirmed among the whole lot,' " the words of R. Yoḥanan b. Nuri.

K. R. ᶜAqiba says, "She brings one for that which confirmed among the whole lot [and] thereby has fulfilled her obigation."

T. 1:10 Z p. 561, ls. 32-36

T. has its own interest, correlative to M.'s. M. has asked about the number of offerings one brings in a case of doubt about five fluxes or miscarriages. T. concurs on that point and agrees also that, if there are five confirmed miscarriages or fluxes, a single offering suffices, T. 1:10A-B, along the lines of ᶜAqiba, K, and M. 1:7Q. Obviously, C, if the woman owes sacrifices for two distinct causes, she brings two offerings. E-G carry this matter forward. H-K then show that M. conforms at M. 1:7Q to ᶜAqiba's view. The story about Simeon b. Gamaliel is congruent to ᶜAqiba's opinion.

CHAPTER THREE

KERITOT CHAPTER TWO

We have another formal construction, two fours and two fives. M. 2.1-2 present (1) four whose atonement is incomplete until they bring an offering (= M 1:7), then (2) four who bring an offering whether they have sinned deliberately or inadvertently. Each construction, M. 2:1C, M. 2:2A-B, appropriately contains four examples. The next presents (1) five who bring a single offering for many transgressions and (2) five who bring a sliding-scale-offering, M. 2:3A-B. M. 2:3C refers to four items; the first of these alludes to a bondwoman, the fourth to a *meṣora*[c] who has been afflicted many times. M. 2:3D-E augment that last item. M. 2:4A-C add a further possibility, not on the foregoing list. The chapter's very sizable appendix, M. 2:4F-M, M. 2:5-6, takes up the theme of the bondwoman and supplies a whole repertoire of rulings on that subject. M. 2:4D-E complete the announced construction, five who bring a sliding-scale-offering. So. M. 2:3A-C, 2:4D-E constitute the second of the two units of fives, and the rest of the chaper is tacked on because of an item alluded to therein.

2:1-2

A. [There are] four whose atonement is not complete [until they bring an offering].

B. And four bring [an offering] for [a transgression done] deliberately as for [one done] inadvertently.

C. These are those whose atonement is not complete [until they bring an offering]:

(1) The *Zab*, and (2) the *Zabah*, and (3) the woman who has given birth, and (4) the *meṣora*[c].

D. R. Eliezer b. Jacob says, "A proselyte is one whose atonement is not complete until the blood will be sprinkled on his behalf."

E. And the Nazir as to [observing prohibitions against] wine, shaving, and uncleanness [has not completed atonement until he has brought his offering].

M. 2:1

A. These bring [an offering for a transgression done] deliberately as for [one done] inadvertently:

B. (1) He who has sexual relations with a bondwoman; and (2) a Nazirite who was made unclean;

C. and (3) for [him who utters a false] oath of testimony, and (4) for [him who utters a false] deposit-oath.

M. 2:2

The lists, M. 2:1A-B, are joined solely [1] because of the common number, four (followed at M. 2:3 by five). B is clear as given. Even though those listed have immersed, they cannot eat Holy Things until they bring their animal in atonement. Eliezer, D, has a fifth item, and E yet another. A proselyte brings a burnt-offering and cannot eat Holy Things before its blood is tossed; the Nazir brings offerings (Num. 6:14), before which time his vow remains in affect. M. 2:2B and C are distinguished in form, in that C's items are expressed as ᶜL + verb. A Nazir who is made unclean by a corpse brings an offering, Num. 6:9-12. The oath of C3 is that the witness claims to have no knowledge of the matter of a loan, while in reality he does (M. Shabu. 4:2-3); and that of C3 is a false oath that one does not have a bailment left in his keeping, when in fact he does and admits it thereafter (M. Shabu. 5:1-2). The bondwoman of M. 2:2B1 is explained in the chapter's appendix, M. 2:5.

A. R. Simeon says, "A Nazir [who has not yet brought his offerings] has not completed atonement in respect to drinking wine" [M. Ker. 2:1E].

B. R. Eliezer b. Jacob says, "A proselyte [who has not yet brought his offerings] has not completed atonement in respect to eating animal-sacrifices" [M. Ker. 2:1D].

T. 1:11 Z p. 261, ls. 36-37

A. All of those who owe pairs [of bird-sacrifices] stated in the Torah—half of them [the sacrifices] are a sin-offering, and half of them are burnt-offerings [M. Qin. 1:1],

B. except for the bird-offering of a proselyte,

C. for even though they [B] are an obligation, both of them were burnt-offerings.

D. [If] he wanted to offer beasts for those which are required, he may offer them [as he wishes].

E. [If] he offered beasts as burnt-offerings for atonement, he has fulfilled his obligation.

F. [If he did so with] meal-offerings and drink-offerings, he has not fulfilled his obligation.

G. They spoke of a pair of birds only to lighten the burden for him.

H. [If] he brought one sort of offering for his purification from *ṣaraᶜat*, let him go and bring the same for his atonement-offering.

I. [If he brought one sort of offering] for his Nazirite-offering, let him go and bring the same for his atonement-offering.

T. 1:12 Z p. 561, ls. 38-40, p. 562, l. 1

---

[1] "The numerical mnemonic is not the sole linking principle here. There is also a common (very general) theme, viz., four *who must bring an offering.*"—R.S.S.

A. *Four [sorts of transgressor] bring [an offering] in the case of deliberate [transgression] as in the case of inadvertent [transgression] [M. 2:1B].*

B. In the case of all of them, if they are under constraint, they are exempt [from liability] except for the Nazir.

T. 1:13 Z p. 562, ls. 1-2 [continued]

T. 1:11 clarifies M. 2:1D, E. Simeon differs from M., and T. explains the meaning of Eliezer's saying in M. [2] T. 1:12 is relevant only in a general way to M., that is, the reference to the proselyte's offering. Apart from that point of contact, T. is autonomous of M. 1:13 then cites and glosses M.

2:3-6

A. Five bring a single offering for many transgressions.

B. And five bring a sliding-scale-offering.

C. These bring a single offering for many transgressions:

(1) He who has sexual relations with a bondwoman many times, and (2) a Nazirite who is made unclean many times, and (3) he who suspects his wife of adultery with many men, and (4) a *meṣoraᶜ* who was afflicted by *negaᶜim* many times.

D. [If] he brought his birds and [then] was afflicted with a *negaᶜ*, they [the birds] do not go to his credit until he brings his sin-offering.

E. R. Judah says, "Until he brings his guilt-offering."

M. 2:3

A. A woman suffered many miscarriages—

B. (1) she aborted a female during eighty days, and went and aborted another female during eighty days following, and (2) she who bore a multiple of abortions ["twins"—each in the period of purifying of the foregoing].

C. R. Judah says, "She [in B2] brings an offering for the first, and she does not bring an offering for the second. She brings an offering for the third, and she does not bring an offering for the fourth."

D. These bring a sliding-scale-offering:

E. (1) for refusing to give evidence ["for hearing the voice" (Lev. 5:1)]; and (2) for an expression of the lips [a rash oath]; and (3) for contaminating the sanctuary and its Holy Things;

and (4) the woman who has given birth, and (5) the *meṣoraᶜ*.

---

2 "Simeon differs from M. only if we assume that M.'s 'shaving and uncleanness' are known to T.'s Simeon and rejected by him. In fact, Simeon's and Eliezer's opinions in T. are formulated together and balance each other syntactically. The implication for T.'s relation to M., whether or not Simeon differs from M. or simply does not address M.'s remaining cases, therefore is less clear."—R.S.S.

F. And what is the difference between the bondwoman and other forbidden sexual relationships (Lev. 18)?

That they are not alike (1) either in punishment or (2) in the offering [required for the transgression]—

I G. For all [other] forbidden sexual relations [are expiated] with a sin-offering, but forbidden sexual relations with a bondwoman, with a guilt-offering.

H. All other sexual relations [are atoned] with a female animal, but the bondwoman, with a male animal [F2].

II I. In respect to all other sexual relations, all the same are the man and the woman. They are equivalent as to stripes and as to an offering.

J. But in respect to the bondwoman, the man is not treated as equivalent to the woman in regard to stripes, and the woman is not regarded as equivalent to the man in respect to an offering [F2].

III K. In respect to all other forbidden sexual relations Scripture has treated him who begins the act as culpable as him who completes it, and he is liable for each and every act of sexual relations [which is not the case here, M. 2:3C1].

L. But this strict rule does the law stringently impose in the case of the bondwoman:

M. that it treats in her regard the man who does the act intentionally as equivalent to the one who does it inadvertently.

M. 2:4

A. What is the bond-woman [to whom reference has been made]?

B. "Any one, half of whom is in bondage and half free [a bondwoman belonging to two partners, one of whom has set her free],

C. "since it is said, *And she has not yet been altogether redeemed* (Lev. 19:20)," the words of R. ᶜAqiba.

D. R. Ishmael says, "This one [the bondwoman] is [simply] a confirmed bondwoman."

E. R. Eleazar b. ᶜAzariah says, "All prohibited sexual relationships are explicitly stated [as wholly free]. What is left to us except one which is half in bondage and half free [= Lev. 19:20]?"

M. 2:5

A. In all forbidden sexual relationships,

B. [if] one is an adult and one is a minor, the minor is exempt.

C. [If] one is awake and one is asleep, the one asleep is exempt.

D. [If] one does the act inadvertently and one deliberately, the one who does it inadvertently is liable to bring a sin-offering, and the one who does it deliberately is subject to extirpation [M. 1:2A].

M. 2:6

The catalogue continues at M. 2:3A-B. C completes A. D-E then form one addition, which is hardly relevant to A, but which expands C4, explaining a secondary issue in that regard. M. 2:4A-C continue the expansion of M. 2:3A-C. M. 2:4A adds a fifth item to M. 2:3C. B then explains A. At C, Judah differs from A. The point of M. 2:3C1-2 is clear as given. C3 refers to a man who warns his wife about involvements with a number of different men. He brings only one meal-offering of jealousy (Num. 5:15ff.). If a *meṣora* suffered from more than one bout of disease, he brings a single offering at the end. D-E raise a secondary point. If a *meṣora*[c] has brought the birds but not completed the rite by bringing the sin-offering (or, as Judah says, the guilt-offering [M. Neg. 14:11]), the birds do not go to expiate the first bout with the disease, and we do not give him credit in line with the ruling of C4. A woman who has produced many miscarriages, M. 2:4A, brings a single offering. This is explained at B. She may, for example, abort a female during the eighty days of purifying of a female, and then abort yet another female; or she may produce "twins" —multiple abortions. In these cases, she brings a single offering. (The House of Shammai, M. 1:6, will concede that if the female is aborted within the eighty days, she does owe an offering.) Judah differs, C. He has the woman bring an offering for the first abortion, not for the one which comes after it during the days of purifying of the first one; but the one (the third) which comes after the completion of the days of purifying of the third, will not.

M. 2:4D takes up M. 2:3B. M. 2:4E refers to M. 2:2C3, using the Scriptural language, Lev. 5:1. It is one who refuses to give testimony. E2 speaks of a promise or an oath with reference to his own person, Lev. 5:4. Lev. 5:2-3 is referred to at M. 2:4E3, Lev. 12:6-8 at E4, and Lev. 14:10ff. at E5.

M. 2:4F begins yet another matter, this time referring us back to M. 2:2B, 2:3C1. ᶜAqiba defines the woman at Lev. 19:20-21 as a bondservant designated to a husband selected by her master. She is not wholly free. Violation of prohibitions against sexual relations in all other cases are punishable by death at the hands of an earthly court or by extirpation, but sexual relations with the handmaiden are punished by stripes. G refers to the difference in the offering that is required. H then explains that the sin-offering may be a female, but the guilt offering is a male. I-J, finally, return us to the first of the two differences specified at F. Accordingly, F is explained by G-J. The rule of K, of course, has been stated by M. 2:3C1, and M. 2:2B, as I said. M. 2:5 continues the exposition inaugurated in the foregoing. M. 2:6 then concludes the construction with three rules in reasonably good balance.

C. *Five bring a sliding-scale-offering* [M. Ker. 2:3A].

D. There are among them poor and rich, there are among them the poorest of the poor.

E. A *meṣora*[c] and one who has given birth [M. Ker. 2:4E4-5] are poor and rich, bringing one for one [infringement].

F. One who contaminates the sanctuary [M. Ker. 2:4E3] is the poorest of the poor, bringing two offerings for one [infringement].

G. On this basis you reckon the tenth of the *ephah* as that which is worth a *peruṭah*.

T. 1:13 [concluded] Z p. 562, ls. 3-5

A. "A *meṣora*[c] who was afflicted with a *nega*[c], then again afflicted with a *nega*[c], then again afflicted with a *nega*[c] brings a single offering for the whole sequence [M. Ker. 2:3C4].

B. "[If] he brought his bird-offering and was afflicted by a *nega*[c] he brings an offering for each and every affliction," the words of R. Eliezer.

D. And sages say, "A single offering for the whole sequence until he brings his guilt-offering [M. Ker. 2:3E].

E. "[If] he brought his guilt-offering and was afflicted by a *nega*[c], brought his guilt-offering [once more] and was afflicted by a *nega*[c], he brings a single offering for each and every affliction."

F. R. Simeon says, "He brings a single offering for the whole sequence, until he completes the offering of his sin-offering [M. Kel. 2:3D." [3]

G. A Nazirite who was made unclean and again was made unclean brings a single offering for the whole [M. Ker. 2:3C2].

H. "[If] he was made unclean on his seventh day and again made unclean on his seventh day, he brings a single offering for each and every time he was made unclean," the words of Rabbi [T. Naz. 4:8: Eliezer].

I. And sages say, "A single offering for the whole sequence, until he will bring his guilt-offering.

J. "[If] he brought his guilt-offering and was made unclean, he brings an offering for each and every one."

K. R. Simeon says, "He brings a single offering for all, until he will bring his sin-offering.

L. "If he brought his sin-offering and was made unclean, and [again] brought his sin-offering and was made unclean, he brings an offering for each and every one" [following *TR* II, pp. 293-294].

T. 1:14 Z p. 562, ls. 5-11 [A-F = T. Neg. 9:7]

A. *A woman who suffered many miscarriages—*

B. *she aborted a female during the eighty days of purifying and went and aborted a female during the eighty days of purifying [or]*

---

[3] "The parallel at T. Neg. 9:7 adds here: 'If he brought his sin-offering and was afflicted by a *nega*[c], he brings a single offering for each and every affliction.' "—R.S.S.

she bore a multiple of abortions ["twins"] [M. Ker. 2:4A-B]—

C. "brings a single offering for the whole sequence," the words of R. Meir.

D. R. Judah says, "*She brings an offering for the first and she does not bring an offering for the second. She brings an offering for the third, and she does not bring an offering for the fourth*" [M. Ker. 2:4C].

T. 1:15 Z p. 562, ls. 11-13

A. These are the points of difference between the betrothed bondwoman and all other forbidden sexual relationships.

B. All other forbidden sexual relationships which are stated in the Torah—lo, these [others] are liable, *in the case of deliberate transgressions, to extirpation, and in the case of inadvertent transgression, to a sin-offering, and in a case of uncertain transgression, to a suspensive guilt-offering* [M. 1:2], which is not the case for the one who has intercourse with a betrothed handmaiden [M. Ker. 2:4M, 2:6D].

C. All [other] forbidden sexual relationships in the Torah treat the one who does the act under constraint as equivalent to the one who does it willingly, *the one who does it inadvertently as equivalent to the one who does it intentionally* [M. Ker. 2:4M [4]], *the one who begins the act [only] as equivalent to the one who completes it* [M. Ker. 2:4K], the one who is sleeping as equivalent to the one who is awake [M. Ker. 2:6C], the one who does it in the normal way as equivalent to the one who does it not in the normal way, [and] imposes a liability for each and every act of sexual intercourse [M. Ker. 2:3C1]—

D. which is not the case with the betrothed handmaiden.

E. In the case of all other forbidden sexual relationships [the law] has treated a minor as equivalent to an adult, to impose the liability solely on the adult [M. Ker. 2:6B].

F. But in the case of a handmaiden, if he [the male who had sexual relations] was a minor, lo, these are exempt from liability.

G. In the case of all other forbidden sexual relationships both of the participants receive stripes.

H. But in the case of a handmaiden, she receives stripes but he does not receive stripes.

I. In the case of all other forbidden sexual relationships both parties bring an offering.

J. But in the case of a handmaiden, he brings, but she does not bring [an offering] [M. Ker. 2:4I-J].

L. *In the case of all other forbidden sexual relationships the penalty is a sin-offering.*

M. *But in the case of a handmaiden, the penalty is a guilt-offering.*

N. *In the case of all other forbidden sexual relationships, one brings a female [sin-offering].*

---

[4] "The wording of T. 1:16C is not the same as that of M. 2:4M. T. rather conflicts with M. 2:6D and C."—R.S.S.

O. *But in the case of a handmaiden, one brings a male [guilt-offering]* [M. Ker. 2:4G-H].

P. In the case of all other forbidden sexual relationships, one is liable for each and every act of sexual intercourse.

Q. But in the case of a handmaiden, one brings a single offering for many acts of sexual intercourse [M. Ker. 2:3C1].

R. In the case of all other forbidden sexual relationships which are stated in the Torah, a court is liable to give instruction in their regard, which is not the case for the betrothed handmaiden.

S. In the case of all other forbidden sexual relationships an anointed priest who gave instruction but did the deed is liable.

T. In the case of the handmaiden, if he did the deed even though he did not give instruction, he brings a guilt-offering on account of a confirmed case.

T. 1:16 Z p. 562, ls. 14-24

A. R. Ishmael says, "Scripture speaks of a Canaanite handmaiden, married to a Canaanite manservant."

B. Others say in his name, "This is one who is married to a free man."

C. R. cAqiba says, "By the Torah-law, it is one who is half a handmaiden and half a free woman, married to a free man [M. Ker. 2:5A-C]."

D. R. Eleazar b. cAzariah said, "She is half a bondwoman and half free" [M. Ker. 2:5E].

T. 1:17 Z p. 562, ls. 24-26

A. He who has sexual relations with any one of all those who are prohibited by the Torah—

he in a single spell of inadvertence but she in five spells of inadvertence—

B. he brings a single sin-offering.

C. And she brings five sin-offerings.

D. [If] she does so in a single spell of inadvertence but he does so in five spells of inadvertence,

E. she brings one sin-offering and he brings five sin-offerings.

F. *In respect to all prohibited relationships, [if] one is an adult and one is a minor, the minor is exempt.*

G. *[If] one is awake and one is asleep, the one asleep is exempt.*

H. *[If] one does it inadvertently and one does it intentionally, the one who does it inadvertently is liable to bring a sin-offering, and the one who does it intentionally is subject to extirpation* [M. 2:6].

T. 1:18 Z p. 562, ls. 26-30

A. There are five guilt-offerings: (1) a guilt-offering for theft, (2) a guilt-offering for sacrilege, (3) a guilt-offering brought for having sexual relations with a betrothed handmaiden, (4) a guilt-

offering of a Nazirite, and (5) a guilt-offering of a *meṣora*ᶜ.
B. R. Eliezer says, "A suspensive guilt-offering."

T. 1:19 Z p. 562, ls. 30-32

T. 1:13 comments on M. 2:4E, and T. 1:14 takes up M. 2:3C4, D-E and augments that matter in a clear way. T. 1:15 cites M. and assigns Meir the now-spelled-out opinion of M. 2:4A-B; here T. represents a considerable improvement and clarification of M. T. 1:16 elaborately restates M.'s propositions, [5] in a formally much improved construction. T. 1:17 restates M. 2:5, allowing for a definition of Ishmael's position. T. 1:18 cites M. 2:6. T. 1:19 is autonomous of M., but runs parallel to M. 2:3A.

---

[5] "The items noted at T. 1:16C state the opposite of M.'s rulings."—R.S.S.

CHAPTER FOUR

KERITOT CHAPTER THREE

The chapter before us focuses upon those liable for a sin-offering for deliberate transgression. These are of two different sorts, described at, respectively, M. 3:1 + 2-3, and M. 3:4-10. In the first set, M. 3:1 + 2-3, we deal with diverse situations in which a man is accused of having eaten forbidden fat and therefore of owing a sin-offering. At M. 3:1, we have two valid witnesses and no contrary claim, then a triplet, first with conflicting testimony, in which case the man brings a suspensive guilt-offering, second, with the man denying what a single witness accuses him of doing, in which case he owes nothing, and finally, a dispute, in which, with two witnesses accusing the man, who denies their testinomy, Meir says the man is liable; sages (= in T.: Judah) declare him exempt. At M. 3:2-3, we consider several acts of transgression in a single spell of inadvertence, in which case the man owes a single sin-offering. In the second, rather arid, set, at M. 3:4-6, by contrast, we show how, by a single act of sexual relations, a man may owe from six to eight sin-offerings, depending on the status of the woman. In the final construction, M. 3:7-9-10, this same sort of issue—whether a person owes one or many sin-offerings for many actions of a single type—is set up now in a more interesting construction, involving ᶜAqiba's questions to Gamaliel and Joshua (3:6-9, a triplet), then Eliezer (3:10). The chapter is reasonably coherent in these two contrasting issues. Its principal formal units, M. 3:4-6, 7-9, present triplets, but I do not think that accounts for the joining of the materials, which in theme have much to say to one another and address a common problem.

3:1

A. [If] they said to him, "You have eaten forbidden fat," he brings a sin-offering.

I B. [If] a witness says, "He ate," and a witness says, "He did not eat"—

C. [or if] a woman says, "He ate," and a woman says, "He did not eat,"

D. he brings a suspensive guilt-offering.

II E. [If] a witness says, "He ate," and he says, "I did not eat"—

F. he is exempt [from bringing an offering].

III G. [If] two say, "He ate," and he says, "I did not eat"—

H. R. Meir declares liable.

I. Said R. Meir, "If two bring upon him the death-penalty which is strict, will they not bring upon him the obligation to an offering, which is lenient?"

J. They said to him, "What if he should choose to say, 'I did it deliberately' [in which case he is exempt from a sin-offering, and the witnesses cannot contradict him]?"

M. 3:1

A is obvious and sets forth a tripartite group, of which the third presents a slightly faulty debate, lacking, after H, *And sages exempt.* This hardly matters, since the consequent debate, I-J, leaves the silent sages the last word, and there can be no doubt as to their position. The issue is liability for a sin-offering as against liability for a suspensive guilt-offering. The former is incurred when one is certain that he has committed a sin, the latter when he is not certain, as at B-D. At E-F there is no uncontested testimony. At G there is, but the man himself denies the testimony of the two witnesses. Meir regards the testimony of two witnesses as paramount, for the reason he gives at I. But the answer of sages, J, is that the cases are hardly the same, because the man could absolve himself from the requirement of a sin-offering by the claim that he did the deed deliberately, in which case, if he instead claims that he did nothing, he also is to be believed.

A. [If] one witnesses says, "He ate forbidden fat," and one witness says, "He ate permitted fat,"

B. [or if] one witness says, "He ate forbidden fat," and a woman says, "He ate permitted fat,"

C. [or if] one woman says, "He ate forbidden fat," and one woman says, "He ate permitted fat,"

D. he brings a suspensive guilt offering [M. Ker. 3:1A-D].

E. [If] one witness says to him, "You ate forbidden fat," and he says, "I ate permitted fat," he is exempt [M. Ker. 3:1E-F].

F. "[If] two say to him, 'You ate forbidden fat,' and he says, 'I ate permitted fat,' they were believed," the words of R. Meir [M. Ker. 3:1G-H].

G. Said to him R. Judah, "How can you say to him, 'Arise and confess,' while he is saying, 'With all my bones I did not sin'? What if he wants to say, 'I did it deliberately,' is he not believed [M. Ker. 3:1J]?"

H. Said R. Simeon, "Under what circumstances? It is when he confessed to that effect at the outset. But if one said to him, 'You ate forbidden fat,' and he says, 'I ate permitted fat,' [but] when they were about to bring contrary evidence against him, he reverted to claim, 'I did it deliberately,' he is not believed."

T. 2:1 Z p. 563, ls. 11-17

T. goes over M.'s materials, as indicated. What is interesting is Simeon's qualification of Judah's position, which effectively leaves matters as Meir wants them.

3:2-3

A. [If] he ate [forbidden] fat and [again ate] fat in a single spell of inadvertence, he is liable only for a single sin-offering.

B. [If] he ate forbidden fat and blood and remnant and refuse [of an offering] in a single spell of inadvertence, he is liable for each and every one of them.

C. This rule is more strict in the case of many kinds [of forbidden food] than of one kind.

D. And more strict is the rule in [the case of] one kind than in many kinds:

E. For if he ate a half olive's bulk and went and ate a half olive's bulk of a single kind, he is liable.

F. [But if he ate two half olive's bulks] of two [different] kinds, he is exempt.

M. 3:2

A. And how much should he who eats them tarry? [Danby: "Within what time must he eat them?"]

B. "As if he ate them as parched corn," the words of R. Meir. [Danby: "(The time that he would need) if he ate a like bulk of parched grains of corn."]

C. And sages say, "[He is not liable] unless he tarries from beginning to end for sufficient time to eat a half-loaf [of bread]."

D. [If] one ate unclean foods [or] drank unclean liquids,

E. drank a quarter-*log* of wine,

F. and entered the sanctuary and tarried there,

G. [the measure of time between entering the Temple having eaten unclean food or drunk wine is] sufficient time to eat a half-loaf [of bread].

H. R. Eleazar says, "If he interrupted it [the act of drinking],

I. "or put into it [the wine] any amount of water,

J. "he is exempt."

M. 3:3

M. 3:2A is matched against B, then C-F comment on the foregoing, also a nicely balanced construction. M. 3:3A-C gloss M. 3:2E, and D-J carry forward the interests of M. 3:3A-C. The contrast between M. 3:2A and B is clear as given. If one repeatedly ate a forbidden food in requisite volume to be liable, that is, an olive's bulk, but these repeated acts of eating were in a single act of inadvertence, in that at no time did the man know he was eating something prohibited, he is liable only for a single sin-offering. But if he ate a number of different forbidden substances in a single spell of inadvertence, B, he is liable for having eaten each one. The point of E-F is that if one ate, in a short period of time (M. 3:3) several distinct quantities of one kind of forbidden food, none of them of requisite volume, he is liable. But if they were of different kinds (as at B), he is exempt. M. 3:3A-C are clear as stated. D-E + F then ask about how long one must stay in the sanctuary to be liable for being unclean therein, D, or being drunk therein, E. G invokes the measure of sages, C. H is then a gloss of E; if one did not gulp the wine or if one diluted it, G is unnecessary.

A. A drunkard invalidates the sacred service, and [if he carries out an act of service in the cult], he is liable to the death penalty.

B. What is a drunkard? Any who has drunk a quarter-*log* of wine forty days old or older than that.

C. [If] he drank [fresh wine] from his press more than a quarter-*log* of wine, he is exempt.

D. [If] he drank less than a quarter-*log* of wine four or five years old, he is liable.

E. Whether he mixed it and drank it in little sips he is liable.

F. R. Eliezer says, "If he drank it in one gulp, he is liable. If he mixed it and drank it, or drank it in little sips, he is exempt" [M. Ker. 3:3H].

G. R. Judah says, "[Those who transgress against the prohibition of drinking] wine [and serving in the cult are subject] to the death-penalty. [But those who transgress against the prohibition of drinking] fermented beverages are subject to warning.

H. "Therefore if he ate a fig from Ke^cilah or drank milk and honey, lo, this one is smitten with forty stripes and transgresses a negative commandment."

I. And just as, if he was a priest, he is invalid for the cult and liable to the death-penalty, so if he was a sage or a disciple of a sage, [1] he is prohibited from teaching or from giving instruction.

J. R. Yosé bar Judah says, "If he was a sage, he is permitted to teach."

T. 1:20 Z p. 562, ls. 32-37, p. 563, ls. 1-2

A. All the same are he who eats [a forbidden food in solid state] and he who dissolves [forbidden food into a liquid] and drinks [it] and he who anoints [himself with it]—

B. if he ate and went and ate again and went and ate again—

[1] "Note here, as in other passages in M.-T., the explicit comparison of priests and rabbis as authority figures."—R.S.S.

C. if there is from the beginning of the first act of eating to the end of the last act of eating sufficient time for the eating for a half-loaf of bread, the several acts of eating join together.

C. And if not, they do not join together [M. Ker. 3:3C].

D. [If] he drank and went and drank again and went and drank again, if there is from the beginning of the first act of drinking to the end of the last act of drinking sufficient time for the drinking of a quarter-*log*, the several acts of drinking join together [to form the requisite volume to render him unclean or culpable].

E. And if not, they do not join together.

T. 2:2 Z p. 563, ls. 17-21
[T. Ter. 7:3, Pes. 1:12, Yoma 5 (4):3]

A. Just as eating involves the requisite volume of an egg's bulk, so drinking involves the requisite volume of an egg's bulk.

B. But eating and drinking do not join together.

C. He who eats an olive's bulk even of five different kinds, lo, these join together.

D. [If] he ate a half-olive's bulk and he was informed [of what he had done], and he went and ate another half olive's bulk of a different kind [of forbidden produce], these do not join together [to form the requisite bulk to impose on him liability].

T. 2:3 Z p. 563, ls. 21-23

T. 1:20 is relevant in a tenuous way to M. 3:3E-F. [2] What T. 2:2 contributes to M. is A, that the same measure applies to the several actions listed by A, a view which, of course, sages will approve, M. 3:3C. Any sort of consumption of prohibited food, in whatever way it is misused (A) must be done in the requisite time. Then T. 2:3 defines the requisite volume that a person must eat to be liable, e.g., to be made unclean by unclean food, a matter of which M. knows nothing. T. 2:3D tells us the opposite of the rule of M. 3:2A about a single spell of inadvertence. Now M. has insufficient volume not joined in a single spell of inadvertence. [3] The rule is obvious.

3:4-6

A. There is he who carries out a single act of eating and is liable on its account for four sin-offerings and one guilt-offering:

B. An unclean [lay-] person who ate (1) forbidden fat, and it was (2) remnant (3) of Holy Things, and (4) it was on the Day of Atonement.

---

[2] "T. 1:20 is directly relevant to M. 3:3H-J."—R.S.S.

[3] "T. 2:3D deals not with M. 3:2A, the single spell of inadvertence, but 3:2F, the issue of joining. The consequence is whether or not the man is liable to bring an offering at all, not how many offerings he must bring."—R.S.S.

C. R. Meir says, "If it was the Sabbath and he took it out [from one domain to another] in his mouth, he is liable [for another sin-offering]."

D. They said to him, "That is not of the same sort [of transgression of which we have spoken heretofore since it is not caused by eating (A)]."

M. 3:4

A. There is he who carries out a single act of sexual intercourse and becomes liable on its account for six sin-offerings:

B. He who has intercourse with his daughter is liable on her account because of violating the prohibition against having intercourse with (1) his daughter, and (2) his sister, and (3) his brother's wife, and (4) his brother's father's wife, and (5) a married woman, and (6) a menstruating woman.

C. And who has intercourse with his daughter's daughter is liable on her account because of violating the prohibition against having intercourse with (1) his daughter's daughter, and (2) his daughter-in-law, and (3) his wife's sister, and (4) his brother's wife, and (5) his brother's father's wife, and (6) a married woman, and (7) a menstruating woman.

D. R. Yosé says, "If the grandfather transgressed and married her, he is liable on her account because of the prohibition of having sexual relations with his father's wife."

E. And so he who has sexual relations with his wife's daughter or with the daughter of the daughter of his wife.

M. 3:5

A. He who has sexual relations with his mother-in-law is liable on her account because of the prohibition against having sexual relations with (1) his mother-in-law, and (2) his daughter-in-law, and (3) his wife's sister, and (4) his brother's wife, and (5) his father's brother's wife, and (6) a married woman and (7) a menstruating woman.

B. And so is the case for him who has sexual relations with the mother of his mother-in-law and with the mother of his father-in-law.

C. R. Yoḥanan b. Nuri says, "He who has sexual relations with his mother-in-law is liable on her account because of the prohibition against having sexual relations with (1) his mother-in-law, and (2) the mother of his mother-in-law, and (3) the mother of his father-in-law."

D. They said to him, "All three in fact fall into a single prohibition."

M. 3:6

Meir and sages, M. 3:4C-D, gloss A-B. Having specified the circumstances in which a person owes a single sin-offering for multiple law-violations, we now spell out those in which he owes many sin-offerings for a single action. The sin-offerings are (1) on account of eating Holy Things in a state of uncleanness, (2) because of eating forbidden fat, (3) because of eating that which is left over beyond its proper time (remnant), and (4) because of eating on the Day of Atonement. The guilt-offering is because of a layman's eating Holy Things, thereby commtting sacrilege. Meir wants to add a violation of the Sabbath, but sages say that the sin-offering which he owes because of removing something from one domain to the other on the Sabbath is not the same as the one owed on account of improper eating. Meir would then give us five, a bridge to the next, six, then seven, sin-offerings.

M. 3:5-6 form a tight unit. M. 3:5B has a man have intercourse with his mother, producing a daughter (1), who also is his sister (2); she has married his brother (from the same mother but a different father) (3), who died, at which point she married his brother's father (4); she, of course, is married, and, it happens, is in her menstrual period. At C we have seven sin-offerings. The granddaughter (1) is married (6) and menstruating (7). She had previously married one of the man's sons (2) then his brother (4), then, the brother of his father (5). *He* was married to his granddaughter's half-sister (3)—another daughter of his granddaughter's husband from another wife. M. 3:6A has the mother-in law (1), a married woman (6) and menstruating (7). She had previously married his son (2), and, when the son died, his brother (4), then his father's brother (5). The man for his part was married to his mother-in-law's sister (3)—again seven. M. 3:6B does not even bother to construct the two cases. Yoḥanan b. Nuri adds to A the notion that the man had been married to his mother-in-law's daughter's daughter and her son's daughter, so she is his mother-in-law's mother and his father-in-law's mother. Sages hold that these are of the same class and subject to a single prohibition, Lev. 18:17, in which case no separate offering is required for each offense.

A. He who has sexual relations with his mother is liable on two counts.

B. He who has sexual relations with his father's sister is liable on two counts.

C. Said R. Yohanan b. Nuri, "He is subject to nine more counts on their account.

D. "How so?

E. "[If] he married a woman, and went and married (1) her sister's daughter, and went and married (2) his sister's daughter and went and had sexual relations (3) with the grandmother, he is liable for transgressing the prohibition against having relations for (4) that count, and (5) on account of his daughter-in-law, and (6) his brother's wife, and (7) his brother's father's wife, and (8) a married woman, and (9) a menstruating woman."

F. Others said to him, "They misled you. They did not say, 'His mother-in-law and the mother of his mother-in-law and the mother of his father-in-law' in the present connection."

T. 1:21 Z p. 563, ls. 2-7

T. expands M. 3:6B, C-D.

3:7-10

A. Said R. ᶜAqiba, "I asked Rabban Gamaliel and R. Joshua in the meat-market of Emmaus, where they had gone to buy a beast for the banquet of Rabban Gamaliel's son:

I B. "He who has sexual relations with his sister, with his father's sister, and with his mother's sister in one spell of inadvertence [M. 1:1E9, 10, 11]—what is the rule?

C. "Is he liable once for all of them, or once for each and every action?

D. "They said to me, 'We have not heard [the rule on that case], but we have heard the rule, He who has sexual relations with his five wives when they are menstruating, in a single spell of inadvertence, that he is liable for each and every act of sexual relations.

E. " 'And we regard the matters [in the former case] as subject to a proof by an argument a *fortiori* [from the latter case].' "

M. 3:7

A. And further did R. ᶜAqiba ask them:

II B. "A limb is dangling from a beast—what is the rule?"

C. They said to him, "We have not heard the rule [for that particular case]. But we have heard the rule concerning a limb which is dangling from a man, that it is deemed clean.

D. "For so did the people afflicted with boils do in Jerusalem:

E. "He goes on the eve of Passover to a physician, and he [the physician] cuts [the boil] until he leaves on it a hair's breath. And he sticks it onto a thorn. And he [the patient] pulls away from it.

F. "And this one would prepare his Passover. And the physician likewise would prepare his Passover.

G. "And we regard the matters as subject to a proof by an argument *a fortiori*,"

[Cashdan, p. 117, n. 2: "Since the limb is considered clean in the case of a man who is susceptible to uncleanness even while still alive, then surely it is so in the case of an animal, which is not subject to uncleanness while alive."]

M. 3:8

A. And further did R. ᶜAqiba ask them:

III B. "He who slaughters five animal-sacrifices outside [the Temple courtyard] in a single spell of inadvertence, what is the law?

C. "Is he liable for one [single] offering for all of them, or for one [offering] for each and every act of slaughter?"

D. They said to him, "We have not heard."

E. Said R. Joshua, "I heard [the rule which applies] in the case of him who eats from a single animal-sacrifice in five dishes, that he is liable on account of each and every act for violation of the laws of sacrilege.

F. "And I regard the matters as subject to proof by an argument *a fortiori*."

G. Said R. Simeon, "Not in this way did R. ᶜAqiba interrogate them but in the case of:

H. "One who eats remnant from five animal sacrifices in a single act of inadvertence—what is the law?

I. "Is he liable for a single offering for all of them, or is he liable for an offering for each and every one?

J. "They said to him, 'We have not heard.'

K. "Said R. Joshua, 'I heard that in the case of:

L. " 'One who eats from a single animal-sacrifice in five dishes in a single act of inadvertence, that he is liable to bring an offering for each and every one on account of violation of the laws of sacrilege.

M. " 'And I regard the matters as subject to proof by an argument *a fortiori*.'

[B. Ker. 15b: "If when one eats five different dishes from one sacrifice, where there are not distinct bodies, he is liable for each dish because there were separate dishes, how much more would one be liable for each act of eating in the case of five sacrifices, where there are distinct bodies."]

N. "Said R. ᶜAqiba, 'If it is law, we shall accept it. But if it is for purposes of argument, there is an answer.'

O. "He said to him, 'Answer.'

P. "He said to him, 'No. If you have so stated in the case of the laws of sacrilege, in which instance the one who gives something to someone else to eat is equivalent to the one who eats, and the one who causes another to enjoy benefit is equivalent to the one who derives benefit himself, joining together a quantity sufficient to be subject to the laws of sacrilege over a long period of time,

Q. " 'will you say so in the case of remnant, to which none of all of these things apply?' "

M. 3:9

A. Said R. ᶜAqiba, "I asked R. Eliezer, 'He who performs many acts of prohibited labor on many Sabbaths but of a single sort of prohibited labor in a single spell of inadvertence—what is the law?

B. " 'Is he liable for a single offering for all of them, or is he liable for an offering for each and every one?'

C. "He said to me, 'He is liable for an offering for each and every such action, on the basis of an argument *a fortiori*:

D. " 'Now if in the case of a menstruating woman, who does not yield many sorts of subdivisions of transgression or many sorts of sin-offerings, one is liable for each and every act of sexual relations,

E. " 'the Sabbath, which yields many sorts of subdivisions of transgression [different types of labor] and many sorts of sin-offerings on their account—is it not logical that he should be liaible for each and every act of labor?'

F. "I said to him, 'No. If you have so stated in the case of having sexual relations with a menstruating woman, who is subject to two distinct warnings—

G. " 'for the man is subject to warning against having sexual relations with a menstruating woman, and a menstruating woman is subject to warning against having sexual relations with the man—

H. " 'will you say the same for the Sabbath, to which applies only a single warning?'

I. "He said to me, 'He who has sexual relations with minors [who are menstruating] will prove the matter. For to them applies only a single warning [that applicable to him, since they are exempt]. Yet he is liable for each and every act of sexual relations.'

J. "I said to him, 'No. If you have so stated in connection with him who has sexual relations with [menstruating] minors, in which instance, even though there is no warning applicable to them now, there will be such a warning applicable to them in due course,

K. " 'will you so rule in the case of the Sabbath, which is subject to a warning neither now nor in due course?'

L. "He said to me, 'He who has sexual relations with a beast will prove the matter.'

M. "I said to him, 'The beast is subject to the same rule as the Sabbath.' "

M. 3:10

The common formal traits shared by M. 3:7-9 are obvious. We proceed directly to the three diverse laws joined by the characteristic that ᶜAqiba reports what others have taught him (+ M. 3:10, joined to M. 3:9 for self-evident reasons). M. 3:7B, D, are the only aspects of the whole relevant to M. 3:4-6, but M. 3:9-10 are congruent to M. 3:2. The problem of B-C is whether the man owes a single sin-offering, because these are deemed a single category, since the prohibition is on account of *sister*, or whether he owes three sin-offerings. D-E are clear as given. Here is a single category, *menstruating women*, and the man owes five sin-offerings, all the more so when we have three distinct women, each in a distinctive relationship. M. 3:8, the second case, shows that flesh dangling from a human being is deemed clean, all the more so for an animal. Flesh dangling from an animal is not deemed unclean as carrion as if it were wholly detached (M. Hul. 9:7-8). Dangling flesh of a human being is clean, though if it were fully removed, it would impart corpse-uncleanness. M. 3:9 varies the pattern somewhat. ᶜAqiba, M. 3:9B, speaks of slaughtering. Joshua, E, brings evidence from the law of sacrilege—that is, *eating*—which is not relevant to *slaughtering*. Simeon revises the matter, G-H, to introduce the issue of *eating* the remnant of a sacrifice left over beyond its time, which *is* relevant to eating and thereby committing sacrilege. Simeon's version then is fully worked out, K-M. ᶜAqiba then rejects Joshua's reasoning on the grounds that the issues of sacrilege and remnant are quite distinct from one another. Even though they have in common the fact that the transgressions in each instance involved eating, either eating what is holy or eating remnant, the differences are too great to permit an appropriate deduction. M. 3:10 is fully spelled out and for our purposes in this context requires no comment, despite its clear contact with M. 3:2.

A. Said R. Simeon, "And what was the connection between slaughtering and eating?

B. "For has R. ᶜAqiba asked about slaughtering, and do they answer him about eating?

C. "But R. Joshua asked about eating by itself, and they answered him [with an argument reasoning by analogy] from eating to eating.

D. "And [while they were talking about about eating], R. ᶜAqiba asked him about a beast on the Sabbath [M. 3:10M]. [4]

E. "But you got the better of me in the time of logical argument."

T. 1:22 Z p. 563, ls. 7-10

Simeon's criticism, M. 3:9G-H, is now explained.

---

[4] "To D, cf. M. 3:10M. I would guess that D-E somehow are supposed to gloss that lemma."—R.S.S.

CHAPTER FIVE

KERITOT CHAPTER FOUR

We come now to the consideration of the situations in which one brings a suspensive guilt-offering, that is, cases in which one is not certain whether or not he has committed a transgression, or, if he is sure he has committed a transgression, exactly what particular one he has done. The chapter is really one long pericope, though I have divided it into two parts, M. 4:1 and M. 4:2-3, since the opening unit, while continued at M. 4:2, may stand by itself. M. 4:1 presents a triplet of cases in which we are not certain whether a person has committed a sin. He brings a suspensive guilt-offering. At M. 4:2A-F we gloss M. 3:2A, B, by pointing out that, if a person is liable in one circumstance to many sin-offerings, in a parallel case of uncertainty he is liable to many suspensive guilt-offerings. M. 4:2G-V and M. 4:3 revert to the issue of M. 4:1, namely, a situation of doubt. But now the doubt concerns which sin, in particular, a person has committed, e.g., eating forbidden fat as against remnant, having sexual relations with his wife, who is menstruating, as against with his sister, violating the Sabbath as against the Day of Atonement. We know he has committed a sin, on which basis Eliezer imposes the requirement of a sin-offering. But we do not know which particular sin he has committed, on which basis Joshua exempts him from the requirement of a sin-offering. There is a further, Ushan dispute, beautifully spelled out in T., on Joshua's opinion as to a suspensive guilt-offering. The chapter is remarkably cogent.

4:1

A. It is a matter of doubt whether or not one has eaten forbidden fat,

B. And even if he ate it, it is a matter of doubt whether or not it contains the requisite volume—

I C. Forbidden fat and permitted fat are before him,

D. he ate one of them but is not certain which one of them he ate—

II E. his wife and his sister are with him in the house—

F. he inadvertently transgressed with one of them and is not certain with which of them he transgressed—

III G. The Sabbath and an ordinary day—

H. he did an act of labor on one of them and is not certain on which of them he did it—

I. he brings [in all the foregoing circumstances] a suspensive guilt-offering.

M. 4:1

The formal traits of M. 4:1 are of principal interest, because the point, I, is self-evident. [1] The reason A-B are distinguished from C-D, E-F, and G-H, is that the opening statement expresses its second clause with the same language as the first, namely, SPQ...SPQ..., while the triplet uses W'YN YDW^{c}... I see no substantive difference between the two formulations.

4:2-3

A. Just as, *if he ate forbidden fat and [again ate] forbidden fat in a single spell of inadvertence, he is liable for only a single sin-offering* [M. 3:2A],

B. so in connection with a situation of uncertainty involving them, he is liable to bring only a single guilt-offering.

C. If there was a clarification in the meantime,

D. just as he brings a single sin-offering for each and every transgression, so he brings a suspensive guilt-offering for each and every [possible] transgression.

E. Just as, *if he ate forbidden fat, and blood, and remnant, and refuse, in a single spell of inadvertence, he is liable for each and every one* [M. 3:2B],

F. so in connection with a situation of uncertainty involving them, he brings a suspensive guilt-offering for each and every one.

I G. Forbidden fat and remnant are before him—

H. he ate one of them but is not certain which one of them he ate [M. 4:1C-D]—

II I. His wife, who is menstruating, and his sister are with him in the house—

J. he inadvertently transgressed with one of them but is not certain with which one of them he has transgressed [M. 4:1E-F]—

III K. The Sabbath and the Day of Atonement—

L. he did an act of labor at twilight, but is not certain on which one of them he did the act of labor [M. 4:1G-H]—

M. R. Eliezer declares him liable to a sin-offering.

N. And R. Joshua exempts him.

O. Said R. Yosé, "They did not dispute about the case [K-L] of him who performs an act of labor at twilight, that he is exempt.

P. —"For I say, 'Part of the work did he do while it was still this day, and part of it on the next.'

Q. "Concerning what did they dispute?

R. "Concerning one who does work wholly on one of the two days but does not know for certain whether he did it on the Sabbath or whether he did it on the Day of Atonement.

S. "Or concerning him who does an act of labor but is not certain what sort of act of labor he has done—

[1] "Note that the cases, though not the problem, of M. 4:1 are those dealt with in Chapter Three, a nice linkage of chapters."—R.S.S.

T. "R. Eliezer declares liable to a sin-offering.

U. "And R. Joshua exempts him."

V. Said R. Judah, "R. Joshua did declare him exempt even from the requirement to bring a suspensive guilt-offering."

M. 4:2

A. R. Simeon Shezuri and R. Simeon say, "They did not dispute about something which is subject to a single category, that he is liable.

B. "And concerning what did they dispute?

C. "Concerning something which is subject to two distinct categories.

D. "For R. Eliezer declares liable for a sin-offering.

E. "And R. Joshua exempts."

F. Said R. Judah, "Even if he intended to gather figs but gathered grapes, grapes but gathered figs,

G. "black ones but gathered white ones, white ones but gathered black ones—

H. "R. Eliezer declares liable to a sin-offering.

I. "And R. Joshua exempts."

J. Said R. Judah, "I should be surprised if R. Joshua declared him wholly exempt. If so, Why is it said, '*In which he has sinned* (Lev. 4:23)?

K. "To exclude him who was occupied [with some other matter and entirely unintentionally committed a transgression]."

M. 4:3

M. 4:2A-F complete the opening unit, linking the whole to M. 3:2, which is explicitly cited, as indicated in italics. The point is clear. If we have a single spell of inadvertence, then, when we are certain what the man has done, he brings a sin-offering, and when we are not certain, he brings a guilt-offering. Further, if in the intervals the man becomes aware of what he has done, e.g., between eating the first olive's bulk and the second, he becomes aware that he has eaten something which may be forbidden fat, he brings a suspensive guilt-offering, D, for each and every transgression. E-F are clear as given.

M. 4:2G-V, continued by M. 4:3, return us to M. 4:1, which is why I regard M. 4:1-3 as a single extended pericope. We systematically cite the triplet of M. 4:1. But there is this difference: while at M. 4:1 we have a possibility that the man has not sinned at all, when we restate the cases, G, I, and K, we make clear that there is no way that the man has *not* sinned. He does not know for sure which sin he has committed, that is, under what category of transgression his sin-offering is brought. Eliezer declares him liable, since, if it is not for one sin, it is for the other (B. Ker. 19a). Joshua exempts, since, in line with Lev. 4:23, he insists that the man who brings a sin-offering know precisely *why* he must do so, that is, for what specific sin or category of sin.

We then have two restatements of the same version of what is subject to dispute, O-U+V and M. 4:3A-I+J. Yosé corrects the statement of K-L, because, P, there is a possibility that the man did not sin at all, since liability must be for an act of completed labor. R, glossed by S (which contributes nothing), then restates the matter essentially in line with the conception of M. 4:2G-N. Judah differs from Yosé, because, in Yosé's view, while the man does know for sure that he has sinned, he does not know what category of sin he has done. But, in Judah's version of Joshua's view, the suspensive guilt-offering is brought only when a man is not sure that he has sinned at all. Accordingly, *declares exempt* means *of any offering at all.* The final version presents a dispute between the two Simeons and Judah, M. 4:3A-E, F-I. The two Simeons go over the ground of Yosé and M. 4:2G-N. The disputants agree that the man is liable who has done a sin which is in a single category, e.g., inadvertently gathering on the Sabbath, with the uncertainty being whether he has gathered figs or grapes. In such a situation, Joshua concedes the man knows that he has committed the sin of gathering on the Sabbath and must bring a sin-offering. But if he has done something which may fall into two different categories, such as the cases given at M. 4:2G-N, eating either forbidden fat or remnant, which are subject to distinct prohibitions, or having intercourse with his wife who is a menstruant, as against having intercourse with his sister, again subject to two distinctive consideration, then we have the stated dispute. Accordingly, the anonymous authority of M. 4:2G-N, Yosé, and the two Simeons, concur.

It is Judah who differs even on the definition of the dispute. At M. 4:3F-I, he states the difference. Even if the man is sure he has done an action subject to a single category of prohibition, but is not certain as to the details of the action, F-G, we have the stated dispute. Judah's second gloss, J, then explains the situation which, in Judah's conception of Joshua's view, leaves the man wholly exempt from an offering. It is one in which the man in no way intended to do something prohibited. But in the case Judah himself gives at F-G, Judah's Joshua will require a suspensive guilt-offering, in contrast to Judah at M. 4:2V. B. 15a's version (= Maimonides, *Comm.*) assigns J to Simeon, which makes more sense.

It is difficult to divide the pericopae of Tosefta which follow among the several units of Mishnah; that is why I present the whole in a single sequence. In general, T. 2:3-12 seem to me relevant to M. 4:1, and the rest, to M. 4:2-3.

A. [If] it is a matter of doubt whether or not one has sinned, he brings a suspensive guilt-offering [M. Ker. 4:1, 2A-B].

B. [If] he has sinned, but is not certain what particular sin he has committed, he brings a sin-offering.

C. [If] he has sinned and is informed of the character of his sin, but he has forgotten what sin he has committed,

D. lo, this one brings a sin-offering, and it is slaughtered for the sake of whichever [sin he has committed], and it is eaten [M. Ker. 4:2C-D].

E. Then he goes and brings a sin-offering for that sin of which he is informed, and it is slaughtered for the sake of whatever [particular sin he has done], and it [too] is eaten.

T. 2:3A Z p. 563, ls. 23-26

A. He who brings one sin-offering for two distinct sins—

B. it is set out to pasture until it is disfigured, then sold.

C. And the man brings with half of its proceeds one for this sin, and with half of its proceeds one for that sin.

D. Two sin-offerings designated for a single sin—let the man offer whichever one of them he prefers.

E. The second then is put out to pasture until it is blemished, and then it is sold, and its proceeds fall [to the Temple-treasury] as a freewill-offering.

F. Two sin-offerings [brought] for two sins—this one is slaughtered for one of them, and that one is slaughtered for one of them.

T. 2:4 Z p. 563, ls. 27-30

A. Two people whose sin-offerings were mixed up in respect to two sins—it is set out to pasture until it is blemished and then sold.

B. And let him bring with the proceeds of half of it a sin-offering for this one, and with the proceeds of half of it a sin-offering for that one.

C. Two sin-offerings for a single sin—let the man offer which ever one of them he prefers.

D. The second is put out to pasture until it is blemished, then it is sold, and its proceeds fall [to the Temple-treasury] as a freewill-offering.

E. Two sin-offerings for two sins—this one is slaughtered for the sake of one of them, and that one is slaughtered for the sake of one of them. [2]

T. 2:5 T p. 563, ls. 30-34

---

2 "T. 2:5C-E repeat T. 2:4D-F. I suspect a copyists error. Lieberman does not comment."—R.S.S.

A. Two sin-offerings which were mixed together—
B. the sin-offering of an individual and the sin-offering of an individual,
C. [or] the sin-offering of the community and the sin-offering of the community,
D. [or] the sin-offering of an individual and the sin-offering of the community—
E. even if they are two distinct sorts—
F. this one is slaughtered for the sake of one of them, and that one is slaughtered for the sake of one of them.

T. 2:6 Z p. 563, ls. 34-36

A. He who brings his sin-offering and slaughtered it—
B. it is a matter of doubt whether or not its blood was [properly] tossed—
C. he has carried out his obligation.
D. If he was lacking the completion of his atonement,
E. it is a matter of doubt whether or not it has gotten dark [so that the blood might have been tossed by night]—
F. lo, this one brings the sin-offering of fowl as a matter of doubt.

T. 2:7 Z p. 563, ls. 36-38

A. "Two people, one of whom has sinned, and it is not known which one of them [has done so],
B. "bring a sin-offering as partners,
C. "[and] make a condition concerning it [that it belongs to the one of them who indeed has sinned],
D. "and it is eaten," the words of R. Simeon.
E. And R. Yosé declares exempt.
F. R. Yosé agrees that this one brings a suspensive guilt-offering and that one brings a suspensive guilt-offering.
G. And R. Yosé agrees in the case of two, of whom one was lacking in the completion of atonement rites, and it is not known which of them, that they bring a sin-offering in partnership and make a condition concerning it [that it is assigned to whichever of them needs it], and then is eaten.

T. 2:8 Z p. 563, l. 38, p. 564, ls. 1-3

A. [If] one forgot the Torah and committed many transgressions, he is liable to bring a sin-offering for each and every one of them.
B. How so?
C. [If] he knew that there is such a thing as forbidden fat but said, "This is not the sort of forbidden fat for which we have been declared liable"—
D. [if] he knew that there is such a thing as blood but said, "This is not the sort of blood for which we have been declared liable"—
E. he is liable for each and every violation of the law.

T. 2:9 Z p. 564, ls. 3-6

A. He who eats an olive's bulk of forbidden fat, an olive's bulk of refuse, an olive's bulk of remnant, and an olive's bulk of that which is unclean, in one spell of inadvertence,

B. brings a sin-offering [M. Ker. 4:2E].

C. If it is a matter of doubt whether or not he has eaten, he brings a suspensive guilt-offering.

T. 2:10 Z p. 564, ls. 6-7

A. He who has sexual relations with his sister and with the sister of his father and with the sister of his mother and with the sister of his wife and with the sister of his father's brother and with a menstruating woman brings a sin-offering.

B. [If] it is a matter of doubt whether or not he had sexual relations therewith, he brings a suspensive guilt-offering.

T. 2:11 Z p. 564, ls. 7-9

T. opens more or less along the lines of M. 4:1, but the whole by no means serves to complement M.'s discussion. The opening pericope, T. 2:3, simply distinguishes the suspensive guilt-offering from the sin-offering, a point which M. of course shares. T. 2:4-9 present a series of rulings on the sin-offering, essentially autonomous of our chapter of M. The main point is that a sin-offering must be brought for some specific transgression and not for two or more. Here, of course, the disputes of Eliezer and Joshua, M. 4:2-3, make the same point. But M.'s interest, in the definition of what constitutes a distinct sin calling for a single sin-offering, is different from T.'s. T. wants to know what one does with a sin-offering in some ambiguous status. T. 2:4 is clear as stated, and so too, T. 2:5-6. The point throughout is that there is a way of rectifying matters. This brings us to another sort of doubt, T. 2:7-8. T. 2:9 completes the construction, which draws to a close with the repetitious, contrasting constructions of T. 2:10-11, a neat and satisfactory set.

A. His wife and his sister—

B. he had sexual relations with one of them and is not certain with which of them he had sexual relations [M. Ker. 4:1E-F]—

C. his two wives, one of them menstruating and one of them not menstruating—

D. *he had sexual relations with one of them and is not certain with which one of them he had sexual relations* [M. 4:2I-J]—

E. *forbidden fat and remnant are before him*—

F. *he ate one of them and is not certain which one of them he ate* [M. Ker. 4:2G-H]—

G. *the Sabbath and the Day of Atonement*—

H. *he did an act of labor on one of them and is not certain on which of them he did the act of labor* [M. Ker. 4:2K-L]—

I. *R. Eliezer declares him liable to a sin-offering.*

J. *And R. Joshua declares him exempt* [M. Ker. 4:2M-N].

K. R. Eliezer says, "*His sin which he sinned*—a sin, whatever it may be."

L. Said to him R. Joshua, "*If the sin which he has committed is made known to him, he shall bring as his offering* ... (Lev. 4:23)—when his sin is clearly known to him."

T. 2:12 Z p. 564, ls. 9-14

A. Said R. Yosé, "Even though R. Joshua did declare the man exempt from the requirement to bring a sin-offering, he declared him liable for a suspensive guilt-offering" [*vs.* Judah, M. Ker. 4:2V].

B. R. Judah says, "R. Eliezer declares him liable to a sin-offering, and R. Joshua declares him exempt."

C. R. Simeon says, "R. Eliezer declares him liable to a sin-offering, and R. Joshua declares him liable to a suspensive guilt-offering."

D. R. Judah said to him, "And not in this case did R. Joshua declare him liable to a suspensive guilt-offering.

E. "But in a case in which it is a matter of doubt whether or not he has sinned.

F. "But in this case, in which he has most assuredly committed a sin, how can he bring a suspensive guilt-offering?" [M. Ker. 4:2V].

G. Said to him R. Simeon, "It is wholly for such a case that Scripture states, *If any one sins, doing any of the things which the Lord has commanded not to be done, though he does not know it, yet he is guilty and shall bear his iniquity. He shall bring to the priest a ram without blemish out of the flock* (Lev. 5:17-18)."

H. Said R. Judah, "R. Eliezer and R. Joshua did not dispute concerning him who intends to do one act of labor and does another along the same lines.

T. 2:13 Z p. 564, ls. 14-21

A. "How so?

B. "His wife and his sister—

C. "He intended to have sexual relations with this one but had sexual relations with that one—

D. "His two wives, one menstruating, one not menstruating—

E. "he intended to have sexual relations with this one but had sexual relations with that one—

F. "Figs and grapes are before him—

G. "*he intended to gather figs and gathered grapes, to gather grapes and gathered figs*—

H. "*black and he gathered white, white and he gathered black* [M. Ker. 4:3F-I]—

I. "R. Eliezer declares him liable to a sin-offering.

J. "And R. Joshua exempts him."

K. Said R. Judah, "R. Joshua did declare him exempt even from a suspensive guilt-offering."

L. R. Simeon Shezuri and R. Simeon say, "They did not differ concerning a matter which is subject to two distinct prohibitions [*vs.* M. Ker. 4:3A], for R. Eliezer declares him liable for a sin-offering and R. Joshua declares him exempt.

T. 2:14 Z p. 564, ls. 21-26

A. "The Day of Atonement which coincided with the eve of the Sabbath,

B. "he did an act of labor at twilight—

C. "R. Eliezer declares liable to a sin-offering.

D. "And R. Joshua declares him exempt" [M. Ker. 4:2K-L].

E. Said R. Yosé, "I do not accept the opinion of R. Eliezer in this case.

F. "For I say, [If] he wrote two letters, one on the Sabbath and one on the Day of Atonement, he is exempt. For the two days do not join together for the completion of a single act of labor."

G. They said to him, "He who smites with a hammer [thereby finishing an act of construction] will prove the matter."

H. He said to them, "The raising up of the hammer was on the Sabbath, and the bringing down of the hammer was on the Day of Atonement."

I. [If] he did an act of labor at the twilight of the Day of Atonement, whether it was before it or after it, he is exempt from a suspensive guilt-offering.

J. For the entire day effects atonement.

K. [If] he did an act of labor at twilight of the Sabbath, whether before it or after it, lo, this one is liable.

T. 2:15 Z p. 564, ls. 26-32

A. The Day of Atonement which coincides with the Sababth,

B. and he did an act of labor, whether before it or afterward,

C. he is exempt from the requirement of bringing a suspensive guilt-offering.

D. For the entire day effects atonement.

E. [If] he did an act of labor in the middle of the day,

F. R. Ishmael declares him liable for two sin-offerings.

G. And R. ᶜAqiba declares him exempt.

H. For R. Ishmael says, "*It is a Sabbath*, so to impose upon him liability for violation of the Sabbath unto itself, *It is the Day of Atonement*, so as to impose upon him liability for violation of the Day of Atonement unto itself."

T. 2:16 Z p. 564, ls. 33-36

T. 2:12-15 go over M.'s versions of the dispute of Eliezer and Joshua. T. 2:12 simply contributes the conflicting exegesis of Lev. 4:23.

Then the unclear point at the end of M. 4:2V is clarified. We now see that Joshua's opinion on the suspensive guilt-offering also is subject to dispute, now between Judah, whom M. knows, and Yosé, whose view M. does not make explicit on this point. This is a real clarification and improvement of M. T. 2:13H, T. 2:14 then spell out Judah's view of what is at issue, on which M. has touched with insufficient detail. T.'s version of Simeon Shezuri and Simeon is faulty at T. 2:13L, as indicated, and, in point of fact, the continuation, T. 2:15A-D, show that their version is the same as M.'s. Yosé then is given a chance to distinguish his picture from their's and to defend his own. On T. 2:15H, see the extended discusson at *TR* II, pp. 295-296. T. 2:16 is complementary.

CHAPTEI SIX

KERITOT CHAPTER FIVE

Our chapter is in three parts, M. 5:1, which is autonomous but introduces M. 5:2-3 and M. 5:4-8, two units which stand in close relationship with one another, spelling out ᶜAqiba's position on a mooted point. M. 5:1 presents ten items, four kinds of blood which one must not eat, and six kinds, for the eating of which one is not liable. The construction is fairly well balanced, but the apodoses—M. 5:1E, G—are somewhat out of phase. M. 5:2-3 work out ᶜAqiba's view that one is liable for a suspensive guilt-offering in the case of a matter of doubt regarding sacrilege, the certain commission of which requires a guilt-offering. Sages maintain that a suspensive guilt-offering is required only in a case in which, if one surely has inadvertently committed a transgression, he brings a sin-offering (M. 1:2). But if in the case of certainty a sin-offering is not required, then in the case of doubt a suspensive guilt-offering is not brought. The continuation of the unit presents ᶜAqiba's view that in any case the act of restitution is not carried out until it is certain that one actually has committed an act of sacrilege. Then, however, the man brings an unconditional guilt-offering, in addition to the conditional one already brought. Ṭarfon proposes an alternative procedure in the present case, and ᶜAqiba points out that the alternative is not invariably advantageous. M. 5:4-8 present a very elegant construction, in five units, in which two distinct issues are intertwined, first, ᶜAqiba's and sages' disagreement as to the requirement of bringing a suspensive guilt-offering in a case in which, if a sin certainly has been committed, one does *not* bring a sin-offering, and Yosé's and Simeon's disagreement on whether or not two people may bring a single guilt-offering or a single sin-offering. Yosé, consistent with M. 1:4, says that two may not do so [1] The chapter as a whole, even including its opening pericope, is redacted with good sense.

5:1

A. (1) The blood of slaughtering in the case of cattle, wild beast, and fowl,

B. whether [said animals are] unclean or clean,

---

[1] "Unless I misunderstand Yosé's opinion at M. 1:4, it is the opposite of the position he holds here."—R.S.S.

C. (2) the blood [shed in the case of] stabbing, and (3) the blood [shed in the case] of tearing [the windpipe or gullet],

D. and (4) the blood let in blood-letting, by which the life-blood flows out—

E. they are liable on its account.

F. (5) Blood from the spleen, (6) blood from the heart, (7) the blood from the eggs [or testicles], (8) the blood of fish, (9) the blood of locusts, (10) blood which is squeezed out [that is, blood which oozes out of the arteries after the life-blood flows out]—

G. they are not liable on their account.

H. R. Judah declares liable in the case of blood which is squeezed out.

M. 5:1

The formal traits are clear. But despite the presence of ten entries, four, then six, in which DM introduces a stich, E does not balance with G—ᶜLYW *vs.* ᶜLYHN.[2] The lists, A-D F, cannot be deemed autonomous compositions, joined only in the redactional stage. Judah's dispute, H against F10, poses no formal problem. In the case of the items of A-D, if one deliberately consumes blood of the stated sorts, he is liable to extirpation (Lev. 7:26-27, 17:14); if he inadvertently does so, he is liable to a sin-offering. In a matter of doubt, he is liable to a suspensive guilt-offering. In the items listed at F-G, there is no such liability. The difference is that the former sorts of blood are produced in the act of killing the animal; the latter are not. The dispute on F10 then is clear: Do we deem blood squeezed out to be produced by human action in the act of killing the animal, as Judah maintains, or to be natural to the condition of the animal, as F-G hold.

The penalty for deliberately eating the blood is extirpation, so Lev. 17:14. If one does so inadvertently, he brings a sin-offering. For whatever act for which one is punishable by extirpation for deliberate commission, one is punishable by the bringing of a suspensive guilt-offering for inadvertent commission (M. 1:1-2). It follows that our pericope by clear implication serves as a prologue to ᶜAqiba's dispute which follows.

A. He who eats an olive's bulk of blood of a clean beast, wild animal, or fowl brings a sin-offering.

B. [If] it is a matter of doubt whether or not he ate [it], he brings a suspensive guilt-offering.

C. But he is liable only for the blood of slaughtering alone.

T. 2:17 Z p. 564, ls. 36-38

---

2 "The issue of number is totally irrelevant to the issue of balanced stichs in this pericope. I do not in any case regard the difference in number (ᶜLYW *vs.* ᶜLYHN) as significant here. For all practical purposes, E and G are identical."—R.S.S.

A. *The blood [shed in the case] of stabbing, and blood [shed in the case of] tearing [the windpipe or gullet], and blood let in blood-letting, by which the life-blood flows out—they are liable on its account* [M. Ker. 5:1C].

B. *Blood which is squeezed out*—one is subject to warning [M. Ker. 5:1F10].

C. R. Judah says, "One is subject to the penalty of extirpation" [M. Ker. 5:1H].

D. *Blood from the spleen, blood from the heart*, blood from the kidneys, blood from the limbs—lo, these are subject to a negative commandment.

E. Blood of those who go on two feet, *blood of eggs* [testicles], [or] blood of creeping things is prohibited. But they are not liable on their account.

F. *Blood of fish and blood of locusts*, lo, this is permitted.

T. 2:18 Z p. 564, ls. 38-39, p. 565, ls. 12

A. He who mashes forbidden fat and swallowed it,

B. he who coagulates blood and ate it,

C. if it is of the volume of an olive's bulk—he is liable.

D. [If] it was mixed up with others, if it is of the volume of an olive's bulk, lo, this one is liable.

E. [If] it was cooked with others, lo, this is prohibited if it is of sufficient quantity to impart a flavor to the whole mixture.

F. [If] one ate a half olive's bulk and drank a half olive's bulk of a single sort [of prohibited fat or blood], lo, this one is liable.

T. 2:19 Z p. 565, ls. 2-5

T. 2:17 differs from M. 5:1B, insisting that we speak of slaughtering a clean beast. T. 2:18 then restates M.'s dispute on blood which is squeezed out, and, concurring with M. 5:1F, T. proceeds to make its own points on the same matters. T. 2:19 supplements M. 5:1. Changing the condition of the blood does not affect its character, so that it remains subject to the original prohibition.

5:2-3

A. R. ᶜAqiba declares [a person] liable to a suspensive guilt-offering in the case of a matter of doubt regarding acts of sacrilege.

B. And sages declare exempt.

C. And R. ᶜAqiba concedes that he does not effect his act of restitution [Lev. 5:15-16] until [his act of sacrilege] actually is made known to him. And he brings with it an unconditional guilt-offering.

D. Said R. Ṭarfon, "How is it that this one brings two guilt-offerings?

E. "But: Let him bring his restitution [for sacrilege] and its added fifth.

F. "And let him bring a guilt-offering worth two *selas* and state, 'If I beyond doubt committed an act of sacrilege, this is restitution for my sacrilege, and this is my guilt-offering.

G. " 'And if it is subject to doubt, then the coins are a freewill-offering, and the guilt-offering is suspended [conditional].' "

H. For the kind of animal that he brings in the case of certainty, he brings in the case of uncertainty.

M. 5:2

A. Said to him R. ᶜAqiba, "Your opinion is sound in the case of an act of small-scale sacrilege.

B. "Lo, in the case of one who is in doubt about causing an act of sacrilege for a hundred *maneh,* is it not better for him to bring a guilt-offering worth two *selas* and not bring a restitution for sacrilege in a matter of doubt which costs a hundred *maneh*?"

C. Thus R. ᶜAqiba concedes the position of R. Ṭarfon in the case of small-scale sacrilege.

D. A woman [after giving birth] who brought a sin-offering of fowl in a case of doubt [as to the character or viability of the foetus],

E. if before the neck was severed, it became known to her that she had certainly brought forth [a viable foetus]—

F. let her make it into an unconditional offering [for certainty].

G. For the kind of animal that she brings in the case of uncertainty she brings in the case of certainty.

M. 5:3

The pericope, in three parts, is well put together. The first part is the dispute, M. 5:2A-B+C, complete in itself. Then we have a kind of debate, M. 5:2D-H, M. 5:3A-C, with a very long statement assigned to Ṭarfon, and a response for ᶜAqiba, with a clear-cut gloss, M. 5:3C. M. 5:3D-G are attached because they make the same point as M. 5:2H. The matter of doubt at M. 5:2A is whether or not a person has derived benefit from Holy Things. If one has without doubt done so, he brings a guilt-offering for sacrilege and also repays the value of what he has misappropriated and an additional fifth thereof (Lev. 5:15-16). ᶜAqiba's position is that in a matter of doubt he brings a suspensive guilt-offering. Sages' position (M. 1:2) is that one brings a suspensive guilt-offering only in the case in which one may or may not have committed a sin for which, in a situation of certainty that one has inadvertently done the deed, he brings a sin-offering. In the case of sacrilege, however, if one surely has done the deed, he brings a guilt-offering for transgression and not a sin-offering. In a case of doubt, sages maintain, he therefore brings no suspensive guilt-offering.

C then clarifies ᶜAqiba's position, and the clarification is important, for it leads to Ṭarfon's criticism, D. ᶜAqiba goes along with sages' position in that, only when the act of sacrilege is established as having certainly taken place does the man effect the act of restitution. At that point he also brings the requisite guilt-offering as well. Here Ṭarfon's criticism is clear. According to ᶜAqiba the man brings two guilt-offerings, one suspensive, when he is unsure that he has committed an act of sacrilege, and one unconditional, when, later, it is clear that he has. Accordingly, Ṭarfon wishes to revise C, while sharing ᶜAqiba's position *vis à vis* A-B. What the man does in a case of doubt is to bring the restitution, E. And, further, F, he brings a guilt-offering worth two *selas*. He then declares that, if it turns out he certainly has committed the act of sacrilege, the restitution has been made (E) and the guilt-offering brought (F). But if the matter should not be clarified, then the money brought for restitution and for the added fifth is to be deemed a freewill-offering; the guilt-offering is to be a suspensive one (= A). H then explains why the guilt-offering may be either unconditional or suspensive. In both instances it is to be a two-year-old ram. That is why he can declare it to be either the one or the other, as the case requires. ᶜAqiba's reply, M. 5:3A-B, is that this solution—M. 5:2E-G— serves for one who is in doubt as to having committed an act of sacrilege worth a small sum. But if one is unsure about having committed an act of sacrilege worth a very large sum, then ᶜAqiba's position—that the man not make restitution until it is certain that he actually has committed the act of sacrilege—is preferable. (The man cannot make the conditional statement, M. 5:2F-G, unless he also makes restitution, which, in the case of a major act of sacrilege, is quite expensive).

The appended unit, D-G, has a woman who is in doubt as to whether or not she has produced a viable offspring. She brings a sin-offering of fowl; but it is not to be eaten (M. Ker. 1:4). Before the sin-offering is sacrificed, it is discovered that the offspring was viable. She declares the bird to be an unconditional sin-offering; it is to be eaten by the priests. Why? Because whether in a case of doubt or in a case of certainty, the sin-offering consists of a pigeon or turtle-dove (M. 6:5). The relevance to the larger setting then is self-evident.

A. He who brings a suspensive guilt-offering on account of an uncertain act of sacrilege, following the opinion of R. ᶜAqiba [M. Ker. 5:2A], and finds out that he has most certainly sinned—

B. [the animal] is [deemed to be] an unconditional [guilt-offering],

C. *for the kind of animal which he brings in the case of uncertainty he brings in the case of certainty* [M. Ker. 5:2H].

T. 2:20 Z p. 565, ls. 5-6

A. The woman who brought a sin-offering of fowl in a case of doubt as to whether or not she has given birth to a viable offspring and learns that she has indeed *not* given given birth [M. Ker. 5:3D-G],

B. lo, this [bird] is unconsecrated. She should give it to her girl-friend [who requires it].

C. *And the one who* [*discovers*] *that she has certainly given birth—let her make it into an unconditional offering* [M. Ker. 5:3F],

D. *for the sort of animal that she brings in a case of uncertainty she brings in a case of certainty* [M. Ker. 5:3G].

T. 2:21 Z p. 565, ls. 6-8

A. In the case of her, the neck of whose bird is wrung, and who [then] is informed [that she certainly has given birth]—let its [the bird's] blood be drained out.

E. Its blood has effected atonement.

C. It is prohibited as to eating.

D. [If this takes place] after its blood has been drained out,

F. it is prohibited for enjoyment.

G. *For to begin with it is brought on account of doubt. It has effected atonement for its matter of doubt and gone its way* [M. Ker. 6:2K].

T. 2:22 Z p. 565, ls. 9-10

T. 2:20 alludes to ᶜAqiba's view, M. 5:2A, and asks the further question of how we dispose of the suspensive guilt-offering when we find out that the person actually *is* guilty. Its answer simply appeals to M. 5:2H, a fine development of M.'s rule. T. 2:21 then jumps to the end of M.'s pericope. M. has spoken of the woman's discovering that she certainly does owe the sin-offering. She simply treats the conditional one as an unconditional one. T. then asks what if she finds out she has *not* given birth. The bird is deemed unconsecrated, having been set aside erroneously. Then, at T. 2:22, we turn to the case of the woman's finding out that she must offer the sin-offering, that is, M.'s case. How do we dispose of the bird? Its blood is drained out against the altar and effects atonement. The bird cannot be eaten. If this takes place after the blood has already been drained—a new point, augmenting M. 5:3E—then the atonement is effected, but the meat cannot be used. The bird remains in the status of one brought in a case of doubt. B. Ker. 26b presents diverse versions of the reading of T. 2:22:

If she learned after the wringing of the neck that the foetus was viable, then, Rab says, "The blood is sprinkled and drained out, atonement is effected, *and it [the fowl] is permitted to be eaten.*" R. Yoḥanan says, "*It is prohibited to be eaten* as a precautionary measure lest it be said that a sin-offering of fowl in a matter of doubt may be eaten."

Sayings assigned to Tannaim then are cited in support of each authority. The issue for our purposes is immaterial.

5:4-8

I A. A piece of meat of unconsecrated food and a piece of meat of Holy Things—

B. [if] one ate one of them, and it is not known which of them he ate—

C. he is exempt.

D. R. ᶜAqiba declares him liable to a suspensive guilt-offering.

E. [If] he ate the second, he brings an unconditional guilt-offering.

F. [If] one person ate the first and another came and ate the second,

G. "this one brings a suspensive guilt-offering and that one brings a suspensive guilt-offering," the words of R. ᶜAqiba.

H. R. Simeon says, "Both of them bring a single guilt-offering."

I. R. Yosé says, "Two do not bring a single guilt-offering."

M. 5:4

II A. A piece of meat of unconsecrated food and a piece of meat consisting of forbidden fat—

B. [if] one ate one of them, and it is not known which of them he ate—

C. he brings a suspensive guilt-offering.

D. [If] he ate the second, he brings a sin-offering.

E. [If] one person ate the first, and another came along and ate the second,

G. this one brings a suspensive guilt-offering and that one brings a suspensive guilt-offering.

H. R. Simeon says, "Both of them bring a single sin-offering."

I. R. Yosé says, "Two do not bring a single sin-offering."

M. 5:5

III A. A piece of meat consisting of forbidden fat and a piece of meat of Holy Things—

B. [if] one ate one of them, and it is not known which of them he ate—

C. he brings a suspensive guilt-offering.

D. [If] he ate the second, he brings a sin-offering and an unconditional guilt-offering.

E. [If] one person ate the first, and another came along and ate the second,

F. this one brings a suspensive guilt-offering, and that one brings a suspensive guilt-offering.

G. R. Simeon says, "Both of them bring [one] sin-offering and [one] guilt-offering."

H. R. Yosé says, "Two do not bring [one] sin-offering and [one] guilt-offering."

M. 5:6

IV A. A piece of meat consisting of forbidden fat and a piece of meat consisting of forbidden fat of Holy Things—

B. [if] one ate one of them, and it is not known which of them he ate—

C. he brings a sin-offering.

D. R. ᶜAqiba says, "He brings a suspensive guilt-offering."

E. [If] he ate the second, he brings two sin-offerings and an unconditional guilt-offering.

F. If one person ate the first, and another came along and ate the second, this one brings a sin-offering and that one brings a sin-offering.

G. R. ᶜAqiba says, "This one brings a suspensive guilt-offering, and that one brings a suspensive guilt-offering."

H. R. Simeon says, "This [one brings] a sin-offering, and that one, a sin-offering. And both of them bring a single guilt-offering."

I. R. Yosé says, "Two do not bring a single guilt-offering."

M. 5:7

V A. A piece of meat consisting of forbidden fat and a piece of meat consisting of forbidden fat which is remnant—

B. [if] one ate one of them, and it is not known which of them he ate—

C. he brings a sin-offering and a suspensive guilt-offering.

D. [If] he ate the second, he brings three sin-offerings.

E. [If] one person ate the first, and someone else came along and ate the second,

F. this one brings a sin-offering and a suspensive guilt-offering, and that one brings a sin-offering and a suspensive guilt-offering.

G. R. Simeon says, "This one [brings] a sin-offering, and that one a sin-offering, and both of them bring a single sin-offering [in addition]."

H. R. Yosé says, "Any sin-offering which is brought on account of sin—two people do not bring it."

M. 5:8

The shared formal traits of the five-part construction are clear. It is the shift in the definition of the problem, M. 5:4A, 5:5A, 5:6A, 5:7A, and 5:8A, which accounts for the fixed differences in the formal articulation of the several units of the construction. The persistent issues are two, first, ᶜAqiba's view that if, for certainly doing a transgression, one brings a guilt-offering, then, in a situation in which one is not sure that he has done so, he brings a suspensive guilt-offering. Sages insist that in a case of doubt one brings a suspensive guilt-offering only for a trangression for which, if one has certainly done the deed, he brings a sin-offering. This view is important at M. 5:4A-D, which go over the ground of M. 5:2-3 and therefore are a perfect joining-unit, at M. 5:7A-D. The second recurrent issue, utterly distinct from the first, is the dispute of Simeon and Yosé, M. 5:4H-I, 5:5H-I, 5:6G-H, 5:7H-I, and 5:8G-H. Simeon will consistently maintain that two people may bring one offering in partnership, with the condition that it will be deemed an offering for the one who requires it. Yosé, consistent with M. 1:4, holds that conditions of this sort are not valid in the case of offerings brought on account of transgression (M. 5:8H). It now remains only to explain the details of the several units.

The first, M. 5:4A, has a doubt as to unconsecrated food as against Holy Things. Here ᶜAqiba repeats his position of M. 5:2A. There may or may not have been an act of sacrilege. Of special interest are F-I, at which ᶜAqiba's position is restated. But G is independent of H-I, which present a separate and distinct solution to the problem. The penalty for eating forbidden fat, M. 5:5, is a sin-offering. There will, then, be no dispute at A-C and the rest follows. The complication at M. 5:6 likewise will not require ᶜAqiba's intervention. If one eats forbidden fat, he must bring a sin-offering. Here, then, sages will agree that the man brings a suspensive guilt-offering, but (obviously) not because of the possibility that he has committed sacrilege ("meat of Holy Things"). Then, M. 5:6D, if he knows he has eaten both, he brings both kinds of offering. The rest is clear as given. At M. 5:7, whether or not the meat was of Holy Things, it certainly was forbidden fat; the man then must bring a sin-offering if he inadverteatly ate it. ᶜAqiba, consistent with his position, wants the man to bring a suspensive guilt-offering because of the possibility that he has eaten forbidden fat *of Holy Things*. ᶜAqiba then requires the suspensive guilt-offering in addition to the sin-offering (C). At E the man eats both, and so all concur that he owes two sin-offerings, as well as the unconditional guilt-offering. F-G have ᶜAqiba repeat his position at D, and H-I are familiar. The final case, M. 5:8A, speaks of two different transgression for which the penalty is a sin-offering: eating forbidden fat and eating left-over sacrificial meat ("remnant"). Since, C, the man certainly has eaten forbidden fat, he must bring a sin-offering. Since, further, he may have eaten remnant, he also brings a suspensive guilt-offering.

Then, D, he ate both. He brings three sin-offerings, one for each piece of forbidden fat, and the third because the second piece, in addition to being forbidden fat, also was remnant. E-H bring no surprises.

A. A piece of meat of forbidden fat of Holy Things and a piece of meat of unconsecrated food—
B. [if] one ate one of them and does not know which of them he ate,
C. he brings [delete: *a sin-offering and*] a suspensive guilt-offering.
D. And in accord with the opinion of R. ᶜAqiba, he brings two suspensive guilt-offerings.
E. [If] he ate the second, he brings a sin-offering and an unconditional guilt-offering.
F. [If] one person ate the first, and another came along and ate the second,
G. here indeed is the rule in accord with the opinion of R. Simeon. Here indeed is the rule in accord with the opinion of R. Yosé [M. Ker. 5:4-8].

T. 3:1 Z p. 565, ls. 11-14

A. *A piece of meat of Holy Things and a piece of meat of unconsecrated food* [M. Ker. 5:4A]—
B. [If] one ate the first and then went and ate the second, [all] in a single spell of inadvertence,
C. he brings a sin-offering and an unconditional guilt-offering.
D. [If he ate them] in two spells of inadvertence,
E. he brings two sin-offerings and one unconditional guilt-offering.

T. 3:2 Z p. 565, ls. 14-16

A. A piece of meat [of forbidden fat] of refuse and a piece of meat of unconsecrated food—
B. [if] one ate one of them and does not know which of them he ate,
C. he brings a suspensive guilt-offering.
D. [If] he ate the second, he brings a sin-offering and a guilt-offering.
E. [If] he ate the first, and another came along and ate the second,
F. "Let them bring a sin-offering in partnership. Let them make a condition concerning it [that it belongs to the one who requires it], and it is to be eaten," the words of R. Simeon.
G. And R. Yosé declares exempt [M. Ker. 5:4F, H-I].
H. R. Yosé concedes [however] that this one brings a suspensive guilt-offering and that one brings a suspensive guilt-offering.

T. 3:3 Z p. 565, ls. 16-20

A. A piece of meat of forbidden fat which is refuse and a piece of meat [of forbidden fat which is] of unconsecrated food—

B. [if] one ate one of them and does not know which of them he ate,

C. he brings two suspensive guilt-offerings.

D. [If] he ate the second, he brings two sin-offerings.

E. [If] one person ate the first, and another came along and ate the second—

F. here indeed is the rule in accord with the opinion of R. Simeon. Here indeed is the rule in accord with the opinion of R. Yosé.

T. 3:4 Z p. 565, ls. 20-23

A. A piece of meat of forbidden fat which is refuse and a piece of meat which is remnant—

B. [if] one ate one of them and does not know which of them he ate,

C. he brings two suspensive guilt-offerings.

D. R. Eliezer says, "He brings a sin-offering and a suspensive guilt-offering."

E. [If] he ate the second, he brings three sin-offerings.

F. [If] one ate the first, and another came along and ate the second—

H. here indeed is the rule in accord with the opinion of R. Simeon. Here indeed is the rule in accord with the opinion of R. Yosé.

T. 3:5 Z p. 565, ls. 23-26

A. A piece of meat of refuse and a piece of meat of remnant—

B. [if] one ate one of them and does not know which of them he ate—

C. R. Eliezer declares him liable to a sin-offering.

D. And R. Joshua declares him exempt.

E. [If] he ate the second, he brings two sin-offerings.

T. 3:6 Z p. 565, ls. 26-28

A. A piece of forbidden fat which is refuse and a piece of forbidden fat which is remnant—

B. [if] one ate one of them and does not know which of them he ate—

C. he brings a sin-offering and a suspensive guilt-offering.

D. And in accord with the opinion of R. Eliezer, he brings two sin-offerings.

E. [If] he ate the second in a single spell of inadvertence, he brings two sin-offerings and an unconditional guilt-offering.

F. [If he did so] in two spells of inadvertence, he brings three sin-offerings and an unconditional guilt-offering.

T. 3:7 Z p. 565, ls. 28-31

A. A piece of forbidden fat which is refuse of Holy Things and a piece of remnant—

B. [if] one ate one of them and does not know which of them he ate,

C. he brings a sin-offering and a suspensive guilt-offering.
D. And in accord with the opinion of R. ᶜAqiba he brings a sin-offering and two suspensive guilt-offerings.
E. And in accord with the opinion of R. Eliezer he brings three sin-offerings.
F. [If] he ate the second in a single spell of inadvertence, he brings three sin-offerings and an unconditional guilt-offering.
G. [If he did so] in two spells of inadvertence, he brings four sin-offerings and an unconditional guilt-offering.

T. 3:8 Z p. 565, ls. 32-35

A. He who eats five pieces of meat from a single animal sacrifice in five dishes in a single spell of inadvertence brings only a single sin-offering.
B. And in a matter of doubt concerning them he brings only a single suspensive guilt-offering.
C. [But if he does so] in five spells of inadvertence, he brings five sin-offerings.
D. And in a matter of doubt concerning them he brings five suspensive guilt-offerings.
E. R. Yosé bar Judah says, and R. Eliezer bar Simeon says, "Even if he ate five pieces [of meat] of five animal-sacrifices in a single spell of inadvertence, he brings only a single sin-offering.
F. "And in a matter of doubt concerning them, he brings only one suspensive guilt-offering."
G. This is the general principle: Whoever brings a sin-offering for a matter of certainty brings a suspensive guilt-offering for a matter of uncertainty. And whoever does not bring a sin-offering for a matter of certainty does not bring a guilt-offering for a matter of uncertainty.
H. But if he ate five pieces of meat from a single animal-sacrifice before the sprinkling of the blood, even in a single spell of inadvertence, he brings a sin-offering for each and every piece [which he ate].

T. 4:1 Z p. 565, ls. 36-39, p. 566, ls. 1-4

T. richly augments M. by supplying further cases in illustration of M.'s basic points. Its complete dependence upon M. hardly requires demonstration. T. 3:1 speaks of forbidden fat of Holy Things and permitted meat. Augmented are M. 5:4A-D, for he who eats Holy Things owes a guilt-offering. Sages then will not require the man to bring a suspensive guilt-offering, since this is not one of the transgressions for which, if one has certainly done it inadvertently, one brings a sin-offering. But eating forbidden fat imposes liability to bring a sin-offering. Hence sages here will require a suspensive guilt-offering, T. 3:1C. Then at T. 3:1E we know that the man has eaten the forbidden fat of Holy Things, and so he offers both a sin-offering and an unconditional guilt-offering. F-G bring us to the dispute of M. 5:4F,

H-I, which as we see, will be alluded to several more times. T. 3:2 proceeds to complicate matters. It introduces the distinction, ignored by M., between a single spell of inadvertence, in which case we have a single sequence of liabilities, and two such spells—a matter intermittently contributed by T. and summarized at T. 4:1. T. wishes to make the point that M. 5:4A, E, speak of a single, uninterrupted spell. But if we have two distinct sequences, then the rule differs, T. 3:2E, for obvious reasons, on the number of sin-offerings to be brought. T. 3:3, refuse and permitted meat, provides a case not in M. But its rule is no different from that of M. 5:5, since any food, eating of which is punishable by bringing a sin-offering, will yield exactly the same rule as T. gives. Since, D, the man brings both a sin-offering and a guilt-offering, A must refer to a piece of meat *of forbidden fat* which also is refuse. Otherwise only a single-offering, the sin-offering, would suffice at D. Yosé's concession, H, is important in augmenting M.'s picture of his opinion. Yosé does not declare both parties entirely exempt, as M. might have led us to suspect, but requires each to take account of his situation by offering a suspensive guilt-offering, for either one may have eaten the forbidden food. T. 3:4 requires no comment, since it repeats established principles, now in connection with a fresh case. What is important at T. 3:5 is Eliezer's intrusion. In his view, the man certainly owes a sin-offering, whichever of the two pieces of meat he ate. Why? Because the penalty for eating refuse and the penalty for eating remnant are the same, the bringing of a sin-offering, and the man therefore surely owes a sin-offering, whichever meat he ate. Joshua, by contrast, will relieve the man of that obligation until he knows for certain which piece of meat he actually ate. So T.'s intent is to link the present problem to M. 4:2-3, a fine piece of redactional exegesis. T. 3:6-8 make the same point in somewhat more complicated cases. Since T. 4:2 cites M. verbatim, it appears to me that T. 4:1 is intended to conclude the discussion of T. Chapter Three by a summary-statement of the matter of spells of inadvertence, one of T.'s principal contributions to the exegesis of M. 5:4-8.

CHAPTER SEVEN

KERITOT CHAPTER SIX

The principal theme of the chapter is worked out at M. 6:1-6; with M. 6:7 joined to M. 6:6, and M. 6:8 a continuation of M. 6:7. The whole, therefore, is an aggregate, built on the basis of an unfolding theme, which is the guilt-offering. M. 6:1-2 are formed by a principal rule, M. 6:1, and a triplet resting thereon, M. 6:2. The problem is the disposition of a suspensive guilt-offering when it is discovered that the person has not, in fact, committed a sin. If this information comes before the animal is slaugthtered, Meir maintains that, since the animal turns out not to have been properly set aside—the man did not sin—the animal is set out to pasture. Sages rule to the contrary that the animal *has* been properly set aside and sanctified. So it is allowed to suffer a blemish and is sold, with the proceeds given to the cult. Eliezer, whose position is restated at M. 6:3, says the animal is to be offered, for it will cover some sin, if not the one for which it has originally been designated. This is consistent with his view at M. 4:2-3, and Joshua's conception at that same pericope will have to have its restatement as well here, at M. 6:7(+8). M. 6:2 then augments the foregoing with reference to an unconditional sin-offering and other offerings which turn out not to be needed. Then, as I said, M. 6:3 will give us its own autonomous version of Eliezer's opinion.

This further serves as a prologue to M. 6:4-5. For M. 6:3 contains a reference to bringing a suspensive guilt-offering even on the day after the Day of Atonement, which is assumed to expiate all such sins. M. 6:4-5 then refers to the disposition of sin-offerings and guilt-offerings owed by people and not brought before the Day of Atonement. Do they then have to be brought thereafter? Indeed, they do. But suspensive guilt-offerings do not have to be brought thereafter. M. 6:5 carries forward this same problem. It follows that M. 6:3-5 are linked to M. 6:1-2 both because of their restatement of Eliezer's view at M. 6:1 and because they have their own deeper congruence to the foregoing.

M. 6:6 is included, I believe, principally because of M. 6:7, which belongs. This latter pericope, M. 6:7, stresses that, if one has set aside a sin-offering and died, his heir should not offer the sin-offering for some other sin. This of course is Joshua's view, M. 4:2-3, and the pericope goes on to make matters still more explicit by stressing that a sin-offering is valid only for a particular sin. M. 6:6, joined because of a common introductory formula, HMPRYŠ, and because of a common interest in the disposition of that which is used for a purpose other than that for which it has been consecrated, nonetheless has its own point of interest. It is in the rules of sacrilege pertinent to one who has set aside two *selas* for a guilt-offering, then purchased animals for some other purpose. The link to the tractate which follows will, of course, be self-evident. But I do not see how the redactor can have included the pericope here without the more relevant formal and thematic connection supplied at M. 6:7. M. 6:8, continuing M. 6:7, presents the obverse side of its rule. If one sets aside funds for the purchase of a sacrifice for a particular sin, he may use those funds for the purchase of a different sacrifice for that same particulair sin—on which Joshua presumably concurs. M. 6:9 is a concluding homily with no relevance whatsover to our tractate.

6:1-2

A. He who brings a suspensive guilt-offering, and is informed that he did not commit a sin—

B. if this was before it was slaughtered,

C. "it [the animal] goes forth and pastures among the flock," the words of R. Meir.

D. And sages say, "It is set out to pasture until it is blemished, then it is sold, and its proceeds fall [to the Temple-treasury] as a freewill-offering."

E. R. Eliezer says, "It is offered up.

F. "For if it does not come an account of this sin, lo, it comes on account of some other sin" [M. 6:3].

G. If after it was slaughtered, he is [so] informed,

H. the blood is to be poured out.

I. And the meat goes forth to the place of burning.

J. [If the man is informed after] the blood is [properly] tossed, the meat is to be eaten.

K. R. Yosé says, "Even if [he is informed while] the blood is in the cup, it is to be tossed, and the meat is to be eaten."

M. 6:1

I A. An unconditional guilt-offering is not subject to the foregoing rule.

B. If [the man is so informed] before it is slaughtered, it goes forth and pastures in the flock.

C. [If the man is so informed] after it has been slaughtered, lo, this is to be buried.

D. [If the man is so informed after] the blood has been tossed, the meat goes out to the place of the burning.

II E. The ox which is stoned is not subject to the foregoing rule.

F. If [it turns out that the ox has not killed a man] before it is stoned, it goes forth and pastures in the flock.

G. [If it turns out that the ox has not killed a man] after it is stoned, it is available for benefit.

III H. The heifer whose neck is broken is not subject to the foregoing rule.

I. If [the murderer is found] before its neck is broken, it goes forth and pastures in the flock.

J. [If the murderer is found] after its neck is broken, it is buried in its place.

K. For on account of a matter of doubt did it come in the first place. It has made atonement for its matter of doubt and goes its way [having served its purpose].

M. 6:2

M. 6:2, a triplet exhibiting acutely disciplined form, depends upon and augments M. 6:1, but M. 6:1 gives no indication of standing at the head of a sizable unitary construction. So M. 6:2 should be regarded as secondary, a rather well-built augmentation of M. 6:1.[1] M. 6:1, for its part, begins with the sort of mild apocopation characteristic of the commencement of a major unit, A-B + C or D. This then makes balance between C and D rather difficult. E-F are distinct from the foregoing, and the gloss at F disposes of all the considerations of C-D. Eliezer, of course, cannot concur on the remainder, since, so far as he is concerned, the animal is suitably offered up to begin with. G-H + I, and J + K, complete the construction. M. 6:2A + B, C = D, are matched at M. 6:2E + F, G, and M. 6:2H + I, J. There can be no match for D, since the blood is not tossed in the second and third cases.

The difference at M. 6:1A-D is that Meir deems the animal to be unconsecrated, since, if the man has not committed a sin, the original dedication is now shown to have been needless and erroneous. Sages deem the animal to have been deliberately consecrated, and so they treat it as sacred, D, and invoke the familiar procedure (M. Tem. 3:3). The difference is how we interpret the intention of the man who has sanctified the animal. E-F of course stand apart from the suppositions of the stated disagreement. G-I are clear as stated. Yosé differs

[1] "M. 6:2 logically is secondary to 6:1, but typical of M.'s organization of materials through comparison and contrast, a highly significant aspect of the phenomenology of M."—R.S.S.

not only from J, but also from G-I. He regards the offering as a valid suspensive guilt-offering. In J's view, when the blood was to be sprinkled, there was a reasonable doubt that the man had sinned, and the tossing effected atonement. Yosé, K, holds that the cup sanctifies the blood for tossing. M. 6:2 then makes its points without disputes, If the man is informed that he has not committed the sin for which he brings the guilt-offering, A, then, if the animal has not been slaughtered, we deem it an animal sanctified in error and therefore not consecrated. If it has been slaughtered, it is buried. C treats the meat as if it were unconsecrated meat slaughtered in the courtyard (M. Tem. 7:4). The only other point of interest is at K. The offering has done its duty and is treated like any other heifer whose neck has been broken.

A. He who brings a sin-offering or a guilt-offering for a sin *and is informed that he did not commit a sin—*

B. [*if this is*] *before it is slaughtered,*

C. *it goes forth and pastures in the flock* [M. Ker. 6:2B].

D. [*If this is*] *after it is slaughtered,* it [the meat's] appearance is allowed to rot and it is taken forth to the place of burning [*vs.* M. Ker. 6:2C].

T. 4:2 Z p. 566, ls. 4-6

A. A beast which is to be stoned,

B. [if] the witnesses against it turn out to be conspirators,

C. is available for benefit.

D. A heifer whose neck is to be broken,

E. [if] the witnesses against it turn out to be conspirators,

F. is available for benefit.

G. Those who owe a heifer whose neck is to be broken,

H. for whom the Day of Atonement passed,

I. are liable to bring it after the Day of Atonement.

J. [If] one found the murderer, one way or the other, they slay him,

K. since it is said, *You shall not thus pollute the land in which you live*; *for blood pollutes the land, and no expiation can be made for the land, for the blood that is shed in it, except by the blood of him who shed it* (Num. 35:33).

T. 4:3 Z p. 566, ls. 6-10

T. 4:2 goes over the ground of M. 6:2A-D. T. 4:3G-I read the considerations of M. 6:4 into M. 6:2H-K. The rest is complementary information.

6:3

A. R. Eliezer says, "A man vows a suspensive guilt-offering any day and any time he wants.

B. "And it is called the guilt-offering of the pious."

C. They said concerning Baba b. Buṭi that he volunteered a suspensive guilt-offering every day,

D. except for the day after the Day of Atonement.

E. He said, "By this sanctuary! If they would allow me, I should bring [one even this day]. But they say to me, 'Wait until you enter the realm of doubt.' "

F. And sages say, "They bring a suspensive guilt-offering only for a matter, the deliberate commission of which is subject to the penalty of extirpation, and the inadvertent commission of which is subject to the penalty of a sin-offering [M. 1:2]."

M. 6:3

The dispute, A vs. F, is in no balance at all, and sages' *they bring* is pointedly out of balance with Eliezer's quite distinct word choices. We have three distinct units, therefore, A-B, C-E, and F. Sages' view (M. 1:2) contradicts ᶜAqiba's, M. 5:4-8. The illustrative materials, C-E, are joined to A by B. The whole is set where it is as a prologue to M. 6:4-5, as we shall now see.

A. *R. Eliezer says, "A man vows a suspensive guilt-offering any day and any time he wants. It is called the guilt-offering of the pious."*

B. *They said concerning Baba b. Buṭa that he would volunteer a suspensive guilt-offering every day, except the day after the Day of Atonement.*

C. *He said, "By this sanctuary! If they would let me, I should offer [one even this day]. But they say to me, 'Wait until you enter the realm of doubt.' "*

D. *And sages say, "They bring a suspensive guilt-offering only for a matter, the deliberate commission of which is subject to the penalty of extirpation, and the inadvertent commission of which is subject to the penalty of a sin-offering"* [M. Ker. 6:3].

T. 4:4 Z p. 566, ls. 10-14

T. cites M. verbatim.

6:4-5

A. Those who owe sin-offerings and unconditional guilt-offerings for whom the Day of Atonement passed [without their making said offerings] are liable to bring [the offerings] after the Day of Atonement.

B. Those who owe suspensive guilt-offerings are exempt.

C. He who is subject to a doubt as to whether or not he has committed a transgression on the Day of Atonement,

D. even at twilight,

E. is exempt.

F. For the entire Day effects atonement.

M. 6:4

A. A woman who owes a bird-offering as a matter of doubt, for whom the Day of Atonement passed [without her making said bird-offering] is liable to bring it after the Day of Atonement.

B. For it renders her fit for eating animal-sacrifices [and it not expiatory in character].

C. A sin-offering of fowl which is brought on account of doubt,

D. if after its neck is pinched it is known [that the woman has not actually sinned at all],

E. lo, this is to be buried.

M. 6:5

At first glance there is no formal link between M. 6:4A-B and M. 6:5A, nor even a pretense that the two substantively identical items have been formulated to stand together. [2] We have the following distinct units: M. 6:4A-B, C-F, M. 6:5A-B, C-E, this last item being a secondary development of M. 6:5A and linking M. 6:5A's interest to that of M. 6:1-2. The point is that the Day of Atonement effects atonement, as M. 6:3 has pointed out, and therefore certain sacrifices, from sages' viewpoint at M. 6:3, are not required. M. 6:4A then limits the matter. What is owed is owed, since the Day of Atonement does not effect atonement for a sin one has certainly committed and which one knew about before the Day. But, B, it does effect atonement in connection with suspensive guilt-offerings. C-F carry this second matter further. M. 6:5A-B then are self-explanatory, since the unit bears its own exegesis at B. If the woman has aborted something which may or may not impose upon her the requirement of bringing a sin-offering as one who has given birth and has not yet brought the bird-offering as a matter of doubt, she must do so. For so long as she has not done so, she cannot eat Holy Things. C-E then generalize on the theme of the sin-offering of fowl, such as the woman may owe at A. A second glance at the whole shows that M. 6:4A-B, like M. 6:5A-B, bear secondary accretions, M. 6:4C-F, M. 6:5C-E, which are only tangentially related to their primary rules. This curious fact provides formal linkage between the two substantively-tightly-joined units.

6:6

I A. He who sets aside two *selas* [Lev. 5:15] for a guilt-offering and purchased with them two rams for a guilt-offering—

---

[2] "Quite to the contrary, the relative clause in the two protases, ŠᶜBR ᶜLYH[M] YWM HKPWRYM, and the two apodoses, ḤYYB[T/YM] LHBYᵓ LᵓHR YWM HKPWRYM, are identical. I would call that a strong formal link. M. 6:4A-B and 6:5A-B comprise a formal unit, each element of which has been glossed and expanded in a different direction."—R.S.S.

B. if one of them [now] is worth two *selas*,

C. let it be offered for his guilt-offering.

D. And the second is set out to pasture until it is blemished, then sold, and its proceeds fall [to the Temple-treasury] as a freewill-offering [M. Tem. 3:3: that is, a guilt-offering, the owners of which have effected atonement].

II E. [If] he purchased with them two rams for unconsecrated use, one worth two *selas* and one worth ten *zuz*—

F. the one worth two *selas* is offered for his guilt-offering [incurred through the act of sacrilege (E)].

G. And the second is for restitution for his sacrilege.

III H. [If] one was for a guilt-offering and one was for unconsecrated purposes,

I. if the one for the guilt-offering was worth two *selas*,

J. it is offered for his guilt-offering.

K. And the second is for restitution for his sacrilege.

L. And let him bring with it a *sela* and its added fifth.

M. 6:6

This is a unitary pericope, linking the tractate in which it is located to that which will follow. There is a tenuous formal and thematic link to M. 6:7-8, as we shall see. The second and third cases, E-G and H-L, are the center of interest. A-D are simple and straightforward. The price of a guilt-offering specified in Scripture is to be two *sheqels*, here stated as two *selas* (four *zuz* to a *sela*). The man has bought two rams, requiring only one of them. If one turns out to be worth two *selas*—eight *zuz*—it is offered in fulfillment of his obligation. The second is treated as a freewill-offering. E introduces an interesting complication. The man set aside money for the purchase of a sacrifice. But he has purchased animals for unconsecrated purposes. This itself constitutes an act of sacrilege to the extent of two *selas* (A). One of the animals is worth the two *selas*; that one is offered. The other is worth ten *zuz*—two *selas* and two *zuz* left over. That is given as restitution. Why? Because he owes two *selas* which he has misappropriated, and the added fifth, that is, a quarter of eight *zuz* (= two *selas*) added on to the two *selas* that is, two *zuz*, or ten in all. The animal is full restitution. In the final case he buys one ram for a guilt-offering and the other for ordinary use. He therefore has misappropriated only one *sela*. He owes a *sela* and a *zuz* (the added fifth). The one ram is offered for the guilt-offering which he owed, and for which he had separated the money. The other is offered for the guilt-offering incurred in the act of sacrilege. And in addition, he has to pay a *sela* and a fifth as restitution.

A. A guilt-offering for thievery, a guilt-offering for sacrilege, a guilt-offering for sexual relations with a betrothed handmaiden,

B. which one brought [when the animal was] at an age of less than thirteen months and one day,

C. not worth [two] silver sheqels,

D. are invalid.

E. [If] one brought them at an age of more than thirteen months and one day, even if they are superannuated, they are valid.

T. 4:5 Z p. 566, ls. 14-17

A. A guilt-offering of a Nazir and a guilt-offering of a *meṣora*[c] which one brought [when the animals were] at an age of more than twelve months are invalid.

B. If one brought them at an age of less than twelve months, even on the eighth day [of their life],

C. they are valid.

D. [If] one brought them at the value of a *sela*, [if] one brought them at the value of a *sheqel*, [if] one brought them at the value of five *denars*, they are valid.

T. 4:6 Z p. 566, ls. 17-19

A. *He who separates two selas for a guilt-offering [and] purchased* [M. Ker. 6:6A] with one of them a ram for a guilt-offering,

B. if it was worth two *selas*, it is to be offered as his guilt-offering.

C. And the [funds for the] second fall to [the Temple treasury] as a freewill-offering.

D. If not, let it be put out to pasture until it is blemished and then be sold, and let him bring with its proceeds a guilt-offering worth two *selas*.

E. And as to the second, let it[s proceeds] fall [to the Temple-treasury] as a freewill-offering.

F. *[If] he purchased with them [the two selas] two rams for a guilt-offering,*

G. *if one of them was worth two selas, it is to be offered as his guilt-offering.*

H. *And the second is to be put out to pasture until it is blemished, then is to be sold, and its proceeds are to fall [to the Temple-treasury] as a freewill-offering* [M. Ker. 6:6A-D].

I. If not, then both of them are to be put out to pasture until they are blemished, then they are to be sold, and let him bring with them a guilt-offering worth two *selas.*

J. And the excess [of the proceeds] fall [to the Temple-treasury] as a freewill-offering.

T. 4:7 Z p. 566, ls. 19-24

A. *[If] he purchased with them two rams for unconsecrated use, one of them worth two selas and one of them worth ten zuz,*

B. *the one which is worth two selas is to be offered as his guilt-offering.*

C. *And the second is his restitution for sacrilege.*

D. *[If] one was for a guilt-offering and one for unconsecrated purposes,*

E. *if the one purchased as a guilt-offering is worth two selas, it is to be offered as his guilt-offering.*

F. *And the second is for the restitution for sacrilege.*

G. *Let him [further] bring a sela and its added fifth* from his own property [M. Ker. 6:6E-L].

T. 4:8 Z p. 566, ls. 24-27

A. [If] he purchased one ram for a *sela* and fattened it up,

B. so that lo, it is worth two,

C. it is valid.

D. Let him [however] bring a *sela* from his own property.

T. 4:9 Z p. 566, ls. 27-28

A. [If] he separated one ram from his flock, worth, at the time of its being separated, a *sela*, and at the time of its being offered up, two [*selas*],

B. it is valid.

C. [If] it was worth two *selas* at the time of its separation and at the time of its being offered up, one *sela*,

D. it is invalid.

T. 4:10 Z p. 566, ls. 28-29

T. 4:5-6 are pertinent to M. 6:6A in their interest in the value of the offerings listed at T. 4:5A, C, T. 4:6A, D. T. 4:5A's guilt-offering for sacrilege, which is to cost two *selas*, is directly relevant to M. T. 4:7-10 then go over the ground of M. 6:6. T. starts with a case prior to M.'s in logic, the purchase of a *single* ram for two *selas*, as against M.'s *two* rams for two *selas*. Then T. cites M. verbatim, T. 4:7F-H, and adds a case contrary to M.'s. That is, one of them is not worth two *selas* and cannot be offered as the guilt-offering (G), so the animals are sold and replaced (I). The next point of interest is T. 4:9. Now the man has spent only a *sela*, though he is supposed to spend two. The animal, being worth two *selas*, is offered, but another *sela* has to be brought in addition. T. 4:10 further complements the foregoing.

6:7

A. He who sets aside his sin-offering and dies—

B. his son should not bring it after him [for a sin the son has committed (M. Tem. 4:1)].

C. Nor should one bring for one sin [a beast set aside in expiation] for another—

D. even [a beast set aside as a sin-offering] for forbidden fat which he ate last night should he not bring [as a sin-offering] for forbidden fat which he ate today,

E. since it is said, *His offering for his sin* (Lev. 4:28)—

F. that his offering should be for the sake of his [particular] sin.

M. 6:7

The formal connection to the foregoing is at A, HMPRYŠ, as at the foregoing. A-B are stated in mild apocopation, M. 6:6A-C are not. The point is familiar from M. 4:2-3 and represents Joshua's view.

A. He who brings a suspensive guilt-offering for a matter of doubt concerning forbidden fat and for a matter of doubt concerning blood,

B. and who is informed that he did not commit a sin—

C. [if this happened] before it was slaughtered,

D. it goes forth to pasture in the flock.

E. [If this happened] after it was slaughtered, its appearance is allowed to rot and it goes forth to the place of burning.

T. 4:11 Z p. 566, ls. 30-31

A. [If] he separated a sin-offering for having eaten forbidden fat but he brought it for having eaten forbidden blood,

B. blood and brought it for fat,

C. lo, this one has not committed sacrilege, but it [the animal] has not effected atonement.

D. [If] he separated coins for a sin-offering for having eaten forbidden fat but brought them for a sin-offering for having eaten forbidden blood,

E. blood, and brought them for a sin-offering for having eaten forbidden fat—

F. if he did so inadvertently, he has committed sacrilege.

G. Therefore it has effected atonement.

H. If he did so deliberately, he has not committed sacrilege.

I. Therefore it has not effected atonement.

T. 4:12 Z p. 655, ls. 31-34

T. 4:11 simply goes over the ground of M. 6:1, as a prologue to T. 4:12. T. now makes a very interesting point. If one separates a sin-offering for one sin but offers it in expiation of some other, M. has told us, it is not a valid offering. What T. then wishes to say is that the man has not committed sacrilege, because, to begin with, the act of sanctification was invalid. Of course the animal does not effect atonement. If one sets aside coins for purchase of a sin-offering on account of one sin but then uses them for a sin-offering in expiation of a different sin, M.'s rule is again invoked, F-I. If this is accidental, then there *is* an act of sacrilege, and, it follows, the offering is valid. If this is done deliberately, it is invalid in the case of coins, just as it is for the animal itself. T. further contributes an exegetical-redactional comment linking M. 6:7 to M. 6:8, for M. will now point out that we may purchase with coins set aside for a sin-offering in expiation for a particular sin a different sort of sin-offering for the expiation of that same sin.

6:8

A. [With funds] consecrated [for the purchase of] a female-lamb [as a sin-offering], they purchase a female-goat.

B. [With funds] consecrated [for the purchase of] a female-goat [as a sin-offering], [they bring] a lamb.

C. [With funds] consecrated [for the purchase of] a female-lamb and a female goat [they purchase] turtle-doves or young pigeons (Lev. 5:7).

D. [With funds] consecrated [for the purchase of] turtle-doves or young pigeons [they purchase] a tenth of an *ephah* [of fine flour, for a meal-offering].

E. How so?

F. [If] one set aside [funds] for the purchase of a female-lamb or a female-goat and then grew poor, he may bring a bird.

G. [If] he grew still poorer, he may bring a tenth of an *ephah* [of flour].

H. [If] he set aside funds for a tenth of an *ephah* [of flour] and got rich, he may bring a bird.

I. [If] he got still richer, he may bring a female-lamb or a female-goat.

J. [If] he set aside a female-lamb or a female-goat and they were disfigured, if he wants, he may bring a bird with their proceeds.

K. [If] he set aside a bird and it was disfigured, he should not bring a tenth of an *ephah* with its proceeds,

L. for a bird is not subject to redemption.

M. 6:8

M. 6:8 is the obverse of the rule of M. 6:7. While one cannot use a sin-offering set aside for the expiation of one sin for the expiation of some other, one may make use of the coins set aside for the purchase of a sin-offering for the expiation of a given sin in the acquisition of a different sort of sin-offering for the expiation of that same sin. The case involves a sliding scale (M. 2:4), in accord with the sinner's resources. The illustration, E-I, serves C at F, then D at G, and reverses the order, reaching A at I. The whole therefore is unitary, and nicely contructed at that. J-L are tacked on but wholly relevant. The man has set aside a lamb or goat; the animal was disfigured. He therefore sells the animal and purchases a bird with the proceeds, in line with C. But, K-L, we cannot reverse the procedure. The bird cannot be redeemed, with the funds received for it used for the purchase of a tenth of an *ephah* of flour, because redemption applies only to beasts, not to birds, as we know from M. Men. 12:1.

A. He who separates a tenth of an *ephah* of fine flour and got rich,
B. [if this happened] before he sanctified it in a utensil,
C. lo, this is deemed equivalent to all [other] meal-offerings.
D. It is to be redeemed and eaten.
E. [If this happened] after he sanctified it in a utensil,
F. its appearance is allowed to rot, and it is taken out to the place of burning.

T. 4:13 Z p. 566, ls. 34-36

A. [If] he separated coins for the tenth of an *ephah* of fine flour and got rich—
B. let him add to them and purchase with it [the money] turtle-doves or pigeons.
C. [If] he separated turtle-doves or pigeons and got rich,
D. [if they have] not [been] expressly designated, let them be left to die, *for fowl is not subject to redemption* [M. Ker. 6:8L].
E. [If] they have been expressly designated, that which is the sin-offering is left to die.
F. But that which has been designated as a burnt-offering is offered as a burnt-offering.
G. [If] he set aside coins for turtle-doves and pigeons and got rich,
H. let him add and purchase with them [the whole sum] a female lamb and a female goat.

T. 4:14 Z p. 566, ls. 36-39

T. complements M. 6:8 by raising some fresh and pertinent questions. What happens if one has set aside the *ephah* of fine flour, but then turns out to be liable to a more expensive offering. We dispose of the fine flour, if it has not yet been sanctified, by redeeming it, then eating that which has been redeemed. If it already has been sanctified in a utensil, T. 4:13E-F, it cannot be redeemed and it is to be burned. Then we ask about the same sort of case, now with respect to coins. Here we can add money and buy a more expensive offering, T. 4:14A-B. What about the case in which one has set aside particular birds, then turns out to be required to bring a lamb or a goat? If we do not know which is to be the sin-offering, D, the birds are left to die. There is no recourse. If we know which is the sin-offering and which is the burnt-offering, then the former is left to die, but the latter is offered. We treat the former as a sin-offering, the owners of which have effected atonement by means of another animal. There is no recourse. Of course, T. 4:14G-H add, if it is a matter of money, we follow the rule of A-B.

6:9

A. R. Simeon says, "Lambs come before goats in all places [in Scripture].

B. "Is it possible [that the reason is] that they are choicer?

C. "Scripture states, *And if* [as an alternative] *he bring a lamb as his offering for a sin-offering* (Lev. 4:32),

D. "teaching that the two are deemed equivalent.

E. "Turtle-doves come before pigeons in all places [in Scripture].

F. "Is it possible [that the reason is] that they are choicer?

G. "Scripture states, *A young pigeon or a turtle-dove for a sin-offering* (Lev. 12:6),

H. "teaching that the two are deemed equivalent.

I. "The father comes before over the mother in all places [in Scripture].

J. "Is it possible [that the reason is] that the honor owing to the father is superior to the honor owing to the mother?

K. "Scripture states, *You shall fear every one his mother and his father* (Lev. 19:3),

L. "teaching that the two are deemed equivalent."

M. But: Sages have stated:

N. The father comes before over the mother under all circumstances, because both he and his mother are liable to pay honor to his father.

O. And so with respect to study of Torah:

P. If the son acquired merit [by sitting and studying] before the master, the master takes precedence over the father under all circumstances,

Q. because both he and his father are liable to pay honor to his master.

M. 6:9

Simeon's pericope is complete in three units, A-D, E-H, and I-L. M-N form a relevant gloss, and O-Q, an irrelevant one.

A. R. Simeon says, "In every place [Scripture] has given precedence to the creation of the heaven over the creation of the earth.

B. "In one place [however] it says, *On the day of the Lord God's creating of earth and heaven* (Gen. 2:4),

C. "teaching that the two are deemed equivalent.

D. "In every place it has given precedence to Abraham over the [other] patriarchs.

E. "But in one place it says, *And I remembered my covenant with Jacob* (Lev. 26:42),

F. "teaching that the three are deemed equivalent to one another.

G. "In every place it has given precedence to Moses over Aaron.

I. "But in one place it says, *It is Aaron and Moses* (Ex. 6:26),

J. "teaching that the two are deemed equivalent.

K. *"In every place it has given precedence to the honor of the father over that of the mother.*

L. *"In one place it says, You shall fear every one his mother and his father* (Lev. 19:3)

M. *"teaching that the two are deemed equivalent* [M. Ker. 6:9I-L].

N. "In every place it has given precedence to Joshua over Caleb.

O. "In one place it says, *Except for Caleb the son of Jephunneh the Kenizzite and Joshua the son of Nun* (Num. 32:12),

P. "teaching that the two are deemed equivalent."

T. 4:15 Z p. 566, l. 39, p. 567, ls. 1-7

T. has its own version.

MEILAH

CHAPTER EIGHT

INTRODUCTION TO MEILAH

While presenting its share of arid, wholly formal constructions, Meilah also raises profound and interesting questions about the nature of the sacred. This tractate pursues its topic with greater intellectual imagination than we have come to expect in the present division of Mishnah. It asks, for example, about the status of that sacred object object or substance which has been subjected to sacrilege, pointing out that, if we punish a person for the commission of sacrilege, then we must treat that which has been subjected to it as secular. It raises issues of agency and, concommitantly, responsibility for an action, joining these issues to the matter of inadvertence. Third, it goes over profound matters of the metaphysics of the cult, familiar at Zebahim and Menahot, and shows the inner logic of several possible positions. These are only three items of its program of inquiry. The tractate unfolds with appropriate attention to matters of form and formal redaction, so that it is the intellectual and aesthetic apogee of our division.

Let us consider first of all the topic, the matter of sacrilege. As usual, Maimonides (*Trespass* 1:1-3, Lewittes, pp. 411-412) provides a fine introduction:

> 1:1 It was forbidden for a private person to make any profane use of the hallowed things of the Lord, both of things that were offered upon the Altar and of things hallowed for the repair of the Temple. Anyone who made such use of hallowed things of the Lord to the extent of a *peruṭah* committed a trespass.
>
> 1:2 Parts of offerings that became permitted to be eaten—such as flesh of a sin offering or a guilt offering after its blood has been sprinkled, or the Two Loaves after the sprinkling of the blood of the Two Lambs—were not included in the law of trespass. Even if a nonpriest ate of these or similar things, inasmuch as some persons were permitted to enjoy them, anyone who enjoyed them did not commit a trespass. Even if hallowed things of this kind became unfit and forbidden to be eaten, as long as there had been a time when they were permitted, the penalty for trespass was not incurred because of them.
>
> 1:3 Anyone who willfully committed trespass incurred flogging and had to pay in full the amount by which he had diminished the value of the holy thing. The admonition against such trespass was inferred from the Scriptural verse: *Thou mayest not eat within thy gates*

the tithe of thy corn ... nor any of thy vows (Deut. 12:17); and it was learned from oral tradition that this was an admonition to one who would eat from the flesh of a burnt offering, since it belonged wholly to the Lord. The same admonition applied to every other holy thing which belonged to the Lord alone, whether it was of the things hallowed for the Altar or of the things hallowed for the repair of the Temple: if anyone enjoyed therefrom a use worth a *perutah*, he incurred flogging.

If one committed a trespass unwittingly, he was required to pay for what he had enjoyed plus an additional fifth. He also was required to bring a ram worth two *sela*[c] and offer it as a guilt offering, and atonement was made for him. This was the offering known as "the guilt offering of trespasses." For it is said: *If anyone commit a trespass, and sin through error, in the holy things of the Lord, then he shall bring his forfeit unto the Lord, a ram without blemish ... for a guilt-offering. And he shall make restitution for that which he hath done amiss in the holy thing, and shall add the fifth part thereto*, etc. (Lev. 5:15, 16). Paying the principal and an additional fifth together with bringing the offering was a positive commandment.

The tractate is unusually cogent. Its two principal units properly arrange, first of all, rules on the applicability of the laws of (1) sacrilege to *sacrifices*, then, with a necessary prologue, principles of (2) sacrilege of *Temple property*.

I. *Sacrilege of sacrifices in particular.* 1:1-3:8

A. *When the laws of sacrilege apply to a sacrifice.* 1.1-4

1:1 The laws of sacrilege apply to a sacrifice which has never been subjected to the private use of the priest but has always remained the possession of the altar. They cease to apply to a sacrifice which at some point has belonged to the priests. If the blood is properly tossed, the laws of sacrilege are suspended. But if not, they remain in effect; this is Johua's view.

1:2-3 Meat of Most Holy Things which went forth beyond the veils before the tossing of the blood—Eliezer: The laws of sacrilege apply [because the tossing of the blood doe not affect the meat]. [c]Aqiba: The laws of sacrilege do not apply [since the blood has been properly tossed in regard to part, if not all, of the meat].

1:4 A deed having to do with the blood in the case of Most Holy Things produces a ruling which is lenient and one which is stringent. But in the case of Lesser Holy Things, the whole result is to impose a stringent ruling. Before the tossing of the blood, Lesser Holy Things are not subject to the laws of sacrilege.

B. *Stages in the status of an offering.* 2:1-9

2:1-9 The point at which the laws of sacrilege apply to various sacrifices, the point at which the sacrifice may be made invalid

by a *Tebul Yom*, the point at which the prohibitions of refuse, remnant, and uncleanness are invoked, and the point at which the laws of sacrilege no longer apply.
2:1-5: Animal offerings.
2:6-9: Meal- and incense-offerings.

C. *Cultic property which is not subject to sacrilege but which also is not to be used for non-cultic purposes.* 3:1-8

3:1-2 Sin-offerings which are left to die because they cannot serve the purpose for which they were designated and cannot serve another purpose. Nazirite's offering: coins set aside for that purpose cannot be used for secular purposes but are not subject to sacrilege.

3:3 Cultic material which at one point is not subject to the laws of sacrilege but which at some other is subject to them.

3:4-5 Ashes of the inner altar, birds too young or too old, which are not subject to sacrilege but which also cannot be used for secular purposes.

3:6 The status of materials dedicated to the Temple or the altar which cannot be used for the altar but the value of which can serve for the upkeep of the Temple: such materials are subject to the laws of sacrilege. Exemplifications.

3:7-8 Roots of trees growing from secular property to the Temple property. He who sanctifies a forest: the law of sacrilege applies to the whole of it. But if the Temple treasurers purchase wood, the laws of sacrilege do not apply to the chips or the foliage.

II. *Sacrilege of Temple property in general.* 4:1-6:6

A. *Sacrilege has been committed only when the value of a peruṭah of Temple property has been used for secular purposes. The joining together of diverse objects for the purpose of reaching the peruṭah's value.* 4:1-2(+3-6)

4:1 Things consecrated for the altar join together to form the requisite volume or value—a *peruṭah's* worth—to be subject to the laws of sacrilege.
Things consecrated for the upkeep of the house join together.
Things consecrated for the altar and things consecrated for the upkeep of the house join together.

4:2 Five things in a burnt offering join together [to form the requisite volume for liability to sacrilege].

[4:3-6 All forms of refuse join together. All forms of remnant join together. All forms of carrion join together, etc. Joshua: General principle. 4:4 Refuse and remnant do not join together, etc.

4:5 All foodstuffs join together to render the body invalid at a volume of half a half-loaf of bread, etc. 4:6 ᶜ*Orlah*-fruit and diverse kinds of the vineyard join together.]

B. *Sacrilege is defined by the one who does it, or by the thing to which it is done.* 5:1-2

5:1-2 He who derives benefit to the extent of a *peruṭah's* value from that which is consecrated, even though he did not cause deterioration through use, has committed an act of sacrilege, so ᶜAqiba. Sages: Anything which is not subject to deterioration through use, once one has derived benefit from it, he has committed an act of sacrilege. Anything which is subject to deterioration through use, one has not committed an act of sacrilege unless he has caused deterioration through use.

If one has derived benefit to the extent of half a *peruṭah* and caused deterioration to the extent of half a *peruṭah*, he has not committed an act of sacrilege—until he will derive benefit to the extent of a *peruṭah* or cause deterioration to the extent of a *peruṭah*.

C. *Sacrilege effects the secularization of sacred property.* 5:3-5

5:3 One does not commit sacrilege after another has done so to the same object, except for a beast or a utensil of cultic service, since in these latter cases the object cannot be secularized.

Rabbi: Anything which is not subject to redemption is subject to a case of sacrilege following sacrilege.

5:4 If one took a stone or beam from what is consecrated, lo, he has not committed an act of sacrilege. If he gave it to his fellow, he has done it. But his fellow has not done it. Thus: Sacrilege applies only where there is enjoyment of consecrated property to the extent of a *peruṭah's* worth.

5:5 What one has eaten and what his fellow has eaten join together, and even over an extended period of time.

D. *Agency in effecting an act of sacrilege.* 6:1-5 (+)

6:1 If the agent carried out his errand and thereby inadvertently committed an act of sacrilege, the householder is responsible. If the agent did not carry out his errand, then he is responsible and the householder is exempt.

6:2 An agent who is not subject to responsibility, e.g., a minor, who carried out his errand leaves the householder responsible. If the agent did not carry out his errand, then the storekeeper becomes responsible, since the householder is not, for the inadvertent act of sacrilege.

6:3 If one gave a *peruṭah* and said to the agent, "With half bring lamps and with half wicks," and he went and brought lamps for the whole of it, both of them—householder and agent—are not held responsible, since by neither has an act of sacrilege to the extent of a *peruṭah* been committed. Half of what the householder instructed has been done, half not.

6:4 If he gave the agent two *peruṭot* and said, "Bring me an *etrog*," and he went and brought him one for a *peruṭah* and a pomegranate for one, both are liable for an act of sacrilege. Judah: The householder has not committed an act of sacrilege, for his instructions have not been carried out.

6:5 He who deposits coins with a money-changer, if bound up—the money-changer should not make use of them. Therefore if they were consecrated and he paid them out, he has committed an act of sacrilege.

[6:6 A *peruṭah* which has been consecrated which fell into a purse containing other money, as soon as one has paid out the first coin, he has committed an act tof sacrilege, so ᶜAqiba. Sages: Only when the last coin has been paid out has he committed an act of sacrilege. ᶜAqiba: The first coin may be that which is consecrated.]

Beginning with the most basic rules affecting sacrifices, the tractate first attends to the question of when an object becomes susceptible to the laws of sacrilege. The second unit then asks about property, not solely animal-sacrifices, the value of which has been consecrated for the altar or for the upkeep of the Temple, but which is not sacrificed in the narrow sense.

The sacrifice is subject to sacrilege so long as that which renders the sacrifice permitted for priestly use has not been properly offered up (M. Zeb. Chapter Two). Secondary issues do not affect that primary principle. The opening unit then provides a very handsome construction, detailing the point at which various sacrifices and offerings become, and cease to be, subject to the laws of sacrilege. Finally we turn to cultic property which is not subject to the laws of sacrilege, on the one hand, but which also cannot be used for secular purposes, on the other. The second unit, turning to Temple property in general, first establishes the fact that sacrilege has been committed only when Temple property to the value of a *peruṭah* has been used for secular purposes. The matter of 'joining together' to reach that value forthwith is raised, with extraneous materials on the same question appended. The second major consideration, II.B, is as stated, a very interesting inquiry, based upon the facts provided by II.A, the importance of the *peruṭah's* value. If something sacred has been used for secular purposes, once we punish the act of sacrilege, we also treat the object as no longer sacred, a logical position. We turn, next, to the matter of agency, with the important consideration that the sacrilege under discussion in our tractate is that which is done inadvertently. The problems of the final unit can be phrased in terms other than the particular facts of our tractate, so we have moved, as we see, from issues particular to the cult and altar to those which are general and, in principle, in no way limited to the matter of sacrilege at all. This is yet another indication of the remarkable care with which the tractate has been formed.

CHAPTER NINE

MEILAH CHAPTER ONE

The opening chapter is conceptually a single, tightly woven fabric, taking up one question and fully exploring its requirements. M. 1:1 makes the fundamental point that the laws of sacrilege apply to a sacrifice which never has been subjected to the private use of the priests but has always remained the possession of the altar. They cease to apply to a sacrifice which at some point has belonged to the priests. It will follow that, if the blood is properly tossed, the laws of sacrilege are suspended. But if the blood is not properly tossed, they remain in effect for the animal under discusson. This viewpoint, which is Joshua's, then is subject to development by Eliezer and ᶜAqiba. The specific issue, as our tractate wishes to phrase it, is the status of the meat of Most Holy Things, part of which is taken out beyond the veils of the courtyard before the blood of the offering is properly tossed against the altar. Is said meat affected by the tossing of the blood? Eliezer maintains that it is not. Therefore the laws of sacrilege continue to apply to the meat, which, it follows, then is not subject to the prohibitions of refuse, remnant, and uncleanness. ᶜAqiba's position is what is interesting. He holds that the tossing of the blood does affect even the part of the meat taken outside the courtyard. M.'s version of his reasoning, which leads to the position that the laws of sacrilege no longer apply, is not clearly stated. But T. makes up for it and shows what ᶜAqiba is thinking. M. 1:3 restates the same dispute, this time with reference to Lesser Holy Things. M. 1:4, tying the whole together, then specifies the general difference between Most Holy Things and Lesser Holy Things, by pointing out that, while in the case of Most Holy Things, before the tossing of the blood the laws of sacrilege apply both to the meat which belongs to the priest and to the sacrificial parts, and afterward they apply only to the sacrificial parts, in the case of Lesser Holy Things, the laws of sacrilege apply to no part of the animal before the tossing of the blood. Afterward they apply to the sacrificial parts. This accounts, of course, for the restatement of the issue of M. 1:2 at M. 1:3. It would be difficult to point to a more satisfying and fully worked out chapter, which, as T. indicates, bears important implications for Zebahim and Menahot as well. I cite here the relevant Tosefta to those tractates, which explicitly depend upon our present pericopae.

1:1

A. Most Holy Things which one slaughtered in the south [side of the altar]—

B. the laws of sacrilege apply to them.

I C. [If] one slaughtered them in the south and received their blood in the north,

D. in the north and received their blood in the south.

II E. [if] one slaughtered them by day and tossed the blood by night,

F. by night and tossed the blood by day,

III G. or [if] one slaughtered them [with the intention of eating that which is usually eaten or offering up that which is usually offered up] outside of their proper time or outside of their proper place—

H. the laws of sacrilege apply to them.

I. A general principle did R. Joshua state: "Whatever has had a moment of availability to [for use by] the priests—the laws of sacrilege do not apply thereto.

J. "And [whatever] has not [yet] had a moment of availability to the priests—the laws of sacrilege do apply thereto."

K. What is that which has had a moment of availability to the priests?

L. That which [after the proper tossing of the blood] has been left overnight, and that which has been made unclean, and that which has gone forth [beyond the veils].

M. And what is that which has not [yet] had a moment of availability to the priests?

N. That which has been slaughtered [with improper intention to eat that which is usually eaten or to offer up that which is usually offered up] outside of its proper time or outside of its proper place,

O. and that, the blood of which invalid men have received or tossed.

M. 1:1

The pericope is in two distinct parts, A-B + C-H, and I-O, which entirely concur with one another. The former is, as indicated, itself divided into A-B and a triplet, C-H. The stichs of the latter are distinguished by use of ŠḤṬN.[1] Joshua's rule, I-J, is systematically spelled out, I at K-L and J at M-O. The point of A-B is that if Most Holy Things are invalidated by being slaughtered at the southern side, rather than at the required, northern side, of the altar (M. Zeb. 5:1-5), they nonetheless are subject to the laws of sacrilege. Even though the sacrifices have been invalidated, they remain consecrated and unavailable for common or even priestly use. C-H make the same point. If the animals are slaughtered in the south but the blood is received in the

1 "The triplet, C-H, is dependent upon A-B for its antecedent. ŠḤṬN also is the operative verb at A-B. The two parts, although formally distinct, have been formulated together."—R.S.S.

proper place, or *vice versa,* or if only partially invalidated, as at E-F, or if slaughtered even with improper intention, which renders them refuse, the laws of sacrilege apply. Joshua's general principle is given a different focus, not the status as to the correct operation of the cult, but the availability to the priests. But the point is the same. Whatever has for one moment become permissible for priestly use—that is, whatever sacrifice, the blood of which has been properly tossed—even though, afterward, the offering has become invalid for some reason, is not subject to the laws of sacrifice. Why not? Because the offering has fallen into the domain of the priests. This is illustrated at K-L. In all three instances the offering was for one moment properly in the possession of the priests, since the blood was correctly tossed. Will Joshua concur with A-H? Of course he will, for at C-D, E-F, the blood has *not* been properly tossed. The priests have never had a right to the offering. The laws of sacrilege continue to apply. Whatever had not yet had a moment of availability to the priests is subject to the laws of sacrilege, J. N then explicitly concurs with G, and O is clear as stated.

A. R. Joshua says, "*Most Holy Things which one slaughtered at the southern [side of the altar]—*

B. "*the laws of sacrilege apply to them.*

C. "*[If] one slaughtered them at the south and received their blood at the north,*

D. "*at the north and received their blood at the south,*

E. "*[if] one slaughtered by day and tossed the blood by night,*

F. "*by night and tossed the blood by day,*

G. "put those drops of blood which are to be put below, above, or those which are to be put above, below,

H. "or those which are to be put [on the altar] at the inside, outside, or those which are to be put outside, inside,

I. "*or [if] one slaughtered them [intending to offer up that which is offered up and to eat that which is eaten] outside of the proper time or outside of the proper place,*

J. "*the laws of sacrilege apply to them*" [M. Me. 1:1A-H].

T. 1:1 Z p. 556, ls. 36-40

A. *A general principle did R. Joshua state: "Whatever has had a moment of availability to the priests—the laws of sacrilege* [read: *do + not*] *apply thereto. And whatever has not [yet] had a moment of availability to the priests, the laws of sacrilege* do [delete: *not*] *apply thereto* [M. Me. 1:1/I-J].

B. "As to that which is made refuse in the case of Most Holy Things, the laws of sacrilege apply thereto. But in the case of Lesser Holy Things, the laws of sacrilege do not apply thereto."

T. 1:2 Z p. 556, l. 40, p. 557, ls. 1-3

A. There is remnant to which the laws of sacrilege apply, and there is remnant to which the laws of sacrilege do not apply.

B. How so?

C. [If] the meat was left overnight before the tossing of the blood, the laws of sacrilege apply to it.

D. [If this happened] after the tossing of the blood, the laws of sacrilege do not apply.

E. But as to that which is unclean, whether it was made unclean before the tossing of the blood or whether it was made unclean after the tossing of the blood, the laws of sacrilege do not apply to it,

F. for the priestly frontlet effects atonement for it [so that the blood *is* acceptable, and the laws of sacrilege are suspended].

T. 1:3 Z p. 557, ls. 3-5

T. of course confirms our surmise that Joshua stands behind both statements in M. and further enriches what is assigned to him. T. 1:3 then refines M. 1:1L. If the meat is left overnight before the blood is tossed, then it never has a moment of availability to the priests and is subject to the laws of sacrilege. But if the blood was tossed, then the meat was left overnight, of course, the meat has been available for a moment to the priests. E-F show that there is a reason behind M.'s position on that which is unclean, a view, as we shall see, vital to ᶜAqiba's larger position in what follows. The priestly frontlet, in ᶜAqiba's view, effects acceptance for a sacrifice which has been made unclean, and this is without regard to when it is made unclean. In that case the meat has a moment at which it is available for priestly use, having been accepted, despite its uncleanness, through the tossing of the blood, and hence having passed into the priests' domain. It follows that, as M. has told us, that which is made unclean is not subject to the laws of sacrilege, for the stated reason.

1:2-3

A. The meat of Most Holy Things which went forth [beyond the veils] before the tossing of the blood—

B. R. Eliezer says, "The laws of sacrilege apply to it. And they are not liable on its account because of violation of the laws of refuse, remnant, and uncleanness."

C. R. ᶜAqiba says, "The laws of sacrilege do not apply to it. Truly are they liable on its account because of violation of the laws of refuse, remnant, and uncleanness."

D. Said R. ᶜAqiba, "Now, lo, he who separates a sin-offering which is lost, and separated another in its stead, and afterward the first turns up, and lo, both of them are available—

E. "is it not so that just as its blood exempts its flesh [from the laws of sacrilege], so it exempts the flesh of its fellow ?

F. "Now if [the proper tossing of] its blood has exempted the flesh of its *fellow* from being subject to the laws of sacrilege, is it not logical that it should exempt its *own* flesh?"

M. 1:2

A. The sacrificial parts of Lesser Holy Things which went forth [beyond the veils] before the tossing of the blood—

B. R. Eliezer says, "The laws of sacrilege do not apply to them. And they are not liable on their account because of violation of the laws of refuse, remnant, and uncleanness."

C. R. ᶜAqiba says, "The laws of sacrilege do apply to them. And they are liable on their account because of violation of the laws of refuse, remnant, and uncleanness."

M. 1:3

M. 1:2 presents a topic-sentence, A, followed by a very nicely balanced dispute, B-C, and a further argument in ᶜAqiba's behalf, D-F. M. 1:3B-C then match M. 1:2B-C, with a fresh, correlated superscription, M. 1:3A.

The case is as follows. A sacrifice of Most Holy Things has been made. We know, M. 1:1, that if the blood is properly tossed, then the meat is available to the priests, so the laws of sacrilege no longer apply. What if, *before* the blood is tossed, some of the meat is taken out of the courtyard, so invalidated, and *then* the blood is tossed? Has there been a moment when the priests have had a right to said meat? No, of course not, Eliezer maintains. Therefore the laws of sacrilege, in line with Joshua's position, M. 1:1, continue to apply. But the meat then is not subject to the rules of refuse, remnant, and uncleanness, which we invoke only for meat which is valid and available. The tossing of the blood has no affect on the flesh which has been invalidated, so there never has been a moment of availability to the priests.

ᶜAqiba, by contrast, maintains that the tossing of the blood does serve to remove the meat from subjection to the laws of sacrilege, even though the meat is invalid for offering. It of course follows that liability to the laws of refuse, remnant, and uncleanness pertains. ᶜAqiba's defense of his position, D-F, is to show that it is possible in principle for tossing of the blood to remove, from liability to the laws of sacrilege, meat which, in point of fact, itself cannot be offered. If ᶜAqiba can establish that principle, he can apply it to our case, in which meat has been invalidated before the tossing of the blood and therefore cannot be offered. If, he points out, we have both sin-offerings—one lost but later on found, another separated in its stead—what do we do?

Slaughtering both, we offer one of them as a sin-offering. This one exempts the flesh of the other from the laws of sacrilege, even though the blood of the other has not been tossed, and even though the other cannot be offered up at all, since it is in the status of a duplicate sin-offering (M. Tem. 4:3). It follows that the tossing of the blood has had the effect of removing from liability to the laws of sacrilege the invalid flesh of the fellow. In the exactly parallel case before us, we deem that the valid tossing of the blood, which serves that portion of the meat which has not been removed from the courtyard, also serves that which has, so far as the present issue is concerned. The tossing of the blood surely is affective for the invalid flesh which has gone forth (F). M. 1:3 goes over the same ground. Now it speaks of the sacrificial parts of Lesser Holy Things. These are subject to the laws of sacrilege only after the tossing of the blood (M. 1:4). If they are taken out of the courtyard before then, Eliezer invokes his position at M. 1:2, and so too does ᶜAqiba.

A. *The meat of Most Holy Things which went forth* [*beyond the veils*] *before the tossing of the blood* [M. Me. 1:2A],

B. and on behalf of which the blood was tossed—

C. *R. Eliezer says, "The laws of sacrilege apply to it, and they are not liable on its account because of violation of the laws of refuse, remnant, and uncleanness."*

D. R. ᶜAqiba says, "The frontlet [of the high priest] effects atonement for that which goes forth.

E. *"The laws of sacrilege do not apply to it.*

F. *"Truly are they liable on its account because of violation of the laws of refuse, remnant, and uncleanness."*

T. 1:4 Z p. 557, ls. 5-8

A. Said R. Simeon, "When I spent the Sabbath in Kefar Bet Pagi, a certain one of the disciples of R. ᶜAqiba came upon me and said to me,

B. " 'Meat which has gone forth beyond the veils and in behalf of which the blood was tossed has been accepted.'

C. "But when I came and laid the matters out before my colleagues in Galilee, they said to me, 'And is it not invalidated? How [does the frontlet] effect atonement for that which is invalid?'

D. "So when I came and laid the matters out before R. ᶜAqiba himself, then he said to me,

E. " '*Lo, he who separates his sin-offering, which is lost, and separated another in its stead, and afterward the first turns up, and lo, both are available* [M. Me. 1:2D]—

F. " 'the laws of sacrilege apply to both of them.

G. " '[If] one slaughtered it, and lo, its blood is setting in cups,

H. " 'the laws of sacrilege apply to both of them.

I. " 'If the blood of one of them is tossed, it has afforded protection for the flesh of its fellow from liability to the laws of sacrilege.

J. " 'If it has afforded protection for the flesh of its fellow from liability to the laws of sacrilege, even though it [the fellow] is invalid, it surely is logical that it should afford protection for its own flesh as well [M. 1:2F]!' "

T. 1:5 Z p. 557, ls. 8-15

A. *The sacrificial parts of Lesser Holy Things which went forth [beyond the veils] before the tossing of the blood* [M. Me. 1:3A],

B. and the blood was tossed in their behalf—

C. *R. Eliezer says, "The laws of sacrilege do not apply to them, and they are not liable on their account because of violation of the laws of refuse, remnant, and uncleanness."*

D. And R. ᶜAqiba says, "The priestly frontlet effects atonement for that which goes forth.

E. *"The laws of sacrilege apply to them, and they are liable on their account because of refuse, remnant, and uncleanness"* [M. Me. 1:3B, C].

T. 1:6 Z p. 557, ls. 15-18

T. 1:4 improves upon M. by adding a very useful clarification at T. 1:4B and, of course, D. Then T. 1:5 beautifully spells out the relevance of the argument in M. The issue, C, is not the affect of the frontlet but the force of the analogy. This is very nicely expanded. We slaughter both sin-offerings simultaneously, but toss the blood of only one of them. That affects the other sin-offering and itself as well. The rest is a restatement of M. 1:3 along the lines of T. 1:4's treatment of M. 1:2.

We turn now to T. Zeb. 4:4-8 and T. Men. 5:9-14, which depend upon the present pericope and read its interests into their tractates. But it will be clear that the issue is primary to Meilah and secondary to Zebahim (and, in the nature of things, tertiary to Menahot).

A. [If] one slaughtered in silence [without improper intention], and [the blood] went forth outside the veils, and one tossed it in silence, lo, this is as it was [valid].

B. [In such a case] the flesh of Holy Things is subject to the laws of sacrilege, but the sacrificial parts of Lesser Holy Things are not subject to the laws of sacrilege.

C. And they are not liable on their account because of [transgressing the law of] remnant or because of [transgressing the law of] uncleanness.

D. [If, however,] the blood was made unclean and one tossed it in silence [without improper intention], the flesh of Most Holy Things is not subject to the laws of sacrilege. But the sacrificial parts of Lesser Things are subject to the laws of sacrilege.

E. And they are liable on their account because of [transgressing the laws of] remnant and uncleanness.

F. For the high priest's front plate effects atonement for that which is unclean, but it does not effect atonement either for that which is kept overnight or on account of that which goes forth [beyond the veil].

T. Zeb. 4:4

A. [If] one slaughtered in silence, and the flesh went outside the veils, and [then] one tossed the blood in silence—

B. R. Eliezer says, "Lo, it is as it was. The flesh of Most Holy Things is subject to the laws of sacrilege. But the sacrificial parts of Lesser Holy Things are not subject to the laws of sacrilege, and they are not liable on their account because of [transgression of the laws of] remnant and uncleanness."

C. R. ᶜAqiba says, "The high priest's front plate appeases for that which goes forth [beyond the veils]. [Therefore] the flesh of Most Holy Things is not subject to the laws of sacrilege, but the sacrificial parts of Lesser Holy Things are subject to the laws of sacrilege, and they are liable on their account because of [transgression of the laws of] remnant and uncleanness."

D. [If] the flesh is made unclean and one [then] tossed the blood in silence, all agree that they do not subject to the laws of sacrilege the flesh of Most Holy Things. But they do subject to the laws of sacrilege the sacrificial parts of Lesser Holy Things, and they are liable on their account because of [transgression of the laws of] remnant and because of [transgression of the laws of] uncleanness. For the high priest's plate effects atonement for that which is unclean but not for that which is kept overnight or for that which goes forth [beyond the veils].

T. Zeb. 4:5

A. [If] one slaughtered in silence, and the blood went outside of the veils, and one tossed it [intending to eat the flesh] outside of its proper time,

B. or [if] one slaughtered [the sacrifice, intending to eat the flesh] outside of its proper time, and the blood went outside of the veils, and one tossed it [intending to eat the fleh] outtside of its proper time,

C. lo, this is as it was.

D. They subject to the laws of sacrilege the flesh of Most Holy Things, but they do not subject to the laws of sacrilege the sacrificial parts of Lesser Holy Things.

E. And they are [not] liable on their account because of [transgression of the laws of] refuse.

T. Zeb. 4:6

A. [If] the blood was made unclean, and one tossed it [intending to eat the flesh of the sacrifice] outside of its proper time, still do they subject to the laws of sacrilege the flesh of Most Holy Things.

B. But they do not subject to the laws of sacrilege the sacrificial parts of Lesser Holy Things.

C. But they are liable on their account because of [transgression of the laws of] refuse.

D. For the high priest's plate effects atonement for that which is unclean, but it does not effect atonement either for that which is kept overnight or for that which goes forth [beyond the veils].

T. Zeb. 4:7

A. [If] one slaughtered in silence, and the flesh went forth outside of the veils, and one [then] tossed the blood [with the intention to eat the flesh] outside of its proper time,

B. or [if] one slaughtered [intending to eat the flesh] outside its proper time, and the flesh went outside of the veils, and one tossed the blood in silence,

C. or [if] one slaughtered [the animal, intending to eat the flesh] outside of its proper time, and the flesh went outside of the veils, and one [then] tossed the blood in silence, [2]

D. or [if] one slaughtered [the animal, intending to eat the flesh] outside of its proper time, and the flesh went outside of the veils, and one tossed the blood [intending to eat the flesh] outside of its proper time—

E. R. Eliezer says, "Lo, it is as it was. They subject to the laws of sacrilege the flesh of Most Holy Things, but they do not subject to the laws of sacrilege the sacrificial parts of Lesser Holy Things. And they are not liable on their account because of [transgression of the laws of] refuse."

F. R. ᶜAqiba says, "The high priest's plate effects atonement for that which goes forth. Still do they subject to the laws of sacrilege the flesh of Most Holy Things, but they do not subject to the laws of sacrilege the sacrificial parts of Lesser Holy Things. But they are liable on their account because of [transgression of the laws of] refuse."

G. [If] the flesh is made unclean, and one tossed the blood [intending to eat the flesh] outside of its proper time,

H. all agree that still do they subject to the laws of sacrilege the flesh of Most Holy Things, and they do not subject to the laws of sacrilege the sacrificial parts of Lesser Holy Things. But they are liable on their account because of [transgression of the laws of] refuse.

I. For the high priest's plate effects atonement for that which is unclean, and the high priest's plate does not effect atonement either for that which is kept overnight or for that which goes forth [beyond the veils].

T. Zeb. 4:8 Z p. 485, ls. 10-34, p. 486, ls. 1-2

T. Zeb. 4:4 rests upon the distinction drawn at M. 1:4 between the point at which the Lesser Holy Things become liable to the laws of

[2] "C repeats B verbatim and is certainly a copyist's error (cf. T. Men. 4:14A-D). Lieberman does not comment."—R.S.S.

sacrilege, which is when the blood is tossed, and the point at which Most Holy Things become liable. The concluding point, F, simply explains the distinction important to T. But the point of interest to our pericope begins at T. Zeb. 4:5. Here we have a statement of the case before us—the taking of the meat outside the veils, followed by the proper tossing of the blood. Both cases—M. 1:2 and M. 1:3—are given at one and the same time. ᶜAqiba's position of course is stated as T. Me. 1:4 has given it. These materials are important to T. Zeb. 4:1ff., because Eliezer's position at M. Me. 1:2-3, in fact, is identical to that which he holds at T. Zeb. 4:1: "If there is no flesh, there is blood." Here the flesh has been spoiled, but the blood-rite nonetheless is properly carried out. The law of sacrilege applies, because the sprinkling of the blood will not affect flesh which has been invalidated by removal from the courtyard; it will not be rendered permissible to the priests and, in line with Joshua's position at M. 1:1, has at no time been permitted to the priests. Eliezer will not then invoke the law of refuse. If at the time of the sacrifice the priest intended to toss the blood or burn the sacrificial parts or eat the flesh outside the proper time, in the case of the flesh which has gone forth, if one eats the flesh, he is not liable on account of eating refuse. Why not? Because the sprinkling of the blood has not affected the meat, and that which renders the offering permissible has not been offered in accord with its requirement (M. Zeb. 2:4). Likewise if the flesh is made unclean, one who eats it is not liable. ᶜAqiba's position, by contrast, is that the law of sacrilege does not apply. Why not? Because the sprinkling of the blood does affect the meat. It removes it from the category of sacrilege, in line, too, with Joshua's position. And the rest follows. The law of refuse is invoked, since we do deem the sprinkling of the blood to have been effective.

What is at issue? Just as at M. Me. 1:2-3, it is the affect of the sprinkling of the blood on the flesh which has been taken out. Eliezer maintains that if there is no flesh, there is still blood, so far as sacrilege (M. 1:1) is concerned. And for the same reason, the law of refuse also does not apply. ᶜAqiba holds that if there is no flesh, there still is blood —just as Eliezer maintains. But, ᶜAqiba adds, since there is *blood*, the sprinkling of the blood does serve to remove the flesh from the category of sacrilege, just as Joshua maintains at M. 1:1. So at issue is whether the tossing of the blood affects the flesh which has been invalidated, and both parties concur on the *opposite* of Joshua's position at T. Zeb. 4:1.

A. [If] one took the handful in silence [without improper intent] and the handful went forth beyond the veils and one offered it up in silence, lo, this is as it was.

B. The laws of sacrilege apply to the residue.

C. But they are not liable on their account because of violation of the laws of remnant and uncleanness.

D. [If] the handful was made unclean and one offered it up in silence, the laws of sacrilege do not apply to the residue.

E. But they are liable on their account because of violation of the laws of remnant and uncleanness.

F. *For the priestly frontlet effects acceptance for that which is unclean, but the priestly frontlet does not effect acceptance for that which is allowed to remain overnight or for that which goes forth beyond the veils* [M. Men. 3:3L].

T. Men. 4:9 Z p. 516, ls. 26-30

A. [If] one took the handful in silence and the residue was taken outside of the veils and one offered up the handful in silence,

B. R. Eliezer says, "Lo, this is as it was. The laws of sacrilege apply to the remnants, but they are not liable on their account because of violation of the laws of remnant and uncleanness."

C. R. ᶜAqiba says, "The priestly frontlet effects acceptance for that which goes forth. And the laws of sacrilege do not apply to the residue. But they are liable on their account because of violation of the laws of remnant and uncleanness."

T. Men. 4:10 Z p. 516, ls. 30-33

A. [If] the residue was made unclean and one offered up the handful in silence, all agree that the laws of sacrilege do not apply to it, but they are liable on their account for violation of the laws of remnant and uncleanness.

B. For the priestly frontlet effects acceptance for that which is unclean, but the priestly frontlet does not effect acceptance either for what remains overnight or for that which goes forth beyond the veils.

T. Men. 4:11 Z p. 516, ls. 33-35

A. [If] one took the handful in silence and the handful went forth beyond the veils, and one offered it up [with improper intention to eat the residue] outside of its proper time,

B. or [if] one took the handful [with the improper intention to eat the residue or offer the handful] outside of its proper time, and if the handful went forth outside the veils, and one [then] offered it up in silence,

C. or [if] one took the handful [with the improper intention to eat the residue or to burn the handful] outside of its proper time,

D. and it went forth beyond the veils, and one [then] offered it up [with the improper intention to eat the residue] outside of its proper time,

E. the laws of sacrilege apply to the residue. Truly they are not liable on its account because of violation of the laws of refuse.

T. Men. 4:12 Z p. 516, ls. 35-37, p. 517, l. 1

A. [If] the handful was made unclean and one offered it up [with improper intention to eat the residue] outside of its proper time,

B. still do the laws of sacrilege apply to the residue, and they are liable on their account because of violation of the laws of refuse.

C. For the priestly frontlet effects acceptance for that which is unclean, but the priestly frontlet does not effect acceptance for that which remains overnight or for that which goes forth beyond the veils.

T. Men. 4:13 Z p. 517, ls. 1-3

A. [If] one took the handful in silence and the residue went forth beyond the veils and one offered up the handful [with the improper intention to eat the residue] outside of its proper time,

B. or [if] one took the handful [with the improper intention to eat the residue or to offer up the handful] outside of its proper time, and the residue went forth beyond the veils, and one offered up the handful in silence,

C. or [if] one took the handful [with the improper intention to eat the residue or to offer up the handful] outside of its proper time, and the residue went forth beyond the veils, and one offered up the handful [with the improper intention to eat the residue] outside of its proper time,

D. R. Eliezer says, "Lo, this is as it was. The laws of sacrilege apply to the residue, but they are not liable on their account because of violation of the laws of refuse."

E. R. ᶜAqiba says, "The priestly frontlet effects atonement for that which goes forth beyond the veils.

F. "Still do the laws of sacrilege apply to the residue, and they are liable on their account because of violation of the laws of refuse."

G. [If] the residue is made unclean and one offered up the handful [with the improper intention to eat the residue] outside of its proper time, all agree that still do the laws of sacrilege apply to the residue, and they are liable on their account because of violation of the laws of refuse.

H. For the priestly frontlet effects acceptance for that which is unclean, but it does not effect acceptance either for that which remains overnight or for that which goes forth beyond the veils.

T. Men. 4:14 Z p. 517, ls. 3-10

A. The two loaves which went forth beyond the veils and the blood of the lambs was tossed [with the improper intention to eat what is to be eaten] outside of its proper time—

B. R. Eliezer says, "They are not liable on account of this bread because of violation of the laws of refuse."

C. R. ᶜAqiba says, "They are liable on account of this bread because of violation of the laws of refuse" [T. Men. 4:9-15 = T. Zeb. 4:4-8, M. Me. 1:1-3].

D. And sages say, "The handful requires [that it be put] into a utensil of service" [M. Men. 3:4C].

E. How so? One takes the handful from a utensil of service and puts it into a utensil of service and sanctifies it in a utensil of service.

F. And if he did not sanctify it in a utensil of service, he has invalidated it.

G. R. Eleazar b. R. Simeon says, "Even if he took the handful from a utensil of service and salted it and put it on the fires, it is valid" [M. Men. 3:4D].

T. Men. 4:15 Z p. 517, ls. 10-15

Reference to the statement of the issues at T. Zeb. 4:4-9 accounts for the version of T. Menahot.

1:4

A. A deed having to do with the blood in the case of Most Holy Things produces a ruling which is lenient and one which is stringent.

B. But in the case of Lesser Holy Things, the whole [tendency] is to impose a stringent ruling.

C. How so?

D. Most Holy Things before the tossing of the blood—

E. the laws of sacrilege apply to the sacrificial parts and to the meat [which is for the priests].

F. After the tossing of the blood, the laws of sacrilege apply to the sacrificial parts, but they do not apply to the flesh.

G. On account of this and on account of that are they liable because of violation of the laws of refuse, remnant, and uncleanness.

H. But in the case of Lesser Holy Things, the whole [tendency] is to impose a stringent ruling—how so?

I. Lesser Holy Things before the tossing of the blood—

J. the laws of sacrilege do not apply either to the sacrificial parts or to the flesh.

K. After the tossing of the blood, the laws of sacrilege apply to the sacrificial parts, but they do not apply to the flesh.

L. On account of this and on account of that they are liable because of violation of the laws of refuse, remnant, and uncleanness.

M. It turns out that a deed having to do with the blood in the case of Most Holy Things produces a ruling which is lenient and one which is stringent, but in the case of Lesser Holy Things, the whole [tendency] is to impose a stringent ruling.

M. 1:4

The elaborate construction is in a familiar form, a generalization, A-B, followed by exemplification of A, at C+D-G, and B, which is restated, at H+I-L; M summarizes the whole. The main point is at B.

Lesser Holy Things are not subject to the laws of sacrilege at all until the blood has been tossed, at which point the sacrificial portions become subject to the laws of sacrilege. But with the sprinkling of the blood, meat of Most Holy Things ceases to be liable to the laws of sacrilege (M. 1:1). D-F make the point clear. Before the blood is tossed, the whole of Most Holy Things is subject to the laws of sacrilege, but not the flesh, which the priests may eat. By contrast, before the tossing of the blood, no part of the Lesser Holy Things is subject to the laws of sacrilege at all. Afterward, the rule is as stated (M). In the case of Most Holy Things, proper tossing of the blood frees the meat from the laws of sacrilege, but in the case of Lesser Holy Things it imposes liability to the laws of sacrilege upon part of that which was formerly exempt.

CHAPTER TEN

MEILAH CHAPTER TWO

The present chapter is a nine-unit construction, in absolutely perfect formal discipline, on the point at which the laws of sacrilege apply to various sacrifices. But the several units supply much more information. In each instance, after telling us that when the item to be offered up has been designated or sanctified, it is subject to the laws of sacrilege, the pericope proceeds to make these points. First, once the sacrifice has been made—e.g., a bird's neck severed, an animal sacrificed, and so on—the sacrifice is subject to be made invalid by a *Tebul Yom* or one lacking in the completion of the rites of atonement or by being left overnight. Second, once the blood is tossed, the prohibitions of refuse, remnant, and uncleanness are invoked. Finally, the point at which, in the end, the laws of sacrilege no longer apply is defined, e.g., in the case of an animal which is not made available to the priests, at the point at which the corpse is fully burned to cinder. Thus we have four stages in the metaphysical 'history' of the sacrifice: susceptibility to sacrilege, at which point the history begins; susceptibility to being invalidated by a person not wholly in a state of cleanness, but also not unclean; third, susceptibility to the prohibitions of refuse, remnant, and uncleanness; and, finally, the end of susceptibility to sacrilege. The first five items cover animal-offerings, the last four, meal- and incense-offerings. Where the mode of expression varies somewhat, it is only because of the facts of the case. The art with which the formalization is effected is shown, among other places, at M. 2:6C's inclusion of a detail substantively out of place in its list of the results of formation of a crust. Tosefta contributes one item only, but that item shows that at least one entry, M. 2:3, takes a position on a rule debated as late as Usha.

2:1-9

I A. The sin-offering of fowl—

B. the laws of sacrilege apply to it once it [the bird] has been sanctified [designated as a sin-offering].

C. [When] its head has been severed, it is rendered fit to be made invalid by a *Tebul Yom* and by one whose rites of atonement have not yet been completed and by being left overnight.

D. [When] its blood has been tossed, they are liable on its account because of violation of the laws of refuse, remnant, and uncleanness.

E. And sacrilege does not apply to it [any longer].

M. 2:1

II A. The burnt-offering of fowl—

B. the laws of sacrilege apply to it once it has been sanctified.

C. [When] its head has been severed, it is rendered fit to be made invalid by a *Tebul Yom* and by one whose rites of atonement have not yet been completed and by being left overnight.

D. [When] its blood has been squeezed out, they are liable on its account because of violation of the laws of refuse, remnant, and uncleanness.

E. And the laws of sacrilege apply to it until it is taken out to the ash-heap.

M. 2:2

III A. Cows which are to be burned and goats which are to be burned—

B. the laws of sacrilege apply to them once they have been sanctified.

C. [When] they have been slaughtered, they are rendered fit to be made invalid by a *Tebul Yom* and by one whose rites of atonement have not yet been completed and by being left overnight.

D. [When] their blood has been tossed, they are liable on their account because of violation of the laws of refuse, remnant, and uncleanness.

E. And the laws of sacrilege apply to them in the ash-heap until the meat is reduced to cinders.

M. 2:3

IV A. The burnt-offering—

B. the laws of sacrilege apply to it once it has been sanctified.

C. [When] it has been slaughtered, it is rendered fit to be made invalid by a *Tebul Yom* and by one whose rites of atonement have not yet been completed and by being left overnight.

D. [When] its blood has been tossed, they are liable on its account because of violation of the laws of refuse, remnant, and uncleanness.

E. And the laws of sacrilege do not apply to its hide.

F. But it will be taken out to the ash-heap.

M. 2:4

V A. A sin-offering, and a guilt-offering, and communal sacrifices of peace-offerings—

B. the laws of sacrilege apply to them once they have been sanctified.

C. [When] they have been slaughtered, they are rendered fit to be made invalid by a *Tebul Yom* and by one whose rites of atonement have not yet been completed and by being left overnight.

D. [When] their blood has been tossed, they are liable on their account because of violation of the laws of refuse, remnant, and uncleanness.

E. The laws of sacrilege do not apply to the meat.

F. But the laws of sacrilege apply to the sacrificial parts until they are taken out to the ash-heap.

M. 2:5

VI A. The two loaves—

B. the laws of sacrilege apply to them once they have been sanctified.

C. [When] they have formed a crust in the oven, they have been rendered fit to be made invalid by a *Tebul Yom* and by one whose rites of atonement have not yet been completed and to have slaughtered the animal-sacrifice [which pertains to them (Lev. 23:18)] on their account.

D. [When] the blood of the lambs has been tossed, they are liable on their account because of violation of the laws of refuse, remnant, and uncleanness.

E. But sacrilege does not apply to them.

M. 2:6

VII A. The show bread—

B. the laws of sacrilege apply to it once it has been sanctified.

C. [When] it has formed a crust in the oven, it has been rendered fit to be made invalid by a *Tebul Yom* and by one whose rites of atonement has not yet been completed and to be laid out on the table.

D. [When] the dishes of incense have been offered, they are liable on its account because of violation of the laws of refuse, remnant, and uncleanness.

E. And sacrilege does not pertain to it [any longer].

M. 2:7

VIII A. Meal-offerings—

B. the laws of sacrilege apply to them once they have been sanctified.

C. [When] they have been sanctified in a utensil, they are rendered fit to be made invalid by a Tebul Yom and by one whose rites of atonement have not yet been completed and by being left overnight.

D. [When] the handful [of the meal-offering] has been offered, they are liable on their account because of violation of the laws of refuse, remnant, and uncleanness.

E. And the laws of sacrilege do not apply to the residue. But the laws of sacrilege apply to the handful [of the meal-offering itself] until it is taken out to the ash-heap.

M. 2:8

IX A. The handful, the frankincense, the incense, the meal-offerings of priests, and the meal-offering of the anointed priest, and the meal-offering which accompanies drink-offerings [M. Zeb. 4:3]—

B. the laws of sacrilege apply to them once they have been sanctified.

C. [When] they have been sanctified in a utensil, they are rendered fit to be made invalid by a *Tebul Yom* and by one whose rites of atonement have not yet been completed and by being left overnight.

D. And they are liable on their account because of violation of the laws of remnant and because of violation of the laws of uncleanness.

E. But the prohibition of refuse does not apply to them.

F. This is the general principle: For whatever is subject to that which renders the offering permitted are they not liable on account of violation of the laws of refuse, remnant, and uncleanness until what renders the offering permitted has been properly offered.

G. And for whatever is not subject to that which renders the offering permitted, once it has been sanctified in a utensil are they liable on account of the violation of the laws of remnant, and on account of violation of the laws of uncleanness.

H. But the law of refuse does not apply to it [at all].

M. 2:9

The formal perfection of this pericope requires no comment. It is only where the facts of the case prevent the repetition of established formularies that we find variation, e.g., at M. 2:6C and 2:7C. The general principle, M. 2:9F-G (which ignores the issue of sacrilege entirely!) pertains to M. 2:9D-E only, therefore cannot be read as an effort to wind up the formal construction with some sort of stunning departure from the norm. Let us briefly comment on the discrete items. Sin-offering of fowl is not ultimately subject to the law of sacrilege because the priests are given the whole of the bird (M. Zeb. 6:4). When the bird is designated for its stated purpose, it is subject to the laws of sacrilege. When the head is severed, it enters its status as a sacrifice. When the blood is tossed, it is permitted for priestly use (M. 2:9E). In the case of burnt-offering of fowl, by contrast, the priest has no portion, therefore the whole bird is subject to the laws of sacrilege until disposed of (M. 2:2E). The same is so at M. 2:3, 4, 5. The point at M. 2:4 is that the priest gets the hide of the burnt-offering. At M. 2:5 the priest has a right to the meat. The shift to the bread- and meal-offerings, M. 2:6-9, simply requires the introduction of a new set of facts. M. 2:6 refers to the two loaves which are offered on the festival of Shabu^cot (^cAṣeret). C refers to the animals sacrificed along with them. M. 2:7C likewise has its important, fresh detail. M. 2:9F depends on M. Zeb. 4:3. M. 2:9's items do not depend upon the acceptable offering of something else to render them permitted to the priests.

A. Cows which are to be burned, once one has slaughtered them and tossed their blood—

B. the laws of sacrilege apply to them.

C. "And they are liable on their account because of violation of the laws of refuse, remnant, and uncleanness," the words of R. Meir.

D. And sages say, "Refuse does not apply [to offerings on the altar] inside."

T. 1:7 Z p. 557, ls. 18-20

M. 2:3D accords with Meir. If at the time of tossing the blood, the officiating priest forms the intention of offering up the sacrificial parts outside of their proper time, the sacrifices are rendered refuse. Sages maintain that the law of refuse does not apply to offerings on the inner altar, but only to those made on the outer altar.

CHAPTER ELEVEN

MEILAH CHAPTER THREE

We turn now to consider cultic property or material which is not subject to the laws of sacrilege, on the one hand, but which also is not to be used for other-than-cultic purposes, on the other. This conception is expressed in the formulary: *they are not available for use [benefit], but the laws of sacrilege do not apply.* M. 3:1-2 make this point with reference to sin-offerings which are left to die because, having been designated, they cannot now serve for the purpose for which they were set aside, and they also cannot be offered for some other. They are not to be offered, therefore are not subject to the laws of sacrilege, but, having been designated as sin-offerings, they retain the sanctity bestowed upon them when they were so designated. They therefore are not available for ordinary use or enjoyment. M. 3:1 has already appeared as M. Tem. 4:1. It serves, however, to introduce M. 3:2, to which the conceptions of M. 3:1 are integral. M. 3:2 concerns several animals set aside as the offerings of a Nazir. Coins set aside for the purchase of such animals are not available for use but are not subject to sacrilege. If the Nazir died before the animals were purchased and the several coins were not specified for a particular purpose, all go to the Temple-treasury. But if the coins are specified, then those for the purchase of an animal for a sin-offering are tossed into the Dead Sea, because they can serve no other purpose, just as we learned at M. 3:1 in connection with the animal designated for a sin-offering itself.

M. 3:3 is a singleton. It is included, I think, because it speaks of a cultic material which at one point is not subject to the laws of sacrilege but at some other is subject to those laws. M. 3:4-5, carrying forward the theme of M. 3:3 but now also the particular principle of our chapter, list a triplet of cultic materials—ashes of the inner altar, birds which are too young or too old, and milk and eggs of consecrated animals—which are not available for general use, but which also are not subject to the laws of sacrilege. M. 3:6 opens with a portentous generalization, but analysis of what follows shows that its illustrative materials go their own way. These introduce a new and interesting question, the status, as to the laws of sacrilege, of materials dedicated to the Temple and to the altar. At issue are accretions to things already dedicated, e.g., a pit, dedicated to the Temple, which fills up with water after it is designated. Judah (T. : Meir) says what comes into the pit after dedication is not subject to sacrilege. Simeon regards what grows in a field or on a tree after it is dedicated as offspring of that which is consecrated.

M. 3:7 and M. 3:8 deal with the established theme of the chapter, things which are not available for ordinary use but which also are not subject to the laws of sacrilege, now, roots of trees growing from secular property to Temple property and the like. The link to M. 3:6 is presumably Simeon's principle, which is rejected. But Judah's also is not wholly accepted, since, as I said, what derives from what is consecrated also is not available for ordinary use.

3:1

A. (1) The offspring of a sin-offering, and (2) the substitute of a sin-offering, and (3) a sin-offering, the owner of which died, are left to die.

B. [The sin-offering] (1) which became superannuated, or (2) which was lost, or (3) which turned out to be blemished,

C. if [this is] after the owner has effected atonement,

D. is left to die, and does not impart the status of substitute [to an animal designated in its stead].

E. And it is not available for enjoyment, but is not subject to the law of sacrilege.

F. And if [this is] before the owner has effected atonement,

G. it is put out to pasture until it suffers a blemish, then is sold, and with its proceeds he [the owner] brings another, and it does impart the status of substitute [to an animal designated in its stead].

H. And it is subject to the law of sacrilege.

M. 3:1

The pericope, which we already have seen as M. Tem. 4:1, stands at the head of its chapter because of the contrast between E and H, and because M. 3:2 will require its law. If the animal is left to die, C-D, it is not to be used for secular purposes, E. But it also is not subject to the law of sacrilege, since it is not designated for offering on the altar and therefore is not deemed sanctified, in line with M. 2:5A. The animal which is available for use in connection with the altar, F-G, is deemed designated for that purpose and is therefore subject to the law of sacrilege, H.

A. All sin-offerings which are left to die [M. Me. 3:1A, B-E]—the funds [set aside for their purchase] go to the Salt Sea [M. Me. 3:2F].

B. They are not available for benefit. But the laws of sacrilege do not apply to them [M. Me. 3:2G].

C. A sin-offering which died of natural causes and a burnt-offering which died of natural causes—

D. the laws of sacrilege do not apply to them.

E. A burnt-offering of fowl, the blood of which one has squeezed out—

F. the down and craw have left the domain of sacrilege [compare *TR* II, p. 289].

G. The laws of sacrilege apply to it [the bird itself] until it is taken out to the ash-heap.

T. 1:8 Z p. 557, ls. 20-23

T. reads the rule of M. 3:2 into the case of M. 3:1A, which is a valuable piece of redactional exegesis and confirms my surmise on why M. 3:1 is included here.

3:2

A. He who sets aside coins for his Nazirite-offering[s] [Num. 6:14: a he-lamb as a burnt-offering, a ewe-lamb as a sin-offering, a ram as a peace-offering]—

B. they [the coins] are not available for benefit.

C. But they [the coins] are not subject to the laws of sacrilege, because they [the sacrifices] are appropriate to be offered wholly as peace-offerings [Lesser Holy Things, not subject to sacrilege before the blood is tossed].

D. [If] he died,

E. [if] they were not designated [for their particular, respective purposes], they fall [to the Temple-treasury] as a freewill-offering.

F. [If] they were designated [for their particular, respective purposes], the money set aside for the sin-offering is to go to the Salt Sea.

G. They are not available for benefit, but they are not subject to the laws of sacrilege.

H. [With] the money set aside for the burnt-offering, they are to bring a burnt-offering.

I. And [with] the money set aside for peace-offerings, they are to bring peace-offerings.

J. And they are eaten for one day [M. Zeb. 5:6] and do not require bread [Num. 6:19].

M. 3:2

The pericope of course is unitary. A-C lay out the basic facts. D then sets forth the problem, the disposition of the coins in the case of the Nazirite's sudden death. E completes one thought, F-G, H, and I-J, the second. Once the coins are set aside for the Nazirite's offering, the coins may not be used for any other purpose. But they also are not subject to the laws of sacrilege. C carries its own reason with it. All of the sacrifices may be offered as peace-offerings, that is, as Lesser Holy

Things, to which the laws of sacrilege do not apply before the blood is sprinkled on the altar (M. 1:4). The Nazirite dies before the offerings are purchased. If the money has not been designated, each coin for its sacrificial animal, then the whole is given to the Temple-treasury as a freewill-offering. If, however, we know that a given coin is to go for the purchase of a specific sacrifice, then in line with M. 3:1A3, C-E, the money for the sin-offering is thrown into the Salt Sea. Through death the owner has effected atonement. Why cannot the money be subjected to the laws of sacrilege? Because—in line with M. 3:1E—no offering will be purchased with it. H and I-J complete the matter. The laws of sacrilege, of course, apply throughout. The meat is eaten over a period of one day, in accord with M. Zeb. 5:6's disposition of the peace-offerings of the Nazirite. They do not require bread, since the Nazirite is no longer available, so the bread cannot be placed in his hands (Num. 6:19).

A. *He who sets aside coins for his Nazirite-offering—they are not available for benefit. But they are not subject to the laws of sacrilege, because they [the animals to be purchased with the coins] are appropriate to be offered wholly as peace-offerings* [M. Me. 3:2A-C, T. Naz. 3:16A].

B. Under what circumstances?

C. When they [the coins] are left undesignated [for the purchase of a particular animal-sacrifice].

D. But if they were designated [for the purchase of a particular animal-sacrifice], the laws of sacrilege apply to the funds set aside for a sin-offering and to the funds set aside for a burnt-offering.

E. But the laws of sacrilege do not apply to the funds set aside for peace-offerings [M. Me. 3:2F-I].

F. If it was a beast, the laws of sacrilege apply to the sin-offering and to the guilt-offering ,but the laws of sacrilege do not apply to peace-offerings.

G. *[If the owner] died, [if] they were not designated, they fall [to the Temple-treasury] as a free-will offering.*

H. *[If] they were designated [for particular purposes], the funds set aside for the sin-offering go to the Salt Sea. The funds set aside for the burnt-offering and the funds set aside for the peace-offerings [are to be spent in the purchase of animals which] are to be offered* [M. Me. 3:2H, I].

I. If it [the beast] was [designated as a] sin-offering, it is left to die.

J. [If] it was designated as a burnt-offering or as peace-offerings, it is to be offered.

T. 1:9 Z p. 557, ls. 23-28

A. If the owner said, "These [coins] are for my burnt-offering and the rest is for the remainder of my Nazirite-offerings," and then died—

B. [with the money set aside for the burnt-offering], [the executor] should bring a burnt-offering.

C. The laws of sacrilege apply to it.

D. And the rest of the money falls [to the Temple-treasury] as a freewill-offering.

E. And the laws of sacrilege apply to them [the coins].

F. [If he said], "These are for my peace-offering, and the rest of the money is for the remainder of my Nazirite-sacrifices," and died—

G. with the money set aside for peace-offerings, let him bring peace-offerings.

H. The laws of sacrilege [do *not*] apply to them.

I. And the rest of the money falls [to the Temple-treasury] as a freewill-offering.

J. And the laws of sacrilege do apply to them.

K. [If he said], "These are for my sin-offering, and the rest is for the other Nazirite-offerings," and then died,

L. the money set aside for a sin-offering goes to the Salt Sea [M. Me. 3:2F].

M. And it is not available for use. But it is not subject to the laws of sacrilege.

N. And [as to] the rest of the money—[if] one wants to bring with them a burnt-offering, he brings [a burnt-offering]. [If he wants to bring] peace-offerings, he brings [peace-offerings].

O. And the laws of sacrilege apply to all of them [the coins], but the laws of sacrilege do not apply to only part of them.

T. 1:10 Z p. 557, ls. 28-32

A. [If] one was liable to offer a sin-offering of fowl and said, "Lo, I pledge myself to bring a burnt-offering,"

B. and he set aside coins and said, "Lo, these are for [purchasing an animal in fulfillment of] my obligation,"

C. [if] he wanted to bring with them a sin-offering of fowl, he may not bring it.

D. [If he wanted to bring with them] a burnt-offering of fowl, he may not bring it.

E. And the laws of sacrilege apply to all of them [the coins], and the laws of sacrilege apply to only part of them [the coins].

F. [If] he died, the coins go to the Salt Sea, because money set aside for a sin-offering is mixed up among them.

T. 1:11 Z p. 557, ls. 33-35

A. [If a Nazirite designated] these [coins] for his sin-offering, and these for his burnt-offering, and these for his peace-offerings,

B. but then they got mixed up together,

C. lo, this one purchases with them three beasts, whether in one place or in three places.

D. He declares the money set aside for the sin-offering to be rendered unconsecrated by means of the animal he has purchased for the sin-offering, the money set aside for the burnt-offering by means of the animal set aside for the burnt-offering, and the money set aside for peace-offerings through the animal set aside as peace-offerings [A-D = T. Naz. 3:16].

E. The laws of sacrilege apply to all of them [the coins], and the laws of sacrilege apply to any part of them [the coins].

T. 1:12 Z p. 557, ls. 35-38

A. The *Zab* and the *Zabah* and the woman after childbirth and the *meṣora*ᶜ and all those mentioned in the Torah who are liable to bring bird-offerings,

B. who separated coins,

C. let one [of the aforenamed] say, "Lo, these are for [the purchase of an animal in fulfillment of] my obligation."

D. [If] he wanted to bring with them a sin-offering of fowl, he may bring it.

E. [If] he wanted to bring with them a burnt-offering of fowl, let him bring it.

F. The laws of sacrilege apply to all of them [the coins], and the laws of sacrilege apply to any part of them.

G. [If] he died, let them fall [to the Temple-treasury] as a freewill-offering.

H. And the laws of sacrilege apply to them.

T. 1:13 Z p. 557, ls. 38-39, p. 558, ls. 1-2

A. [If one said], "A purse among my purses is consecrated," or, "An ox among my oxen is consecrated"—

B. the laws of sacrilege apply to all of them [the coins or oxen], and the laws of sacrilege apply to any one of them.

C. What is he to do?

D. He brings the largest among them and says, "If this one is consecrated, lo, it is the consecrated one. If not, then that which is consecrated in any place is to be deemed as unconsecrated in exchange for this one [which is now consecrated]."

T. 1:14 Z p. 558, ls. 2-4

A. The bones and the sinews and the hooves and the horns which separated from consecrated animals before the tossing of the blood—

B. the laws of sacrilege apply to them.

C. [If they separated] after the tossing of the blood, the laws of sacrilege do not apply to them.

D. But a coal which burst from off the altar, whether before midnight or after midnight, lo, this one should not return it.

E. It is not available for benefit, but the laws of sacrilege do not apply to it.

T. 1:15 Z p. 558, ls. 4-7

T. 1:9 essentially restates M.'s points, clarifying what M. has left entirely clear. T. 1:10 then proceeds to specify a number of situations invited by M.'s general rule. The point of T. 1:10/0 is that if one has derived benefit from all of them, then he has derived benefit also from the funds for the burnt-offering included in the money in hand. Then the laws of sacrilege apply. But if he derived benefit from only part of the money, then he may have derived benefit only from the funds set aside for peace-offerings, and that money is not subject to the laws of sacrilege. Hence he is not liable for the misappropriation of only part of the available money. T. 1:11 goes on to a parallel but distinct case, stated at A. If the man says he wants to bring an offering with the coins, he thereby indicates his intent to fulfill all of his obligations, not only for the one specified at A. The problem of T. 1:12 is clear as stated. If the coins are designated for the purchase of particular animals but then mixed together, there is a remedy, as specified at D. T. 1:13-15 are relevant, but supplementary. T. 1:15 would be better situated at M. 1:4; its point of contact is at D-E.

3:3

A. R. Simeon [so Pa, C, M, K, P, Vat 119, Maimonides, *Comm.*, B. Me. 11a; printed texts, N: *Ishmael*] says, "Blood is subject to a lenient law at the outset and to a strict law at the end, and the drink-offerings are subject to a strict rule at the outset and to a lenient rule at the end.

B. "The blood at the outset: the laws of sacrilege do not apply to it.

C. "[When] it has gone forth to the Qidron Brook, the laws of sacrilege apply to it.

D. "Drink offerings at the outset: the laws of sacrilege apply to them.

E. "[When] they have gone forth to the pits, the laws of sacrilege do not apply to them."

M. 3:3

Simeon simply sets up facts into a paradox. Before blood is tossed on the altar, it is not subject to the laws of sacrilege (M. Hul. 8:6). The remnants of the blood, poured onto the base of the altar, flow down into the Qidron Brook and are sold to farmers for manure. Those who use it without paying for it are guilty of sacrilege (M. Yoma 5:6). The drink-offerings are subject to the laws of sacrilege. When they flow down to the foundations of the altar, they cease to be subject to those laws. The relevance of this pericope to its larger setting is not self-evident since the established theme—things not available for enjoyment but also not subject to the laws of sacrilege—is not stated.

A. *R. Simeon says, "Blood is subject to a lenient law at the outset and to a strict law at the end"* [M. Me. 3:3A].

B. It is mixed together in the gutter and rolls on downward to Qidron Brook and is sold to the farmers for manure.

C. "And the laws of sacrilege apply to them [the coins]," the words of R. Meir and R. Simeon.

D. And sages say, "Sacrilege does not pertain to the money."

E. And so did R. Simeon say, "He who sanctifies money for the upkeep of the house—

F. "The laws of sacrilege apply to them [the coins]."

G. *And drink-offerings are subject to a strict rule at the outset and to a lenient rule at the end* [M. Me. 3:3A].

H. R. Eleazar bar Ṣadoq says, "There was a little channel between the *ᵓUlam* and the altar, on the west of the ramp.

I. "Once in every sixty or seventy years, the young priests would go down there and collect from there wine, which was congealed like dried figs.

J. "They bring them up and burn it them in a state of sanctity,

K. "since it is said, *In the holy place you shall pour out a drink offering of strong drink to the Lord* (Num. 28:7).

L. "Just as it is poured out in a state of holiness, so it is burned in a state of holiness."

M. And it says, *He built a watchtower in the midst of it and hewed out a wine vat in it* (Is. 5:2)—

N. *He built a watchtower*—this is the *Hekhal.*

O. *He hewed out a wine vat in it*—this is the altar.

P. *And* also *he hewed out a wine vat in it*—this is the pit.

T. 1:16 Z p. 558, ls. 7-15

T. systematically cites and glosses M., as indicated, M. does not know the secondary dispute of C-D.

3:4

I A. The ashes [of the incense] of the inner altar and [of the wicks that remain] of the candelabrum—

B. are not available for benefit, but the laws of sacrilege do not apply.

C. He who sanctifies the ash to begin with—

D. the laws of sacrilege apply to it.

II E. (1) Turtledoves which have not yet reached their maturity and (2) pigeons which have become superannuated

F. are not available for benefit, but the laws of sacrilege do not apply.

G. R. Simeon says, "Turtledoves which have not yet reached their maturity—the laws of sacrilege apply to them. But pigeons which have become superannuated are not available for benefit, but the laws of sacrilege do not apply."

M. 3:4

We have two distinct units, A-B + C-D and the dispute, E-F *vs.* G. The point of A-B is that, unlike the ashes of the outer altar, the ashes of the inner altar and of the wicks of the candelabrum, once removed from the inner altar, are no longer deemed holy. (Those of the outer altar are held to retain their holiness.) While they cannot be used, they also are not subject to the law of sacrilege. C-D are an interpolated gloss. If one collected such ashes after they are removed from the inner altar to the ash-heap and dedicated them to the Temple, they of course are sacred and subject to the law of sacrilege as is anything else dedicated to the Temple. The point of E-F is that while these birds cannot be offered, they also cannot be enjoyed. Simeon's view is that the turtle-doves may be used later on, so they remain subject to the law of sacrilege. The stated rule (E2) applies to pigeons, which cannot be used again. It seems to me that M. 3:4A-B, E-F, and M. 3:5A form a triplet of items belonging in some measure to the cult which are not to be used but not subject to the laws of sacrilege.

3:5

III A. The milk of animal-sacrifices and the eggs of turtledoves are not available for benefit, but the laws of sacrilege do not apply to them.

B. Under what circumstances?

C. In the case of what is made holy for the use of the altar.

D. But in the case of what is made holy for the upkeep of the Temple-house—

E. [If] one has sanctified a chicken, the laws of sacrilege apply to it and to its egg.

F. [If he sanctified] an ass, the laws of sacrilege apply to it and to its milk.

M. 3:5

The important side to this unitary pericope is the distinction of C-D. The eggs and milk, A, cannot be offered on the altar. They are not subject to the laws of sacrilege. But if one has sanctified something for the upkeep of the Temple house, then the *value* is what is consecrated, so that whatever pertains to that which has been dedicated belongs to the Temple and is deemed consecrated on that account until it has been redeemed. This same matter is continued in the following, far more ambitious statement.

Since M. 3:6A-D are clear that something which is not appropriate for use on the altar *is* subject to the laws of sacrilege, and M. 3:5A excludes milk and eggs of animal-sacrifices from liability to the laws of sacrilege on the ground that they are not appropriate for use on the altar, there is an obvious contradiction between the conceptions of the two pericopae. This is eliminated by Papa (B. Me. 12b), who explains M. 3:5A by revising M. 3:5 with the italicized words as follows: "*This is so only for things themselves consecrated for use on the altar. But if their value is dedicated for the altar, it is considered as if they have been dedicated for the upkeep of the house.* If one consecrated a chicken, both it and its eggs are subject to the law of sacrilege..."

3:6

A. Whatever is appropriate for [use on] the altar but not for the upkeep of the house,

B. for the upkeep of the house and not for the altar,

C. not for the altar and not for the upkeep of the house—

D. the laws of sacrilege apply thereto.

E. How so?

F. [If] one sanctified (1) a hole full of water [B], (2) a dung-heap full of dung [C], (3) a dovecot full of pigeons [A], (4) a tree covered with fruit, (5) a field full of herbs—

G. the laws of sacrilege apply to them and to what is in them.

H. But if he sanctified (1) a hole, and afterward it filled with water, (2) a dung-heap, and afterward it was filled with dung, (3) a dovecot, and afterward it was filled with pigeons, (4) a tree and afterward it filled with fruit, (5) a field and afterward it was filled with herbs—

I. "the laws of sacrilege apply to them, but the laws of sacrilege do not apply to what is in them," the words of R. Judah.

J. R. Simeon [B. Me. 13a, Maimonides, *Comm.*: *Yosé*] says, "He who sanctifies a field and a tree—the laws of sacrilege apply to them and to what grows in them,

K. "for they are the offspring of that which has been consecrated" [Danby: "since their growth is from what belongs to the Temple"].

L. The offspring of the tithe of cattle may not suck from [a beast that is] tithe [of cattle].

M. And others donate [their beasts] thus [on condition that, if the tithe of their cattle should be a female beast, its milk should not be deemed consecrated but should be available for its offspring].

N. The offspring of a consecrated beast should not suck from consecrated beasts.

O. And others donate their beasts thus.

P. Laborers should not eat of dried figs which have been consecrated.

Q. And so: A cow should not eat of vetches which have been consecrated.

M. 3:6

We have what appear to be two distinct units, M. 3:6A-K, and L-Q. But A-K present two quite separate parts, A-D and F-K. L-M, N-O, then P, Q, by contrast, form a unity. A-D are clear as stated. The illustrative materials, F-K, joined by E, are curiously out of phase. For without A-D, we should not have interpreted F-K as a statement of the issue of A-D. F-K address a quite distinct issue, specifically, that which is spelled out by I-K. What is important to F-H is the distinction—which is so pointedly stated—between sanctifying a hole filled with water and one which is empty but which afterward fills up. Then the dispute is very clear. Judah distinguishes what is sanctified, the hole, from what later on accrues to what is sanctified. Simeon (*Yosé:* Pa, C, M, K, P, Vat119) deems the latter to be the offspring of the former and to be sanctified. Now what has the operative distinction to do with A-D? Nothing whatsoever! Indeed, on second glance it is difficult to align F's items with A-C. Clearly, F1 illustrates B, in that water can be used to make mud for construction; F2 falls under C; and F3 falls under A. But what shall we say of F4 and F5? Grapes and olives will serve for making wine and oil for the altar; other fruit is not used on the altar. Herbs are not used on the altar. It would appear that F4 may illustrate either A or C, and F5 repeats F2 in illustrating C—a strange state of affairs. If, however, we drop E, then F-K stand all by themselves, and, of course, nicely introduce L-Q. For L conforms to Simeon's conception at J-K, carrying his position to its logical extreme. The same is so of N, of course. M and O complete their respective units and the whole is certainly a single construction. P and Q refer to workers or animals in the Temple-service. They further illustrate the point of L.

A. *Whatever is appropriate for [use on] the altar but not for the upkeep of the house,*

B. *for the upkeep of the house and not for the altar,*

C. *not for the altar and not for the upkeep of the house* [M. Me. 3:6A-C]—

D. even milk, even cheese, and even brine—

E. the laws of sacrilege apply to them.

F. [If] he consecrated a cow, the laws of a sacrilege apply to it, to its offspring, and to its milk.

G. [If he consecrated] an ass, the laws of sacrilege apply to it and to its milk [M. Me. 3:5F].

H. If he consecrated a chicken, the laws of sacrilege apply to it and to its egg [M. Me. 3:5E].

T. 1:17 Z p. 558, ls. 15-18

A. The egg of a turtledove [M. Me. 3:5A] and the crop of fowl and the offerings of gentiles

B. are not available for use, but are not subject to the laws of sacrilege.

C. He who sanctifies turtledoves for the upkeep of the house—

D. the laws of sacrilege apply to their eggs [M. Me. 3:5E].

T. 1:18 Z p. 558, ls. 18-19

A. A dung-heap—

B. the laws of sacrilege apply to it and its dung.

C. A pit—

D. the laws of sacrilege apply to it and to its water.

E. A dovecot—

F. the laws of sacrilege apply to it and to its doves.

G. [If] one sanctified them empty and afterward they were filled up,

H. *"the laws of sacrilege apply to them, but the laws of sacrilege do not apply to what is in them"* [M. Me. 3:6I], the words of R. Meir.

I. R. Eleazar b. R. Simeon says, "Also: the laws of sacrilege apply to what is in them."

T. 1:19 Z p. 558, ls. 19-22

A. Said R. Yosé, "I prefer in all cases [M. 3:6H] the opinion of R. Meir,

B. "except for the case of the field and the tree,

C. "because in these cases it is usual for them to be filled up [with herbs or fruit, and hence that was to be expected at the outset]."

T. 1:20 Z p. 558, ls. 22-23

A. Laborers who work in the sanctuary should not eat dried dates which are consecrated.

B. But others donate [food] for them.

C. And so: A cow which was working in the sanctuary [or: Temple properly] should not eat from vetches which have been consecrated.

D. But others donate for them [M. Me. 3:6P-Q].

T. 1:21 Z p. 558, ls. 23-25

A. [If] one sanctified a cow, vetches, and sheaves,

B. they do not say, "Let this cow eat the vetches and the sheaves."

C. But others donate for it.

T. 1:22 Z p. 558, ls. 25-27

A. A laborer who did work [for the sanctuary], whether for a *maneh* [a hundred] or for two hundred *zuz*, should not say, "Give me this cow for the *maneh* [which you owe me] and this cloak for fifty *zuz*."

B. For that which has been consecrated is not rendered unconsecrated in exchange for an act of labor but only in exchange for money alone.

C. How do they carry out the procedure?

D. They set aside the payment for the craftsmen. They render them [what is set aside] unconsecrated in exchange for the coins of craftsmen, and they [then] give them [the objects desired] to the craftsman as their salary.

E. Then they go and take them from the contribution fund of the chamber.

F. Manure and dung of consecrated animals—lo, these are prohibited.

G. And funds paid for them fall to the Temple treasury.

T. 1:23 Z p. 558, ls. 27-31

T. 1:17 provides a better expansion of the cited pericope of M. than does M. itself. T. 1:18 concurs with M. 3:5, as indicated. T. 1:19A-F restate M. 3:6F-G, omitting F4-5, which, as we noted, are ambiguous. T. further expresses Yosé's position at T. 1:20. T. 1:21 restates M. 3:6P-Q, which then T. 1:22-23 proceed to expand and augment.

3:7

A. [If] the roots of a privately-owned tree come into consecrated ground,

B. or those of a tree which is consecrated come into privately-owned ground,

C. they are not available for enjoyment, but they are not subject to the laws of sacrilege.

D. A well which gushes forth from a field which is consecrated—[the water] is not available for enjoyment, but the laws of sacrilege do not apply.

E. [If] it went outside of the field, they derive benefit from it.

F. Water which is in a golden jar—

G. is not available for benefit but is not subject to the laws of sacrilege.

H. [If] one put it into a glass, the law of sacrilege applies to it.

I. The willow-branch [set beside the altar]

J. is not available for benefit but is not subject to the law of sacrilege.

K. R. Eleazar b. R. Ṣadoq says, "The elders would take some of it for their *lulabs.*"

M. 3:7

The pericope is in the following parts: A-C, D-E, and F-K. The point of A-C is that if the roots spread out from unconsecrated to consecrated ground or *vice versa*, we invoke the rule that one may not make use of the tree, but the tree is not subject to the law of sacrilege, since it does not wholly fall within the domain of the Temple. The same rule is stated at D, but E gives an important qualification. F-K turn to cultic materials. F refers to water in the golden jar kept for the animal-sacrifice.

A. That which is located in the shadow of a dovecot or in the shadow of a cave [belonging to the sanctuary]—
B. they are not available for use, but the laws of sacrilege do not apply.
C. And [to] that which is on the lands [of the Temple]
D. the laws of sacrilege apply.
E. Water which is in the pitcher—
F. the laws of sacrilege do not apply to it.
G. [When] *one poured it into a glass, the laws of sacrilege apply to it* [M. Me. 3:7H].
H. But as to the pitcher and the glass itself,
I. the laws of sacrilege apply to them,
J. because they themselves are consecrated.

T. 1:24 Z p. 558, ls. 31-34

A-B go over the ground of M. 3:7A-C. E-J augment M. 3:7F-H. Maimonides (*Trespass* 5:6, Lewittes, pp. 428-9) states the present set of materials as follows:

The law of trespass applied to what grows from consecrated things. How was this? If one consecrated a field and it grew grass, or a tree and it produced fruit, trespass was committed with the produce. But if one consecrated an empty cistern and then it was filled with water or a dunghill and then it was filled with dung or a dovecote and then it was filled with pigeons, no trespass was committed with the contents, since they did not grow from the consecrated things.

Likewise, no use might be enjoyed of the dung and the refuse in a court belonging to the Temple, but no trespass was committed therewith. What was to be done with them? They were to be sold, and the money accrued to the Temple treasury.

It was forbidden to make any use of the water that flowed out of a spring welling in a consecrated field while it was still in the field, but if one did make use of it, no trespass was committed. If the water flowed outside the field, it was permitted to make use thereof. No use might be enjoyed of a willow growing in a consecrated field, but no trespass was committed therewith.

If a tree belonging to a private person was near a consecrated field and its roots spread into the field, then if between the tree and the consecrated field there was a distance of less than sixteen cubits it was forbidden to enjoy any use of the roots in the field, but no trespass was committed with them. If the tree was more than sixteen cubits distant, trespass was committed by anyone who enjoyed a use of the roots (in the consecrated field).

If a tree belonging to the Temple was near a private person's field and its roots spread into the field, then trespass was committed with the roots if the tree was within sixteen cubits (of the field). If the tree was more than sixteen cubits distant, the roots in the private person's field might not be used, but no trespass was committted with them.

3:8

A. A nest which is up at the top of a tree which has been consecrated

B. is not available for benefit, but is not subject to the law of sacrilege.

C. And that which is on an *asherah*-tree—

D. one may flick it off with a reed.

E. He who sanctifies a forest—

F. the law of sacrilege applies to the whole of it.

G. And the Temple-treasurers who bought wood—

H. the laws of sacrilege apply to the wood.

I. But the laws of sacrilege do not apply to the chips and [they do] not [apply] to the foliage.

M. 3:8

A-B do not continue the foregoing, because they are matched with C-D. [1] E-I form a second pericope. The nest is built of wood and leaves deriving from unconsecrated domain. Since the tree is consecrated, however, the nest is not to be used. The one on the *asherah*-tree may be used. The rule in the case of the consecrated tree is more strict. If one consecrated a forest, everything in it is deemed set apart. But if the Temple-treasurers bought the forest intending to make use of the wood for beams, only the usable wood is purchased by them. What they cannot use for beams they do not sanctify.

A. He who sanctified a forest for beams [for the Temple]—

B. the laws of sacrilege apply to the beams and the laws of sacrilege apply to the chips and to the foliage [M. Me. 3:8E-F].

C. *But the Temple-treasurers who purchased a forest for wood—*

D. *the laws of sacrilege apply to the wood, but the laws of sacrilege do not apply to the chips nor to the foliage* [M. 3:8G-I].

T. 1:25 Z p. 558, ls. 34-35

T. clarifies M. 3:8E-I.

---

[1] "That is to say, A-D are prior to the larger construction. Formally, of course, A-B *do* continue the foregoing."—R.S.S.

CHAPTER TWELVE

MEILAH CHAPTER FOUR

Only at the opening pericope, M. 4:1, does sacrilege occur. It is taken for granted (but not explicitly stated) that an act of sacrilege must involve a substance of at least the value of a *peruṭah*. If one misappropriates less than that value of a sacrifice, he is not liable. M. 4:1 rules that diverse consecrated materials join together to form the requisite amount of material. Things consecrated for the altar and those consecrated for the upkeep of the house join together to form the requisite bulk (in line with the theory of M. 3:6). The remainder of the chapter consists of a sequence of statements listing things which do or do not join together to form the requisite volume for various purposes, none of them dealing with sacrilege. There is a formula, recurring in the fixed predicate, *join together with one another*, but this language is necessary for what is to be said, and I do not see the chapter as the product of a single hand.

4:1

I A. Things consecrated for the altar join together with one another [for making up the requisite quantity—a *perutah's* worth—to be subject to] the law of sacrilege.

B. and to impose liability on their account for transgression of the laws of refuse, remnant and uncleanness.

II C. Things consecrated for the upkeep of the house join together with one another [in regard to sacrilege].

III D. Things consecrated for the altar and things consecrated for the upkeep of the house join together [for making up the quantity to be subject to] the law of sacrilege.

M. 4:1

This triplet—A, C, D—of declarative sentences takes for granted the fact that the minimum requisite for misappropriating consecrated materials is the value of a *peruṭah*. If one misappropriates less than that value, he has not incurred the liability to bring a guilt-offering for sacrilege. That is the point of A and D. B refers to the quite separate, minimum requisite for consuming sacrificial meat which is refuse or which has been left overnight or which is unclean. That minimum is an olive's bulk of said meat. If, then, one eats less than an olive's bulk, or misappropriates less than a *peruṭah's* value, of three or four different sorts of things consecrated for the altar, these different things join together to make up the requisite amount. C makes the same point for things consecrated for the upkeep of the house. D then joins A and C, but not B. There can be no doubt that the whole is a unitary pericope.

4:2

A. Five things in a burnt-offering join together [to form the requisite volume for liability to sacrilege]: (1) the meat, (2) the forbidden fat, (3) the fine flour, (4) the wine, and (5) the oil.

B. And six in the thank-offering [join together]: (1) the meat, (2) the forbidden fat, (3) the fine flour, (4) the wine, (5) the oil, and (6) the bread.

C. (1) Heave-offering, and (2) heave-offering of tithe, and (3) heave-offering of tithe of *demaʾi*, and (4) dough-offering, and (5) first fruits join together

to impose a prohibition and to impose liability to the added fifth on their account.

M. 4:2

A and B form a doublet. [1] C is independent. A falls under the rule of M. 4:1A-B. But B is subject only to M. 4:1B, since sacrilege does not apply to Lesser Holy Things. C's five items are deemed equivalent, all being called heave-offering. Dough-offering (C4) is called heave-offering at Num. 15:20, and so too, first-fruits, at Deut. 12:6. That is why all five are treated as a single category which join together. If a *seah* of one of these, or a *seah* made up of small parts of all five, should fall into less than a hundred *seahs* of unconsecrated produce, that will prohibit use of the unconsecrated produce. He who inadvertently eats from such a mixture is liable to pay the priest the principal (what he has eaten) and an added fifth.

A. A half-*peruṭah* in value of things consecrated for the altar and a half-*peruṭah* in value of things consecrated for the upkeep of the house join together with one another for purposes of sacrilege [M. Me. 4:1D].

B. A burnt-offering and its sacrificial parts join together with one another [to impose liability for] offering them up outside and to impose liability on their account because of violation of the laws of refuse, remnant, and uncleanness.

C. A burnt-offering and its drink-offerings join together with one another [to impose liability for] offering them up outside and to impose liability on their account because of violation of the laws of refuse, remnant, and uncleanness [M. Me. 4:2A].

---

1 "Note also the numerical mnemonic, 5/6."—R.S.S.

D. A thank-offering and its bread join together with one another [to impose liability for] offering them up outside and to impose liability on their account because of violation of the laws of refuse, remnant, and uncleanness [M. Me. 4:2B].

E. A half olive's bulk of meat and a half olive's bulk of bread join together with one another to impose the status of refuse on the bread, but not on the meat.

F. That which has been rendered refuse in the case of Most Holy Things joins together [M. 4:3A].

G. That which has been rendered remnant, whether in the case of Most Holy Things or in the case of Lesser Holy Thing, does not join together [*vs.* M. 4:3B].

T. 1:28 Z p. 559, ls. 3-9

T. goes over the propositions of M. 4:1-2. It raises the further, and secondary, question of joining together in connection with offerings made outside of the Temple. If one offers up a half-olive's bulk of meat outside of the Temple, he is not liable. If he offers up a half-olive's bulk of meat and a half-olive's bulk of bread (D), then the two join together to make up the requisite bulk, and he is liable. T. 1:26-27 are at M. 5:4.

4:3

A. All forms of refuse join together.
B. All forms of remnant join together.
C. All forms of carrion join together.
D. All forms of creeping things join together.
E. The blood of a creeping thing and its flesh join together.

F. A general principle did R. Joshua state, "All things that are alike in the [duration of] uncleanness of each and in the requisite measure of each join together.

G. "[If they are alike] (1) in [duration of] uncleanness but not in requisite measure, (2) in requisite measure but not in [duration of] uncleanness, (3) neither in [duration of] uncleanness nor in requisite measure,

"they do not join together [to form the volume that is necessary to convey uncleanness]."

M. 4:3

The five items—A-E—are distinct from F-G, but they say the same thing in detail which F-G say in general. The fresh point of A is that refuse of Most Holy Things and Lesser Holy Things joins together. That of C is that refuse of an unclean and that of a clean beast join together. The different creeping things (D) of Lev. 11:29-30 join together in the volume of a lentil. Joshua's statement allows all things alike in the affects and character of their uncleanness and in the requisite measure to impart uncleanness to join together. G/1 is illustrated by a limb of carrion which imparts uncleanness at any measure, as against the flesh of carrion, which must be of the volume of an olive's bulk. G2 is exemplified by carrion and corpse-matter, both of which impart uncleanness in the volume of an olive's bulk, but are of a different sort, since the former's uncleanness lasts until evening, but the latter's for seven days (and also: in a tent). G3 speaks of corpse-matter and a creeping thing, different in affect, for the creeping thing imparts uncleanness by contact, but its uncleanness lasts only to the evening, and its measure is a lentil's bulk, while corpse-matter imparts uncleanness by overshadowing; its uncleanness lasts a week; and its measure is an olive's bulk.

4:4

A. Refuse and remnant do not join together, because they are of two [different] categories.

B. The creeping thing and carrion,

C. and so too, carrion and the flesh of a corpse—

D. do not join together with one another to impart uncleanness,

E. even in accord with the lesser of the two of them.

F. Food which has been made unclean by a Father of uncleanness and that which has been made unclean by an offspring of uncleanness join together to impart uncleanness in accord with the lesser remove of uncleanness of the two of them.

M. 4:4

We continue M. 4:3. A clarifies M. 4:3A and B; B, M. 4:3C and D. C is inserted. The reason this statement—A-D—is required is at E, which forms the bridge to the contrast of F. We do not impose uncleanness even in accord with the lesser measure of the two, or in accord with the more lenient form of uncleanness of the two. F is clear as stated and is spelled out at M. Toh. 1:5. If we have food unclean by a Father of uncleanness, hence in the first remove, and other food unclean by an offspring, hence in the second remove, they join together in the volume of an olive's bulk to impart uncleanness at the second remove, that is, heave-offering food which touches such a mixture is in the third remove and therefore invalid.

4:5

A. All foodstuffs join together—

B. to render the body invalid, at a volume of half a half-loaf of bread;

C. in the case of food, two meals for an ᶜ*erub* [M. Erub. 8:2];

D. in the volume of an olive's bulk to impart uncleanness as food,

E. in the volume of a fig's bulk in connection with removal [from one domain to another on] the Sabbath [M. Shab. 7:4],

F. and in the volume of a date's bulk [for the volume prohibited for eating] on the Day of Atonement [M. Yoma 8:2].

G. All liquids join together—

H. to render the body invalid, at a volume of a quarter-*log*;

I. and for the mouthful [which it is forbidden to drink] on the Day of Atonement.

M. 4:5

A-B are matched by G-H. C is formally distinct. Forming a subunit, D, E, and F are balanced against one another. I balances F. The whole complex, of course, is artificial, a catalogue made up of available formulas. The main point is that unclean foods which add up to half of a half-loaf (two eggs' bulks) invalidate a person's body so that he cannot eat heave-offering; and all sorts of unclean liquids do the same at a volume of a quarter-*log*. M. Ker. 3:3 is relevant.

4:6

A. ᶜ*Orlah*-fruit and diverse kinds of the vineyard join together.

B. R. Simeon says, "They do not join together."

C. Cloth and sacking, sacking and leather, leather and matting join together with one another.

D. R. Simeon says, "That is because they are suitable to be made unclean as that which is used for sitting [with *moshab*-uncleanness].

M. 4:6

ᶜOrlah-fruit—fruit of trees in their first three years of growth—is not to be eaten. Produce growing as diverse kinds in a vineyard is not to be eaten. A then wishes to treat the two together, so that if a *seah* made up of the two should fall into two hundred *seahs* of permitted food, the whole is prohibited (M. Orl. 2:1). Simeon does not regard as decisive the fact that there is a common requisite volume—two hundred *seahs*. C refers to making up the requisite area of fabric for receiving *midras*-uncleanness as something which is used for sitting, e.g., to be made unclean by a *Zab*'s sitting down thereon. M. Kel. 27:1-2 has told us that these different sorts of fabric are subject to different measures, cloth—three by three handbreaths; sacking—four by four; leather—five by five; matting—six by six. They will join together to be made unclean in accord with the measure of the more lenient of the two, as explained at M. Kel. 27:3. Simeon spells out how this rule does not violate the principle of Joshua, M. 4:3 (compare Albeck, pp. 283, 421). Even though the basic measures are not the same, these join together because, so far as receiving uncleanness as a seat, the measures *are* the same for all fabrics: a handbreadth by a handbreath of any one of them can be made into a seat.

A. *All liquids join together to form a quarter-log* [M. Me. 4:5G-H] and for the measurement of pouring out on the Sabbath [M. Shab. 8:1].
B. A creeping thing—its blood and its flesh and its limbs join together to form the requisite volume of a lentil [M. Me. 4:3E].
C. All those things which are prohibited in the case of a Nazir join together with one another to form the requisite volume of an olive's bulk.
D. A half olive's bulk from a clean beast while it is alive and a half olive's bulk of the same after it has died—lo, these join together.
E. A half-olive's bulk of an unclean beast while it is alive and a half-olive's bulk of an unclean beast after it has died do not join together.
F. A half-olive's bulk of a clean beast and a half-olive's bulk of an unclean beast, whether alive or dead, do not join together.

T. 1:29 Z p. 559, ls. 9-14

A. All corpses join together with one another to form the requisite volume of an olive's bulk.
B. A half olive's bulk of flesh and a half-olive's bulk of corpse-matter join together with one another [M. Me. 4:3F].
C. But all other sources of uncleanness in connection with a corpse do not join together with one another,
D. for they are not equivalent in respect to the requisite volume of them required for imparting uncleanness [M. Me. 4:3G].
E. A half-olive's bulk of meat and a half-olive's bulk of milk join together to impose liability on their account because of [eating forbidden] food and because of cooking [the two together].
F. The stones of a house afflicted by a *nega*[c] and its wood and dirt join together with one another.
G. R. Simeon says, "Cloth and sacking and hide and matting join together with one another because their measurement, a handbreadth by a handbreadth, is equivalent on account of being cut off [and used for sitting]" [M. Me. 4:6C-D].

T. 1:30 Z p. 559, ls. 14-19

T. augments M. as indicated.

CHAPTER THIRTEEN

MEILAH CHAPTER FIVE

The conceptual aridity of the foregoing chapter contrasts with the interesting propositions laid before us in the present and following ones. First, ᶜAqiba introduces the distinction, in regard to sacrilege, between deriving benefit from, and causing damage or deterioration to, consecrated property. In his view, either the one or the other imposes liability to sacrilege. For sacrilege depends upon the one who does it, not upon the thing to which it is done. Sages maintain that if something can deteriorate through use, then if someone derives benefit from that object but the object itself is unaffected, he is not liable to bring an offering on account of sacrilege. This proposition is handsomely spelled out at M. 5:1-2.

M. 5:3 turns to a second interesting idea, carried forward at M. 5:4. If someone commits sacrilege, then what is the status of that which is subject to his act? Since the man is guilty, he surely has effected the secularization of the object. It follows that to the same object only one act of sacrilege can be done, and a person who, after the first man has committed his act of sacrilege, comes along and also commits a similar act, is not guilty of an act of sacrilege. He has, after all, derived benefit merely from an ordinary, unconsecrated object, that is to say, an object which has suffered sacrilege and so been rendered unconsecrated by the action of the prior party. M. 5:4 makes this point and yet one more, which is that merely taking a consecrated object but not deriving any benefit from it does not constitute an act of sacrilege. This, of course, is precisely where we began. It would be difficult to construct a more cogent and formally and conceptually unified statement than this one. M. 5:5, finally, provides a suitable formal conclusion for the whole excellent construction.

5:1-2

A. "He who derives benefit to the extent of a *perutah's* value from that which is consecrated,

B. "even though he did not cause deterioration [through use of it],

C. "has committed an act of sacrilege," the words of R. ᶜAqiba.

D. And sages say, "Anything which is subject to deterioration through use—he has not committed an act of sacrilege unless he has caused deterioration through use.

E. "But anything which is not subject to deterioration through use—once he has derived benefit from it, he has committed an act of sacrilege."

F. How so?

G. [If a woman] put a chain around her neck,

H. a ring on her finger,

I. drank from the cup of gold [M. Tamid 3:4B, used for water for the animal to be offered as the whole-offering of the day],

J. once she has derived benefit from it, she has committed an act of sacrilege.

K. [If a man] put on a shirt,

L. covered himself with a cloak,

M. used an axe to split wood—

N. he has not committed sacrilege unless he has caused deterioration through use.

O. [If] he pulled wool out of a sin-offering [lamb] when it was alive, he has committed an act of sacrilege only if he has caused deterioration.

P. But if this was after it was dead, once he has made use of it, he has committed an act of sacrilege.

M. 5:1

A. [If] one derived benefit to the extent of a half-*peruṭah* and caused deterioration to the extent of a half-*peruṭah*,

B. or [if] he derived benefit to the extent of a *peruṭah* from one thing and caused deterioration to the extent of a *peruṭah* in some other thing—

C. lo, this one has not committed an act of sacrilege—

D. until he will derive benefit to the extent of a *peruṭah* and [or] cause deterioration to the extent of a *peruṭah* in the very same thing.

M. 5:2

The dispute, M. 5:1A-C *vs.* D-E, is not balanced, but the two sayings, A-C and D-E, themselves are phrased in extremely tight discipline. Sages' position gets two illustrations, G-N and O-P. G-N give three instances each, then O-P supply yet one more contrast. The point of the dispute is clear as stated at A-E. The position of ᶜAqiba is that sacrilege depends upon the user, not the thing used. Sages do not wholly reject that position, E, but cannot entirely agree, D. (T. of course will phrase this fact in its own distinctive way.) G-J exemplify E, K-N, D; and then O reverts to D, P to E. So the illustrations run E, D, D, E, a neat construction indeed. Causing deterioration means to diminish the value of the object. The enjoyment of J is the use of the objects; people would, it is assumed, be willing to pay a *peruṭah* to wear such things. The dead sin-offering (P) has to be buried (M. Tem. 7:3) so it has no value, hence is not subject to deterioration. M. 5:2 carries forward sages' position and clarifies the matter. They require benefit to the extent of a *perutah* or deterioration to the extent of a *perutah*, since the one does not join together with the other in sages' view.

A. He who derives benefit and he who causes deterioration to the extent of a *perutah* from that which is consecrated commits an act of sacrilege.

B. [If] he derived benefit but did not cause deterioration,

C. caused deterioration but did not derive benefit,

D. lo, this one has not committed an act of sacrilege—

E. until he will derive benefit and intend to derive benefit,

F. so that his act of deriving benefit and his causing deterioration should be simultaneous,

G. in regard to something which is usually subject to deterioration,

H. and at the time that he has derived benefit, he has caused deterioration,

I. and, in the case of an agent, that he has carried out his agency [M. 6:1A].

J. *R. ᶜAqiba says, "If one derived benefit, even though he did not cause deterioration, he has committed an act of sacrilege"* [M. Me. 5:1A-C].

K. R. ᶜAqiba [sages] concedes to sages [ᶜAqiba] in respect to things which are not subject to deterioration, for example, bracelets, nose-rings, chains, and finger-rings, that if he derived benefit, even though he did not cause deterioration, he has committed an act of sacrilege.

L. Sages [ᶜAqiba] concede to R. ᶜAqiba [sages] in respect to things which are subject to deterioration, that if he derived benefit but did not cause deterioration, he has not committed an act of sacrilege.

T. 2:1 Z p. 559, ls. 20-25

A provides a rather ambitious introduction to T.'s treatment of the issues of Chapters Five and Six, at I, including as it does the consideration of M. 6:1 in its prologue to M. 5:1-2. But when we come to the center of the matter—J-L—there are no surprises. B. Me. 18a has ᶜAqiba concede in the case of things which do deteriorate that sages, M. 5:1D, are correct, in which case K should have sages agree with ᶜAqiba, and L, ᶜAqiba with sages. [1]

A. *One cannot commit sacrilege after another has committed sacrilege [in the same thing] in the case of consecrated things, except*

[1] "Logically, this is an odd construction. When both parties have conceded to each other, they wind up stating the same position. Either K or L by themselves would suffice, but both together create a problem."—R.S.S.

for a beast [M. Me. 5:3A-B].

B. R. Neḥemiah says, "*A beast and a utensil of service*" [= M. 5:3B].

C. *He who derives benefit from a sin-offering while it is alive has committed sacrilege only if he causes deterioration.*

D. *But if it is dead, once he has made use of it, he has committed sacrilege* [M. Me. 5:1/O-P],

E. for deterioration does not pertain to that which is dead.

F. [If] he derived benefit but did not cause deterioration,

G. caused deterioration but did not derive benefit,

H. lo, this one has not committed an act of sacrilege—

I. until he will derive benefit and cause deterioration,

J. and intend to derive benefit—

K. until his deriving benefit and his causing deterioration should be simultaneous,

L. and should pertain to that which is detached from the ground,

M. and in the case of an agent, that the agent should perform his agency.

T. 2:6A, Z p. 559, ls. 33-37 (continued)

T. cites and glosses M., as indicated, returning to T. 2:1A-I.

5:3

A. One does not commit sacrilege after another has committed sacrilege [in the same thing] in the case of consecrated things,

B. except for a beast or a utensil or service.

C. How so [B]?

D. [If] he rode on a beast and his fellow came along and rode on it, and yet another came and rode on it—

E. drank from the golden cup [M. 5:1/I] and his fellow came along and drank from it, and yet a third party came along and drank from it—

F. pulled wool out of a sin-offering [M. 5:1/O], and his fellow came along and pulled wool from the sin-offering, and yet a third came along and pulled wool from the same sin-offering—

G. all of them have committed an act of sacrilege.

H. Rabbi says, "Anything which is not subject to redemption *is* subject to a case of sacrilege following sacrilege."

M. 5:3

B is illustrated by D, E, and F+G. Rabbi rejects the narrow view of A-B and broadens it. Whatever one cannot redeem—not merely the items of B—is exempt from the rule of A, by analogy to D-G's illustrations. The logic of A+H is clear. If something is subject to sacrilege, it is profaned and therefore cannot then be subjected to another act of sacrilege, no longer falling into the category of the sacred (Maimonides, *Comm.*). But that which cannot leave the status of sanctity can be subjected to successive acts of sacrilege, never ceasing to fall into the category of the sacred (H).

5:4

A. [If] one took a stone or a beam from what is consecrated, lo, this one has not committed an act of sacrilege.

B. [If] he gave it to his fellow, he has committed an act of sacrilege.

C. But his fellow has not committed an act of sacrilege.

D. [If] he built it into the structure of his house, lo, this one has not committed an act of sacrilege—

E. until he actually will live under it [and enjoys its use] to the extent of a *perutah's* worth.

F. [If] he took a *perutah* of consecrated money, lo, this one has not committed an act of sacrilege.

G. [If] he gave it to his fellow, he has committed an act of sacrilege.

H. But his fellow has not committed an act of sacrilege.

I. [If] he gave it to a bath-keeper, even though he did not take a bath, he has committed an act of sacrilege.

J. For he [the bathkeeper] says to him, "Lo, the bath is open to you. Go in and take a bath."

M. 5:4

Carrying forward M. 5:3, this is a nicely executed pericope from a single hand, which makes the same point twice, A-E, F-J, ten distinct stichs in matched groups of five. [2] The point is not a development of M. 5:1-2, for here the sole possibility is enjoyment, not deterioration. The focus is on the culpability of the person to whom consecrated property is handed over. At A there is no enjoyment. At B the malefactor gains the pleasure of his fellow's thanks for the stone or beam. But, in line with M. 5:3, the stone or beam is now deemed secular, having been subject to the act of sacrilege, so the fellow commits no further act of sacrilege, in connection with the same stone or beam. D-E set up a second case. The man takes said stone or beam and builds it into his house. He is liable to violation of the law of sacrilege only when there is some concrete enjoyment from the stone or beam. The only fresh point in F-J is at J, which is E's parallel.

A. [If] one took an ax which had been consecrated and cut wood with it [M. Me. 5:1M].

---

2 "More precisely, D-E and I-J constitute a substantive, but not a formal pair." —R.S.S.

B. if he derived benefit and caused deterioration to the value of a *perutah*,

C. he has committed an act of sacrilege.

D. If not, he has not committed an act of sacrilege.

E. [If] his fellow came and cut wood with it,

F. both of them have committed sacrilege.

G. [If] the first took it and gave it to the second, the first has committed an act of sacrilege, and the second has not committed an act of sacrilege [M. Me. 5:4B-C].

T. 2:2 Z p. 559, ls. 26-28

A. [If] he took an ass which had been consecrated and rode on it,

B. if he derived benefit and caused deterioration to the extent of the value of a *perutah*,

C. he has committed an act of sacrilege.

D. And if not, he has not committed an act of sacrilege.

E. [If] his fellow came and rode on it,

F. both of them have committed an act of sacrilege.

G. [If] the first one took it and gave it to the second, the first has committed an act of sacrilege, and the second has not committed an act of sacrilege.

T. 2:3 Z p. 559, ls. 28-30

A. [If] one took a stone which had been consecrated and built it into his house,

B. a beam *and built it into his house,*

C. *lo, this one has not committed an act of sacrilege,*

D. *until he will live under it* [*and enjoy its use*] *to the extent of a perutah's worth* [M. Me. 5:4D-E].

T. 2:4 Z p. 559, ls. 30-31

A. If he took a *perutah* which had been consecrated and said, "Lo, it is mine,"

B. he has said nothing—until he will take it out and spend it for secular purposes.

C. [If] he gave it to a barber, even though he [the barber] did not cut his hair, he has committed an act of sacrilege [M. Me. 5:4/I-J].

D. And in the case of a burnt-offering, [if] he gave it to his fellow, and his fellow to his fellow, all of them have committed an act of sacrilege [M. Me. 5:3H].

T. 2:5 Z p. 559, ls. 31-33

What is important at T. 2:2 is its rule on the repeated act of sacrilege. T. 2:2 conforms to the view of M. 5:5B-C. The same recurs at T. 2:3. T. 2:4 simply restates M.'s rule. T. 2:5 makes the further point that merely stating that one plans to make secular use of a consecrated object is null. One must actually commit a deed.

Maimonides (*Trespass* 6:4, Lewittes, pp. 432-3), states the proposition of T. 2:2-4 as follows:

> One trespass after another was committed with a consecrated thing only if it was a beast or a vessel put to use by the Temple [M. 5:3A-B]. Thus, if one split wood with a hatchet belonging to the Temple and enjoyed it a *perutah's* worth and diminished its value, and then another came and split with it and enjoyed it and diminished its value, both committed a trespass. But if one took the hatchet and gave it to another, he committed a trespass and his fellow did not. If one drank from a cup of gold and enjoyed it a *perutah's* worth, and then another came and drank therefrom and enjoyed it, all of them committed a trespass. But if one took the cup and gave it to another as a gift or sold it to him, he committed a trespass and the other did not. If one rode upon an ass and enjoyed it a *perutah's* worth and diminished its value, and another came and rode upon it and enjoyed it and diminished its value, and then still another came and rode upon it and enjoyed it and diminished its value, all of them committed a trespass. But if one gave the ass to his fellow as a gift or sold it or gave it for hire, he committed a trespass and the other did not ....

The point of T. 2:2, therefore, is that an act of sacrilege can be committed more than once with a utensil of service (M. 5:3A-B). But if the first party takes the object and hands it over to the second, then the second is not responsible for sacrilege, which has been caused by the first. The same point is made repeatedly. [3]

A. He who separates his *sheqel* and spent it—
B. lo, this one has committed an act of sacrilege.
C. He who separates his sheqel for his fellow [who spent it],
D. lo, this one [who set aside the sheqel] has committed an act of sacrilege.
E. [If] he purchased with it [consecrated money] bird-offerings for *Zabin* and bird-offerings for *Zabot* and bird-offerings for women who have given birth—

T. 1:26 Z p. 558, ls. 36-37

A. he who brings his sin-offering or his guilt-offering or his Passover-offering from that which is consecrated—
B. he who pays his *sheqel* of a *zuz* from a *zuz* which he has consecrated—

[3] "The same rule is given at M. 5:4A-C with a different rationale. If an item is not subject to repeated acts of sacrilege, the recipient obviously will not have committed an act of sacrilege in receiving it. If an item is subject to repeated acts of sacrilege, the recipient must actually benefit from it (not merely receive it) for sacrilege to have been committed by him."—R.S.S.

C. "once he has taken it, he has committed an act of sacrilege," the words of R. Simeon.

D. And sages say, "He has committed an act of sacrilege only after the blood has been tossed."

E. On this basis did they say:

They do not bring meal-offerings, drink-offerings, meal-offerings of cattle, the bread of the thank-offering,

from that which has not yet been tithed or from heave-offering, from first tithe from which the heave-offering [of the tithe] has not yet been removed, from second tithe and from that which has been sanctified which have not been redeemed, from that which is mixed up with heave-offering or from that which is new, from fruit which has been grown in the seventh year.

F. But if one brought from such sources, he has not committed an act of sacrilege.

G. And one need hardly say, [one should not bring] from *ᶜorlah*-fruit and from produce which has grown as mixed seeds in a vineyard [= T. Men. 8:30].

T. 1:27 Z p. 558, ls. 37-39, p. 559, ls. 1-3

T. 1:26-27 pertain to the issues of M. 5:4. T. insists that one actually carry out a deed of desecration in order to be guilty of an act of sacrilege. A-B are clear as stated. C surely conforms to the view of M. 5:4A-C, assuming that T. 1:26D refers to the one who separated the *sheqel* for his friend, not the friend. T. 1:26E, T. 1:27A, B, set up three separate cases for dispute by Simeon and sages. Simeon takes the view that taking the consecrated funds makes the person liable. Sages' view is interesting. There is no sacrilege until the coin actually is used for a secular purpose. Here, it is only after the misappropriation is confirmed by the sacrifice of the animals purchased with the already-consecrated funds that the person is guilty of sacrilege. T. 1:27E-G are familiar from T. Men. 8:30. [4]

5:5

A. What he has eaten and what his fellow has eaten,
B. what he has used and what his fellow has used,
C. what he has eaten and what his fellow has used,
D. what he has used and what his fellow has eaten
E. join together with one another—
F. and even over an extended period of time.

M. 5:5

Continuing the inquiry of M. 5:4, we now ask, If a person eats less than a *peruṭah* of consecrated food and gives his fellow less than that

[4] "Although the formulation there is slightly varied. Specifically, F there deals with invalidation, not sacrilege."—R.S.S.

value, is he liable? Yes, E says, he is, since the two join together to form the requisite value for the sacrilege of which the person himself bears responsibility. F adds the consideration of an extended spell of inadvertence, M. Ker. 3:9, as [c]Aqiba says.

CHAPTER FOURTEEN

MEILAH CHAPTER SIX

A worthy continuation of the excellent foregoing chapter, this one addresses itself in a rather subtle way to the problem of agency in connection with sacrilege, which is, we recall, an inadvertent act to begin with. Obviously, if the agent does what he is told, then the employer is liable. If the agent does not do what he is told, then the agent is responsible for his own deeds (M. 6:1). But when we introduce some variables, matters become more interesting.

The first has to do with degrees of carrying out what one is told. If the owner specifies that the agent tell the guests to take one piece of meat, the agent tells the guests to take two, and the guests take three, how do we apportion responsibility for the sacrilege inadvertently committed upon the consecrated meat? The householder is liable, since what he has said has been done; so too is the agent; but the guests also are responsible for that third piece. This viewpoint, M. 6:1, turns out to be that of sages *vis à vis* Judah at M. 6:4. Judah will insist that the exact instructions of the employer be carried out to the letter, or the employer is exempt from the consequences. M. 6:2 stresses the matter of inadvertence, as I said above. If the employer realizes that he has sent a consecrated coin, then he no longer is responsible for sacrilege, which by definition is totally unintentional. The agent is not responsible. It is the storekeeper who inadvertently misappropriates sacred property, and he becomes liable when he, for his part, pays out the coin.

M. 6:3 states a further, rather subtle distinction. We know that one is liable for sacrilege only if he has misappropriated sacred property at least to the value of a *peruṭah*. What if, then, the agent misappropriates property to the value of a half-*peruṭah*, but the instructions of the employer are carried out to the extent of the value of a half-*peruṭah*? Neither is liable for having committed an act of sacrilege. M. 6:4, already alluded to, presents Judah's position that the employer may claim he wanted his instructions carried out to the letter, so that, if the agent has exceeded them, the employer no longer is liable even to the extent that his instructions *have* been carried out.

M. 6:5 makes the obvious point that if a money-changer is ordinarily permitted to make use of coins, and among them are coins which are consecrated, he is responsible for his actions. But if he is not ordinarily permitted to do so, and he does so, he is not responsible. M. 6:6 presents the quite separate issue of the point at which liability to sacrilege begins in the case of a single pouch containing a *peruṭah* which has been consecrated and ordinary coins. ᶜAqiba's view is that as soon as one coin out of said pouch is used, since it may be the holy one, the user is guilty of sacrilege. Sages maintain that all of the coins are to be used before we are sure that the person has committed sacrilage. T. improves the statement of the issue by having ᶜAqiba require a *suspensive* guilt-offering with the use of the first and subsequent coins, and an unconditional guilt-offering only with the last—a much more refined version of the matter.

6:1

A. The agent who carried out his errand [and thereby inadvertently committed an act of sacrilege]—

B. the householder [who appointed the agent is responsible and] has committed the act of sacrilege.

C. [If the agent] did not carry out his errand [in committing an act of sacrilege],

D. the agent [is responsible and inadvertently] has committed the act of sacrilege.

E. How so?

F. [If] he said to him, "Give out meat to the guests," but he gave them liver,

G. "Liver," and he gave them meat—

H. the agent has committed the act of sacrilege.

I. [If] he said to them, "Give them one piece each," and he [the agent] said, "Take two each," but they took three each,

J. all of them are guilty of committing an act of sacrilege.

K. [If] he said to him, "Bring [such and such a thing] from the window," or, "From the chest," and he brought it to him,

L. even though the householder said, "I meant *only* from here, and he brought it from there,"

M. the householder has committed the act of sacrilege.

N. But if he said to him, "Bring it to me from the window," and he brought it from the chest,

O. or "From the chest," and he brought it from the window.

P. the agent has committed the act of sacrilege.

M. 6:1

The opening construction, A-D, begins with mild apocopation, A-D, then an understood *if*, C-D. There are two sets of illustrations, F-H+I-J, K-M+N-P. The latter serves both rules, A-B and C-D. The householder instructs his agent to make use of something which is consecrated, not knowing that the thing is consecrated. If it then turns out that the thing was consecrated, who is responsible? If the agent did what he was told, then the householder is responsible. But if the agent in some way has not accurately done precisely what the householder told him to do, he no longer is deemed the agent of the householder. The agent himself inadvertently has committed the act of sacrilege. F-H illustrate C-D.

I-J do not. They present a special case. Why do all three bear responsibility, the householder, the agent, and the guests? When the guests ate the first piece, they carried out the errand of the householder, so he is responsible for an act of sacrilege. At the second, they did what the agent told them, so he now bears responsibility. And when they ate the third, they themselves inadvertently have committed an act of sacrilege as well. Accordingly, at this point—I-J—there is no illustration of either A-B or C-D, but of a quite separate proposition. [1]

K-M serves A-B and N-P, C-D, a more satisfactory construction. Here, moreover, there is a useful exegesis of the generalizations. The fresh point of K-M is that the agent has brought the object, and the householder has not made explicit the position outlined at L. The original instructions at N, by contrast, are explicit. At L the claim is not substantiated by an actual command, and at N it is.

A. [If] there is consecrated meat and ordinary meat for guests,
B. *and he said to him,* [*the waiter*], *"Give them each a piece,"*
C. *and he says to them, "Take two each,"*
D. *and they took three each—*
E. *all of them have committed an act of sacrilege* [M. Me. 6:1/I-J].
F. But in the case of a burnt-offering, only those who eat have committed an act of sacrilege.

T. 2:6B Z p. 559, ls. 33-39

T's appended item, F, is explained by Maimonides (*Trespass* 7:2) as follows:

> But if they were flesh of a burnt-offering and the like, only the one who ate committed a trespass. For the latter was guilty of another prohibition in addition to that of trespassing, and in all of the law of Scripture no transgression by an agent made the sender culpable except in the case of a trespass if no other prohibition was involved with it.

6:2

A. [If] he sent by means of [an agent who was] a deaf-mute, an imbecile, or a minor [to purchase goods with money which unbeknowst to the sender, was consecrated],
B. if they carried out their errand,

[1] "I-J is a typical Mishnaic 'third case', which takes up the logic of the preceding two and advances it one step further in a different direction."—R.S.S.

C. the householder has committed the act of sacrilege.
D. [If] they did not carry out their errand,
E. the storekeeper has committed the act of sacrilege.
F. [If] he sent something by means of a person of sound senses,
G. and realized before he reached the storekeeper [that the coins are consecrated and therefore regretted having sent those coins],
H. the storekeeper will have committed the act of sacrilege when he pays out [the coins].
I. What should he [F-G] do?
J. He should take a *peruṭah* or a utensil and state, "A *peruṭah* which is consecrated, wherever it may be, is made unconsecrated by this."
K. For that which is consecrated is redeemed by money or by something which is worth money.

M. 6:2

Developing the foregoing, the pericope, with its additions, is unitary, since A-C+D-E are balanced by F-H, then I-K complete the matter. We come to a case, A-E, of an agent who is exempt from responsibility, therefore liability. The responsibility now can be only the householder's or the storekeeper's. Of course if the errand has been carried out properly, then the one who sent the minor bears responsibility, as he would (M. 6:1) for the deeds of his adult-agent. But if the minor-agent has not done what he was told, then, when the storekeeper inadvertently pays out the coins he has received, he becomes culpable for sacrilege. For it is only at that point that the storekeeper has converted for secular purposes that which has been sanctified. F need not tell us that the agent who carried out his agency shifts the liability to the one who sent him. It raises a separate issue. The employer (householder) has sent coins, but then realizes that he sent coins which had been sanctified. This is before the agent reaches the store. Once the householder knows that the coins are sanctified, he no longer is liable to a guilt-offering for sacrilege, which is owed solely in a case of inadvertence. H then gives us the expected rule, which is, as above, that when the storekeeper makes secular use of the coins, he becomes liable. I-J revert to F-G, and K explains J. The householder should exculpate the storekeeper, before the coins reach him, by redeeming the coins. This is done by the process of substitution described at J. K explains why J says he may make use of a utensil.

A. [If the father said,] "*A peruṭah* which has been consecrated do I have in the window,"
B. and the son went and [inadvertently] paid it out—
C. the son has committed an act of sacrilege, and the father has not committed an act of sacrilege.

D. If his father said to him, "Go and take it," the father has committed an act of sacrilege, and the son has not committed an act of sacrilege.

E. [If] he gave him a *peruṭah*, and said to him, "Go and buy me goods from the market,"

F. and the householder realized that it has been consecrated,

G. but the agent did not realize it,

H. the agent has committed an act of sacrilege [M. 6:2F-H].

I. If both of them realized [that the money was consecrated], both of them have not committed an act of sacrilege.

J. But the storekeeper has committed an act of sacrilege when he will have paid it out.

L. [If] all three of them [now including the storekeeper] realized [that it was consecrated], none of them has committed an act of sacrilege [M. Me. 6:2F-H].

M. But the goods belong to the sanctuary.

N. What should he do to remove his fellow from the grip of sacrilege?

T. 2:7 Z p. 559, ls. 39-40, p. 560, ls. 1-4

A. He takes a *peruṭah* or a utensil, saying, "The *peruṭah* which has been consecrated, wherever it may be, is rendered unconsecrated by means of this *sela*, or by means of this pitcher, or by means of this cloak" [M. Me. 6:2/I-K].

B. For the status of consecration applies to everything.

C. But it does not apply to slaves, deeds, or real estate.

T. 2:8 Z p. 560, ls. 4-6

The point of T. 2:7A-D is obvious. If the son does not carry out the father's errand, then the father is not liable to sacrilege. If the son does what the father says, then the father is liable. It goes without saying that in all instances we have inadvertence. F-L go over the ground of M. 6:2F-H. All three are exempt, at L, because for none is the situation one of inadvertence. N, continued at T. 2:8, conforms to M.'s picture.

6:3

A. [If] he gave him a *peruṭah* [and] said to him,

B. "With half of it bring me lamps, and with half of it wicks,"

C. and [if] he went and brought back lamps for the whole of it or wicks for the whole of it—

D. or if he said to him, "Bring me lamps for the whole of it," or, "Wicks for the whole of it,"

E. and he went and brought him lamps for half of it and wicks for half of it,

F. both of them have not committed an act of sacrilege.

G. But if he said to him, "Bring me lamps for half of it from such-and-such a place, and wicks for half of it from such-and-such a place,"

H. and he went and brought for him lamps from the place in which he was supposed to get the wicks, and wicks from the place from which he was supposed to get the lamps,

I. the agent has committed the act of sacrilege.

M. 6:3

The formal traits of this beautifully balanced and unitary pericope require no comment. The point of A-F is that neither party is guilty of sacrilege, the employer because his wishes have been carried out only in respect to the disposition of half a *peruṭah* of value (C, E); and the agent, because he has failed to carry out his instructions only to the extent of half a *peruṭah* (B, D). G-I bring us back to M. 6:1N-P. The agent is responsible because he has revised the terms of his agency and committed sacrilege with the whole of the *peruṭah*, being responsible for both halves (H).

A. [*If*] *one gave him a peruṭah and said to him,*

B. *"With half of it bring me lamps, and with half of it wicks,"*

C. *but he went and brought him lamps for the whole of it, or wicks for the whole of it,*

D. *both of them have not committed an act of sacrilege* [M. Me. 6:3A-C]—

E. the householder, because his errand has not been carried out;

F. and the agent, because he has not changed the terms of his errand to the value of an entire *peruṭah.*

G. But [if] he gave him a hundred pieces of silver and said to him "With the whole of it bring me lamps," "with the whole of it bring me wicks,"

H. and he went and brought him lamps with half of it and wicks with half of it

I. both of them have committed an act of sacrilege:

J. the householder, for his errand has been carried out to the extent of [much more than] a *peruṭah* of value;

K. and the agent, because he has changed the terms of his errand to the value of a *peruṭah.*

L. But if he said to him, "Bring them to me from Joseph," and he brought them to him from Simeon,

M. "[Bring me] from Shiḥin," and he brought him from Sepphoris,

N. it is the agent who has committed an act of sacrilege.

T. 2:9 Z p. 560, ls. 6-12

T.'s exegesis of M. is clear and self-evidently persuasive.

6:4

A. If he gave him two *peruṭot* [and] said to him, "Bring me an *etrog*,"

B. and he went and brought him an *etrog* for a *peruṭah* and a pomegranate for a *peruṭah*,

C. both of them have committed the act of sacrilege.

D. R. Judah says, "The householder has not committed an act of sacrilege.

E. "For he says to him, 'I wanted a big *etrog*, and you brought a small and poor one.' "

F. [If] he gave him a golden *denar* [= six *selas*] [and] said to him, "Bring me a shirt,"

G. and he went and brought him a shirt for three *selas* and a cloak for three,

H. both of them have committed an act of sacrilege.

I. R. Judah says, "The householder has not committed an act of sacrilege.

J. "For he says to him, 'I wanted a large shirt, and you brought me a small and poor one.' "

M. 6:4

The view of the anonymous rule, A-C, F-H, is that the householder's wishes have been carried out to the extent of a *peruṭah*, and the agent has changed the terms of his agency to the extent of a *peruṭah*. Judah's view is clear as stated: the householder has a valid claim that his instructions have not been carried out. It goes without saying that M. 6:1/I-J conform to sages' view here.

A. *[If] one gave him two peruṭot and said to him, "Bring me an etrog,"*

B. *and he went and brought him an etrog for a peruṭah and a pomegranate for a peruṭah,*

C. *both of them have committed an act of sacrilege.*

D. *R. Judah says, "The householder has not committed an act of sacrilege, for [he may claim], 'I wanted a large etrog, and you brought me a small, poor one.' "*

E. *[If] he gave him a golden denar and said to him, "Bring me a shirt,"*

F. *and he went and brought him a shirt for three [selas] and a cloak for three [selas],*

G. *both of them have committed an act of sacrilege.*

H. *R. Judah says, "The householder has not committed an act of sacrilege, for he may say to him, 'I wanted a large shirt, but you brought me a small, poor one' "* [M. Me. 6:4A-J].

I. But R. Judah concedes in the case of pulse that both of them have committed an act of sacrilege,

J. for pulse which sells for a *sela* is like that which sells for a *perutah*.

T. 2:10 Z p. 560, ls. 12-18

T.'s gloss is clear.

6:5

A. He who deposits coins with a money-changer—
B. if they were bound up, he [the money-changer] should not make use of them.
C. Therefore if he paid [them] out, he has committed an act of sacrilege.
D. If they are loose, he may make use of them.
E. Therefore if he paid them out, he has not committed an act of sacrilege.
F. [If the owner of the coins] deposited [them] with a householder,
G. one way or the other, he [the householder] should not make use of them.
H. Therefore if he paid them out, he has committed an act of sacrilege.
I. "A storekeeper is deemed equivalent to a householder," the words of R. Meir.
J. R. Judah says, "He is equivalent to a money-changer."

M. 6:5

The point of this triplet (A-C, D-F, G-H) is that if the bailee behaves contrary to the norm, then the bailee, like the agent, has changed the terms of bailment (A-C) and bears liability for committing an act of sacrilege.

A. *He who deposits coins with a money-changer—*
B. *if they were bound up, he should not make use of them.*
C. *Therefore if he paid them out, he has committed an act of sacrilege.*
D. *If they are loose, he may make use of them.*
E. *Therefore if he paid them out, he has not committed an act of sacrilege.*
F. *[If he deposited them] with a householder,*
G. *one way or the other, he should not make use of them.*
H. *Therefore if he paid them out, he has not committed an act of sacrilege.*
I. *"A storekeeper is equivalent to a householder," the words of R. Meir.*
J. *R. Judah says, "He is equivalent to a money-changer."*

T. 2:11 Z p. 560, ls. 18-21

T. = M. 6:5.

6:6

A. A *perutah* which has been consecrated, which fell into a purse [containing other money],

B. or if one said, "A *perutah* in this purse is consecrated"—

C. "as soon as one has paid out the first [coin in the purse],

D. "he has committed an act of sacrilege," the words of R. ᶜAqiba.

E. And sages say, "[He has not committed an act of sacrilege] until he has paid out all the money in the purse."

F. And R. ᶜAqiba concedes in the case of one who says, "A *perutah* in this purse is consecrated," that he goes along and pays out the money [without having committed an act of sacrilege] until he will have paid out all the money which is in the purse.

M. 6:6

The point of the dispute, A-E, is that, in ᶜAqiba's view, the first coin may be that which is consecrated. [2] When, therefore, the man pays out that first coin, he has committed the act of sacrilege. But all subsequent coins may or may be consecrated, so call for a suspensive guilt-offering (M. Ker. 5:3), except for the last, which requires an unconditional one. If, however, *any* one coin is designated (F), then all are deemed unconsecrated except for the last, which, willynilly, is consecrated.

A. *A perutah which has been consecrated which fell into a purse,*

B. *or he who says, "A perutah in this purse is consecrated,"*

C. *"once he has paid out the first* [M. Me. 6:6A-C], he brings a suspensive guilt-offering.

D. "And once he has paid out the second, he brings an unconditional sin-offering," the words of R. ᶜAqiba.

E. And sages say, "He brings a suspensive guilt-offering only on account of something which is subject to extirpation [and] for the inadvertent doing of which one is liable to a sin-offering" [M. Ker. 1:2].

T. 3:1 Z p. 560, ls. 22-25

A. To whose benefit does this [money paid for] sacrilege fall?

B. He who makes use of a sin-offering or a guilt-offering, lo, this one adds [the added fifth], bringing [with the funds] another sin-offering or another guilt-offering.

C. [If] his sin-offering already has been offered, then it [the money for the new one] goes to the Salt Sea.

D. [If] his guilt-offering already has been offered, then it [the money] falls to the Temple treasury as a freewill-offering.

---

2 "In light of F, B is a poor gloss for ᶜAqiba, and serves only sages' opinion, E."—R.S.S.

E. [If the foregoing pertains to making use of] Most Holy Things before the tossing of the blood, Lesser Holy Things after the tossing of the blood [M. 1:4], a burnt-offering and sacrificial parts, a handful [of the meal-offering] and an incense-offering, the meal-offering of an anointed priest and the meal-offering which accompanies drink-offerings,

F. let the funds [set aside for that purpose] fall to the Temple treasury.

G. [If the foregoing pertains to making use of] community offerings, let them [the funds] fall to the Temple treasury as a freewill-offering.

H. [If the foregoing applies to making use of] that which is sanctified for the altar, let the coins fall to the benefit of that which is consecrated for the altar [= B].

I. [If the foregoing applies to] that which has been sanctified for the upkeep of the house, let the coins fall to the benefit of that which is sanctified for the upkeep of the house.

T. 3:2 Z p. 560, ls. 25-29

T. 3:1 expands M. 6:6C-D and goes over the familiar ground of M. Ker. 5:2-3. T. 3:2 asks how we dispose of the money for the principal and added fifth which one brings with the offering owed on account of sacrilege. B. Me. 9b reads, at B, *He who makes use of money destined for his sin or guilt-offering*. The rule then is that if the sin-offering has not been offered, the man adds a fifth and offers his sin-offering for the whole sum. If the guilt-offering has been offered, the funds are paid over, as T. says. For T., then, if the sin-offering has not been offered, he adds the funds and buys another fatter than the first. If it has been offered, then the money has to be disposed of. The rest of the rules are as expected. Maimonides (*Trespass* 4:7) states the opening rule as follows:

> If one made use of money set aside for a sin-offering, then before his sin-offering was to be offered up, he was obligated to add a fifth to the amount of his trespass and to bring with the sum his sin-offering.... For the rule was that restitution for a trespass committed with offerings for the altar was devoted to offerings for the altar, and restitution for a trespass committed with things hallowed for the repair of the Temple was devoted to the repair of the Temple. However, if he became aware that he had trespassed, but his sin-offering was then offered up before he set aside his restitution, or if he set it aside but did not include it in the money [paid out] for his sin-offering, he had to take the money for restitution plus a fifth and throw it into the Salt Sea....

TAMID

CHAPTER FIFTEEN

INTRODUCTION TO TAMID
TAMID CHAPTERS ONE THROUGH SEVEN

Nothing in our Order, and little enough in the whole of Mishnah, prepares us for the distinctive character, both literary and substantive, of the present tractate and its immediate successor. For instead of a collection of rules, together with controversies thereon, we now come to what is essentially a narrative, along the lines of M. Parah Chapter Three and of M. Yoma Chapters One through Seven. The topic of the narrative is how the priest offers the daily burnt-offering described at Numbers 28:3-4: *This is the offering made by fire which you shall bring to the Lord: male lambs of the first year, unblemished, two each day, for a continual burnt-offering. One lamb you shall offer in the morning, the other lamb you shall offer at dusk.* The narrative which follows tells how the morning-part of the rite was carried out. There is Babylonian Gemara for Chapters One, Two, and Four, but no Tosefta for this or the following two tractates.

Let us now consider the sequence of topics through which the narrative unfolds.

I. A. *The priests arise in the morning.* B. *Clearing the altar of ashes.* 1:1-4, 2:1-5

A. *Priests*

1:1	In three places do the priests keep watch.
1:2	He who wants to take up the ashes from the altar gets up early.
1:3	He took the key and opened the door. Inspection of the area.
1:4	He who won the right to take up the ash from the altar does so. He is given instructions.

B. *Clearing the altar.*

2:1	Priests then help clear the altar, removing unburned meat.
2:2	They heap up ashes in the ash-pile in the middle of the altar.
2:3	They heap up twigs for the altar-fire.
2:4	Priest arranges the altar fire.
2:5	Continuation of foregoing.

II. *Selecting the lamb for the daily burnt-offering.* 3:1-5

3:1 Superintendent casts lots to see who carries out the various acts of the rite.
3:2 Superintendent finds out that the time of the rite has come.
3:3 Lamb is selected.
3:4 Utensils for slaughter are taken out.
3:5 Lamb is brought to the shambles.

III. *Clearing the ashes.* 3:6-9

3:6-8 Procession of those who remove the ashes of the inner altar and the other priests.
3:9 The ashes are removed from the inner altar. The candlestick is cleaned and rekindled.

IV. *Slaughtering the lamb.* 4:1-3

4:1 The lamb is tied, slaughtered. The blood is tossed. The lamb is butchered.
4:2 Continuation of 4:1.
4:3 Continuation of 4:2.

V. *The priests bless the congregation. The limbs are brought to the altar.* 5:1-4

A. *Blessing*

5:1 The priests say a blessing, the Ten Commandments, and bless the people.

B. *Carrying the limbs*

5:2 The superintendent casts lots to find out who will carry the limbs from the ramp to the altar.
5:3 The priests who are not chosen by lot are dismissed.
5:4 The incense is offered.

VI. *Clearing the ashes.* 5:5-6:2+3

5:5 The ashes are removed from the altar.
5:6 The ashes are disposed of.
6:1 The ones who are in charge of the incense and of removing the ashes go up and to their work [repetition of M. 3:9].
6:2 The one who uses the firepan heaps up cinders.
6:3 The one who prepares incense mixes it and puts it onto the altar.

VII. *Conclusion of rite. The limbs are tossed on the altar.*

7:1 The high priests goes in and prostrates himself.
7:2 The priests who had participated line up on the steps of the porch.

7:3 The high priest burns the offerings on the altar. Each of the priests hands him the part which he has carried in. When this rite is completed, the prefect signals the Levites, who proceed to say Psalms.

7:4 What Psalms the Levites said.

The narrative appears more coherent and continuous than it is, because we have three separate points at which the clearing of the altar is treated, IB, III, and VI, and incense is offered at M. 5:4 and 6:3. Certainly unit VI is confusing, since the proper movement of the story is from IV through V to VII, that is, from slaughtering the lamb, to the public rite, and finally to the placing of the limbs of the burnt-offering on the altar-fires. Why we again should be told about clearing the ashes, moreover, between unit II and unit IV is no more obvious. So we have to take account of a somewhat more complicated literary situation than appears at first glance. This is clear not only from the awkward sequence of topics but also from the repetition of M. 3:9 at M. 6:1, concrete evidence of the problem. I am inclined to see as the basic version of the story, Ia, II, IV, and VII, since the materials on the blessing of the congregation and the bringing of the limbs to the altar, V, are somewhat confusing as well. [1]

In order to emphasize how successfully the redactor has strung together these materials into a stylistically harmonious account, I have used italics not only for citations of Scripture, but also to indicate glosses and interpolations. These, set into italics, will show clearly what I believe to be the essential narrative intended by the ultimate narrator-redactor.

1:1-4

A. In three places do the priests keep watch in the sanctuary: (1) in the room of Abtinas, (2) in the room of the flame, and (3) in the room of the hearth.

B. The room of Abtinas and the room of the flame were upper rooms.

C. And youngsters keep watch there.

D. The room of the hearth is vaulted.

E. And it was a large room surrounded by a raised pavement of stone.

F. And the mature members of the [priestly] household [of the day] sleep there [on the raised pavement],

[1] "I totally disagree with this theory of the tractate, and view the narration (excluding interpolations) as basically continuous. The plethora of ashes to be cleaned out is not so hard to account for as Neusner suggests. See my remarks below, M. 6:1, p. 163."—R.S.S.

G. with the keys to the courtyard in their charge, [2]

H. and [there sleep] the fledgling priests, each with his mattress on the ground.

I. They [the priests] did not sleep in the consecrated garments.

J. But they spread them out, doubled them over, and lay them down under their heads, and cover themselves with their own clothes.

K. [If] one of them should have a nocturnal emission of semen, he goes out, proceeding along the passage that leads below the building—

L. and lamps flicker on this side and on that—

M. until he reaches the immersion-room.

N. And there was a fire there,

O. and a privy in good taste.

P. *And this was its good taste:* [3] *[if] he found it locked, he knows that someone is there; [if he found it] open, he knows that no one is there.*

Q. He went down and immersed, came up and dried off, and warmed himself by the fire.

R. He came and sat himself down with his brothers, the priests [in the house of the hearth],

S. until the gates were opened.

T. He goes out, proceeding on his way [home].

M. 1:1

A. He who wants to take up [the ashes] from the altar gets up early,

B. and immerses before the superintendent comes by.

C. *And at what time does the superintendent come by?*

D. *Not all the times are the same.*

E. *Sometimes he comes at cockcrow, or near then, earlier or later.*

F. The superintendent came and knocked on their door.

G. And they opened it to him.

H. He said to them, "Let him who has immersed come and cast lots."

I. They cast lots.

J. Whoever won won.

M. 1:2

A. He took the key and opened the door and entered *via* the room of the hearth into the Temple courtyard.

B. And they entered after him with two lighted torches in their hands.

C. And they divided into two parties.

D. These go along the colonnade eastward, and those go along the colonnade westward.

---

[2] So Ginzberg, Tamid, p. 200.

[3] Ginzberg treats the present passage as a gloss "based on an erroneous reading, and, of course, [it] cannot be attributed to the original compiler." This same conclusion is reached here on form-analytical grounds, which are equally self-evident.

E. They would go along and inspect [to make sure everything was in order], until they reach the place where they make the baked cakes.

F. These met up with those.

G. They said, "Is it in order?"

I. "All is in order."

J. They had those who make the baked cakes begin to make baked cakes.

M. 1:3

A. He who had won [the right] to take up [the ash] from the altar [Lev. 6:3]—he will take up the ash from the altar.

B. And they say to him, "Be careful not to touch a utensil [the fire-shovel] before you sanctify your hands and your feet in the laver."

C. And lo, the fire-shovel is placed in the corner between the ramp and the altar, at the westward side of the ramp.

D. No one goes in with him, nor is there a light in his hand.

E. But he goes along by the light of the altar-fire.

F. They did not see him, nor did they hear a sound from him until they hear the noise of the wooden device which Ben Qaṭin made for the laver [M. Yoma 3:10].

G. And they say, "The time has come."

H. He sanctified his hands and feet with the laver.

I. He took the silver fire-shovel and went up to the top of the altar, and he cleared away the cinders from one side and the other, scooped up the innermost ashes, and came down.

J. He reached the pavement.

K. He turned his face northward [toward the altar].

L. He went along ten cubits to the east of the ramp.

M. He heaped up the cinders together on the pavement, three handbreadths from the ramp,

N. the place in which they toss the crops of fowl, and the ashes of the innermost altar and the candlestick.

M. 1:4

M. 1:1A is expanded by B-C, D-H. The mature priests and the fledgling ones sleep in the house of the hearth where a fire kept them warm, A3, D-G. K-T are integral to the narrative (excluding the minor glosses, L, P). After immersion, the priest (K) remains unclean until sunset, so he cannot serve that day. He goes back to the house of the hearth (R) and remains until he can go home. M. 1:2A-B, F-I carry forward the narrative: C-E gloss B. M. 1:3's baked cakes (M. 1:3H) are for the meal-offering of the high priest (Lev. 6:13-14, M. Men. 4:5). At M. 1:4 the one who is selected, M. 1:2, to clear the altar of ashes takes up to work. M. 1:4C may be seen to gloss B, that is, the utensil he is not to touch before washing his hands and feet, since it certainly breaks the flow of thought, which goes on from

B through D-F. I is the first point at which we need to know about the fire-shovel. The purpose of the device, F, is to bring fresh water for washing his hands. When the wheel was drawing up the water, the priests in the dark could hear the sound. The priest cleared away the cinders and scooped up the ashes, containing the fully burned offerings.

2:1-5

A. His brothers saw that he came down, and they came running.
B. They hastened and sanctified their hands and their feet from the laver.
C. They took the shovels and the rakes and went up to the top of the altar.
D. The limbs and the fat pieces which had not been consumed the preceding night they raked to the sides of the altar.
E. If the sides did not hold them, they arranged them on the circuit by the ramp.

M. 2:1

A. They began heaping up ashes on the apple [ash-pile].
B. And the apple was in the middle of the altar.
C. *Sometimes there were three hundred kors [of ashes]*
D. *And at festivals they did not clear away the ashes,*
E. *for they are an ornament to the altar.*
F. *The priest never through neglect failed to remove the ashes.*

M. 2:2

A. They began heaping up the twigs to prepare the altar-fire.
B. *And are all sorts of wood valid for the altar-fire?*
C. *Yes.*
D. *All sorts of wood are valid for the altar fire,*
E. *except for olive-wood and wood of the vine.*
F. *But with these were they used [to light the fire]: boughs (1) of the fig-tree, or (2) of the walnut-tree, or (3) of oleaster-wood.*

M. 2:3

A. He arranged the altar-fire, the larger one on the east side, with its open side [at which side it was tended] facing east.
B. And the tips of the inner twigs were touching the apple.
C. And there was a space between the twigs, through which they set fire to the kindling-wood.

M. 2:4

A. They selected from there fine pieces of fig-wood [= M. 2:3F1] [with which] to arrange the second altar-fire, [the one] for the incense,
B. toward the south-western corner, four cubits to the north of the corner.
C. *[On weekdays, they took] sufficient [wood to produce] an amount of five seahs of cinders, and on the Sabbath, sufficient for an amount of eight seahs of cinders.*

D. For there [A] did they place the two dishes of frankincense which accompany the show-bread.

E. The limbs and pieces of fat which had not been consumed the preceding evening they put back onto the altar-fire.

F. They kindled the two altar-fires.

G. And they came down.

H. And they went to the office made of hewn stone.

M. 2:5

Chapter Two continues the narrative, with important glosses or interpolations at 2:2C-F, 2:3B-F, 2:5C. Once the ashes are cleared off, the priests go up and arrange the altar-fires, the large one for the sacrificial parts, the small one for incense. M. 2:2C-F explain why a large "apple" or mound of ashes was left on the altar. This "apple" was deemed an ornament, indicating how large a number of sacrifices had been made. It therefore would be left there and heaped upward. It was, M. emphasizes, not through neglect that the priests left it there (M. 2:2F), but because it was regarded as an ornament (M. 2:2E). M. 2:3B-C certainly are curious. [4] M. 2:4-5 then describe the arranging and kindling of the two altar-fires.

3:1-9

A. The superintendent said to them, "Come and cast lots [to determine] (1) who executes the act of slaughter, (2) who tosses the blood, (3) who removes the ashes of the inner altar, (4) who removes the ashes of the candlestick, (5) who carries up the limbs to the ramp:

B. *"(1) the head, (2) the [right] hind-leg, (3) the two fore-legs, (4) the rump, and (5) the [left] hind-leg, (6) the breast, (7) the neck, (8) the two flanks, (9) the innards, (10) the fine flour, (11) the cakes, (12) the wine* [see Sarason to M. 4:3, below, p. 159]."

C. They drew lots.

D. Whoever won won.

M. 3:1

A. The superintendent said to them, "Go and see whether the time for carrying out the act of slaughter has come."

B. If it had come, the one who sees it says, "It is daylight."

C. Matya b. Samuel says, "[He who sees it says,] 'The whole eastern horizon is light.'

D. " 'Up to Hebron?'

E. "And he says, 'Yes.' "

M. 3:2

---

[4] "M. 2:3B-C ideed are curious. They look like an attempt at a transition to the (previously formulated?) rule of D-E (+F)."—R.S.S.

A. He said to them, "Go and bring a lamb from the lamb-office."
B. *Now lo, the lamb-office was located at the north-western corner.*
C. *And there were four offices there:*
(1) *one was the lamb-office;*
(2) *and one was the seal-office;*
(3) *and one was the hearth-office;*
(4) *and one was the office in which they would prepare the show-bread.*

M. 3:3

A. They went into the office for utensils and brought out from there ninety-three silver and gold utensils.

B. They gave [the lamb which was to be] the daily whole-offering a drink from a golden cup. [5]

C. Even though it was inspected the preceding night, they inspect it again by the light of the torches.

M. 3:4

A. He who had won [the right to carry out the rite] of the daily burnt-offering drags it along down to the shambles, and those who had won the right to offer up the limbs go after him.

B. The shambles was located at the north of the altar, and on it were eight short pillars, and square blocks of cedar-wood were on them.

C. And iron hooks were set into them.

D. And there were three rows [of hooks] on each one [block], on which they would suspend [the slaughtered beasts].

E. And they flay them on marble tables between the pillars.

M. 3:5

A. Those who had won the right to remove the ashes of the inner altar and of the candlestick would go first,

B. with four utensils in their hand, the ash-bin, the oil-jar, and two keys.

C. *The ash-bin is like a large golden three-qab measure. It holds two and a half qabs.*

D. *The oil-jar is like a large golden flagon.*

E. *The two keys—one goes down [into the lock] as far as its arm-pit, and one opens [the door] forthwith.*

M. 3:6

A. He came to the northern door.

B. *And the great gate had two [such] doors, one at the north, and one at the south.*

C. *Into that at the south no man ever entered. And this is expressly stated concerning it by Ezekiel: And the Lord said to me, This gate shall be shut, it shall not be opened, neither shall any man enter in*

[5] See Saul Lieberman, *Hellenism in Jewish Palestine* (N.Y., 1950), pp. 150-1.

by it, for the Lord, the God of Israel, hath entered in by it: therefore it shall be shut (Ez. 44:2). 6

D. He took the key and opened the door.

E. He went into the cell, and from the cell into the *hekhal*, until he came to the great gate.

F. He came to the great gate.

G. He removed the bolt and the locks and opened it up.

H. The one who was going to execute the act of slaughter did not perform the act of slaughter until he heard the sound of the great gate opening.

M. 3:7

A. (1) *From Jericho did they hear the sound of the great gate opening.*

B. (2) *From Jericho did they hear the sound of the shovel* [M. 5:6].

C. (3) *From Jericho did they hear the sound of the wooden device which Ben Qaṭin made for the laver.*

D. (4) *From Jericho did they hear the sound of Gabini, the crier.*

E. (5) *From Jericho did they hear the sound of the flute.*

F. (6) *From Jericho did they hear the sound of the cymbal.*

G. (7) *From Jericho did they hear the sound of the singing.*

H. (8) *From Jericho did they hear the sound of the shofar.*

I. *There are those who say, "Also the voice of the high priest when he made mention of the divine name on the Day of Atonement."*

J. (9) *From Jericho did they smell the scent of the compounding of the incense,*

K. *Said R. Eleazar b. Diglai, "My father's house and goats were on the mountain of Mikhwar. And they sneezed from the smell of the compounding of the incense."* 7

M. 3:8

A. He who had won the right to collect the ash of the inner altar entered in.

B. And he took the ash-bin, put it down before him, and scooped up ashes with both hands and put them into it.

C. And at the end he swept the rest into it.

D. And he left it and went out.

E. He who had won the right to clean the candlestick entered, and, [if] he found the two eastern lights flickering, he cleaned the rest and left those flickering in their place.

F. [If] he found that they had gone out, he cleaned them and lit them from those which were [yet] flickering.

---

6 "In the context of the narrative, M. 3:7B-C are an explanatory gloss, since the action moves smoothly from A to D. B-C, on the other hand, are integral to M. Midd. 4:1, where they also occur."—R.S.S.

7 Ginzberg, *Tamid*, p. 40, states, "The remark of R. Elazar ben Daglai...—not in the Munich manuscript!—is certainly of post-Talmudic time."

H. A stone was before the candlestick, and on it were three steps, on which the priest stands and fixes up the lamps.

I. And he left the oil-jar on the second step and went out.

M. 3:9

Apart from the massive interpolation at M. 3:8, there is one point of interest, the dispute at M. 3:2. Here we see that the opinion contrary to B is stated in exactly the same narrative style as the materials which surround it. How will Matya b. Samuel have stated matters? He would simply add to A what is in his name at C, D, and E. There is no shift in diction; the powerful narrative current proceeds unaffected. [8] The contrast to M. 3:8 hardly needs comment. The rest is fairly routine. M. 3:1A lists five items, then B augments A5 with a dozen. The augmentation is not very precise, since A5 asks for the *limbs*, and B tells us too much. On that basis I am inclined to see M. 3:1B as a rather extensive interpolation. [9] M. 3:6A announces that it is out of place. [10] We should have expected it after M. 3:4. But, I suppose, since M. 3:4 includes its reference to the animal and giving it water from the golden cup, the redactor has preferred first to dispose of the animal. Since the other utensils are not systematically afforded a description, I should suppose M. 3:6C-E are a useful gloss. But this is not so certain as other such judgments. There is a serious break, however, at M. 3:7.

---

8 "Although it certainly is possible to view Matya b. Samuel's lemma as disputing the previous lemma, I am more inclined to view it as a part of the narrative (as do Albeck, p. 298, and Ginzberg, "The Mishnah Tamid", pp. 41-42, and note 24 on p. 42), since M. Sheq. 5:3 lists a Matya b. Samuel as the Temple attendant in charge of the lottery. Albeck would read the pericope as follows:

B. ...the one who sees it says, 'It is daylight.'

C. [Then] Matya b. Samuel says [i.e., asks], 'Is the whole eastern horizon light up to Hebron?'

D. And he [the priest at B] says [i.e., responds], 'Yes.'

In other words, what we have here is a ritualized exchange. [Ginzberg reads the passage differently: 'Matthatias, the son of Samuel is (or was) in the habit of announcing the time of the slaghtering of the daily sacrifice by using these words.' I think Albeck's reading makes better syntactic sense, but the net result is the same.]" —R.S.S.

9 "This interpolation is related to M. 4:3, as I will spell out below."—R.S.S.

10 "M. 3:6A certainly is not out of place. The chapter proceeds according to the order of the lots cast at M. 3:1—executing the slaughter [M. 3:2-5], (tossing the blood), removing the ashes from the inner altar and from the candlestick [M. 3:6-9], then, in Chapter Four, carrying the limbs up to the ramp. This accounts for the account of the ash-removal between the preparations for the act of slaughter and the carving-up of the limbs. The thematic order is articulated through the repetition of the formulary, MY ŠZK[H/W] B..., at M. 3:5 ('He who won the right to slaughter the daily offering'), 3:6 ('Those who won the right to remove the ashes from the inner altar and the candlestick', and again at 3:9), 4:2-3 ('...those who won the right to the various portions')."—R.S.S.

We have no idea who comes to open the door. A doorkeeper has not been referred to.[11] We have no clear notion of the place of the opening of the door in the larger rite. As matters stand, however, M. 3:7 is carried forward at M. 3:9. The door is opened, M. 3:7, then, M. 3:9, through that door pass those who are to clean the inner altar. M. 3:9 is thus tied closely to M. 3:7; those who are to clean the inner altar and the candlestick go through the opened door. The responsible priest collects the ashes but does not remove them. Then the one who takes care of the candlestick does the same. He cleans the candlestick and adds oil if needed, then leaves the oil-jar in place and leaves.

4:1-3

A. They did not [wholly] bind up the lamb, but [only] tied it[s foreleg and hindleg].

1 B. Those who had won [the privilege of taking] the limbs take hold of it.

C. And thus was the manner of tying it:

D. its head to the south [toward the altar], and its face to the west [toward the *heikhal*].

E. He who effects the act of slaughter stands in the east with his face to the west.

F. And that [daily whole-offering] of the dawn was slaughtered at the northwestern corner, at the second ring.

G. That [daily whole-offering] of twilight was slaughtered at the northeastern corner [of the altar], at the second ring.

H. The slaughterer slaughtered.

I. The one who receives the blood received the blood.

J. He came to the northeastern corner.

K. He tosses [the blood] in a northeasterly direction,

L. [Then he came] to the southwestern corner.

M. He tosses [the blood] in a southwesterly direction,

N. The residue of the blood did he pour out on the southern base [of the altar].

M. 4:1

A. He [who slaughtered the daily whole-offering] did not break the hind-leg. But he pierces it at the knee-joint and hangs it up therewith.

B. He did flay it downward, until he reached the breast.

2 C. [When] he reached the breast, he cut off the head and gave it to him who had won it.

---

[11] "There is no doorkeeper. The door is opened by the priest who is to clean the inner altar. That is why he is given two keys (at 3:6B). The narrative moves from M. 3:7A to D. B-C, integral at M. Mid. 4:2, are extraneous here. From M. 3:7H, the narrative resumes at 3:9. Ignoring the interpolation at 3:8, the action is continuous." —R.S.S.

3 D. He cut off the shanks and gave them to him who had won them.
E. He stripped off the hide.
F. He cut open the heart and removed its blood.
4 G. He cut off the fore-legs and gave them to him who had won them.
5 H. He came up to the right hind-leg, cut it off, and gave it to him who had won it, and the two testicles with it.
I. He cut it [the carcass] open, so that all of it was open before him.
J. He took the fat and put it at the place at which the head had been cut off above.
6 K. He took the innards and gave them to him who had won them, for the purpose of washing them.
L. And as to the stomach: they wash it in the swilling-room, so much as was required.
M. And as to the innards: they wash them three times at the very least, on the marble tables which are between the pillars.

M. 4:2

A. He took the knife and separated the lungs from the liver, and the lobe of the liver from the liver.
B. But he did not move it from its place.
7 C. He pierced the breast and give it to him who had won it.
D. He proceeded to the right flank and did cut it down-wards to the backbone—
E. *but he did not touch the backbone—*
F. until he reached the two thin ribs.
8 G. He cut it off and gave it to him who had won it, with the liver suspended from it.
H. He came to the neck, and left with it two ribs on this side and two ribs on that side.
9 I. He cut it off and gave it to him who had won it, with the windpipe, heart, and lungs hanging from it.
J. He came to the left flank and left with it two thin ribs above and two thin ribs below.
K. And so did he leave them on the other side.
L. It turns out that he left on both of them two each above and two each below.
10 M. He cut it off and gave it to him who had won it, and the backbone with it, and the spleen hanging from it.
N. *This was the larger part, but that of the right side do they call the larger part, for the liver is suspended on it.*
11 O. He came to the rump, cut it off, and gave it to him who had won it, with the fat tail, and the lobe of the liver, and the two kidneys with it.
12 P. He took the left hind-leg and gave it to him who had won it.
Q. All of them turned out to be standing in a row, and the limbs in their hands:
(1) the first, with the head and a hindleg, the head in his right

hand, with its muzzle along his arm, and its horns in his fingers, and the place at which it was slaughtered turned upwards, and the fat set on top of it [that place], and the right hind-leg in his left hand, and the flayed end outermost;

(2) the second, with the two fore-legs, that of the right hand in his right hand, and that of the left in his left, with the flayed end outermost;

(3) the third, with the rump and the [other] hind-leg, the rump in his right hand, and the fat-tail hanging down between his fingers, and the lobe of the liver and the two kidneys with it, the left hind-leg in his left hand, with the flayed end outermost;

(4) the fourth, with the breast and the neck, the breast in his right hand, and the neck in his left, and with its ribs between his fingers;

(5) the fifth with the two flanks, that of the right in his right hand, that of the left in his left, with the flayed ends outwards;

(6) the sixth, with the innards put in a dish, and the shanks on top of them, above;

(7) the seventh, with the fine flour;

(8) the eighth, with the baked cakes;

(9) the ninth, with the wine.

R. They went and put them on the lower half of the ramp, on the west side of it.

S. And they salted them [the limbs and meal-offering].

T. Then they came down and came to the office of hewn stone to recite the *Shema*ᶜ.

M. 4:3

The narrative bears virtually no gloss, since M. 4:3E, N may or may not be integral to the narrative. It appears to me that the story has twelve priests (indicated in bold-face Arabic numerals) who had won the right to take hold of various parts of the offering, but it then, M. 4:3Q, enumerates nine priests, and of these only six, instead of the expected twelve, handle parts of the animal. It does not seem to me that the list of "all of them" (Q) is harmonious with what precedes. [12]

5:1-6

A. The superintendent said to them, "Say one blessing."

B. They said a blessing, pronounced the Ten Commandments, the *Shema*ᶜ [Hear O Israel (Deut. 6:4-9)], *And it shall come to pass if you*

---

[12] "The first part of this pericope deals with the order of carving up the sacrifice. It does not indicate one way or the other *how* the various limbs are to be distributed, merely that he who is to receive a specified limb is awarded that limb at a particular moment in the rite. Q then informs us how the limbs are distributed. So the two parts of the pericope are not *necessarily* in conflict with each other, and I am inclined to believe that they do not conflict at all. Note that the gloss at M. 3:1B follows exactly the order of the sacrificial parts at 4:3Q (twelve items distributed among nine priests). 3:1B, extraneous in its own context, is secondary to 4:3Q."—R.S.S.

shall hearken (Deut. 11:13-21), and *And the Lord spoke to Moses* (Num. 15:37-41).

C. They blessed the people with three blessings: *True and sure*, ᶜ*Abodah*, and the blessing of priests.

D. And on the Sabbath they add a blessing for the outgoing priestly watch.

M. 5:1

A. [The superintendent] said to them, "Those who are new to [the preparation of] the incense, come and cast lots."

B. They cast lots.

C. Whoever won won.

D. "Those who are new with those who have had a chance [compare Song of Songs 7:14], come and cast lots on who will bring up the limbs from the ramp to the altar."

E. *R. Eliezer b. Jacob says, "He who brings up the limbs to the ramp [without another lottery] is the one who brings them up onto the altar."* [13]

M. 5:2

A. They handed them [who had no assignment] to the ministers.

B. They did remove their clothing from them.

C. And they left them only their underpants alone.

D. And there were wall-niches there, on which were written [the names] of the various pieces of clothing.

M. 5:3

A. He who won [the right to offer] the incense did take the spoon.

B. *And the spoon was like a large gold three-qab measure, holding three qabs.*

C. *And the dish was in it, full and heaped up with incense.*

D. *And it had a cover.*

E. *And there was a kind of covering on it.*

M. 5:4

A. He who won [the right to the ashes with] the firepan took the silver firepan and went up to the top of the altar and cleared away the cinders in either side and scooped up [ashes with the firepan].

B. He came down and emptied them out into that [firepan] of gold.

C. About a *qab* of cinders scattered from it, and he swept them out into the water-channel.

D. And on the Sabbath he covered over them with a psykter.

E. *And a psykter was a large utensil, holding a letekh, and two chains were on it, one with which he pulled to lower it, and one with which it was held firm from above, so that it should not roll.*

---

[13] Ginzberg, *Tamid*, pp. 40-41, observes that M. 5:2E "is quoted in Yoma 26a as a Baraita and not as a Mishnah, which proves that it was not in the text of Tamid at the time of the Amoraim."

F. *And three purposes did it serve:*
(1) they turn it over on top of cinders;
and (2) on a creeping thing on the Sabbath;
and (3) they lower the ashes from on the altar with it.

M. 5:5

A. [When] they reached the area between the porch and the altar, one man took the shovel and tosses it between the porch and the altar.

B. *No one in Jerusalem hears the voice of his fellow on account of the noise of the shovel.*

C. *And three purposes did it serve:*

(1) *a priest who hears its sound knows that his brethren the priests enter in to prostrate themselves, and he then runs and comes along;*

(2) *And a son of a Levite who hears its noise knows that his brethren, the Levites, enter to say their song, and he then runs and comes along;*

(3) *and the head of the priestly watch then had the unclean people stand at the eastern gate.*

M. 5:6

In the context of the narrative, the saying of blessings takes place in the office made of hewn stones. But the narrative breaks at M. 5:1. M. 5:2 completes the assignments of the various tasks. The dispute, M. 5:2D-E, of course, is utterly out of balance; Eliezer's saying ignores the narrative style to which we are accustomed. M. 5:3 then accounts for the removal of priests with no task for the day. The priestly garments then are given up by those who have no use for them at that time. The narrative begun at M. 5:2 resumes at M. 5:4. But only M. 5:4A advances the discussion. The rest clearly is gloss, by analogy to M. 5:5E-F, M. 5:6B-C (though B may deserve a place within the narrative). M. 5:6 refers to the two priests, one who takes charge of the incense, the other, the ashes. The *shovel*, some sort of musical instrument, is sounded for the purposes listed below, C. [14] The story continues at M. 6:1A.

[14] "Despite the Amoraic tradition, attributed to Rab and Samuel (y. Sukk. 55d, b. Arakh. 10b), that the MGRPH ('shovel') was a musical instrument, the evidence at M. Tam. 5:6 and 3:8 (and of course 2:1) suggests that we deal here with a real shovel. At M. 5:6 the shovel is not 'played', but thrown between the porch and the altar. This presumably produces the loud (clanging) noise, on account of which 'no one in Jerusalem could hear the voice of his fellow.' M. 3:8 attributes noises of legendary proportions to other Temple fixtures and utensils as well: the sound of the great door opening, the sound of the wooden device which Ben Qaṭin made for the laver (cf. M. 1:4F-G). The shovel is listed at M. 3:8B in the context of these Temple utensils, *not* in the context of musical instruments (E-H). In neither pericope, then, does the context suggest that the MGRPH is a musical instrument."—R.S.S.

6:1-3

A. They [the priests who were in charge of the incense and of removing the ashes] began to go up onto the steps of the porch.

B. *Those who had won [the right to remove] the ashes of the inner altar and the candlestick went before them* [= M. 3:6A].

C. *He who had won [the right to clean] the ashes of the inner altar went in* and took the basket [left at M. 3:9] and prostrated himself and went out.

D. *He who had won [the right to remove] the ashes of the candlestick entered in.*

E. *And [if] he found the two eastern-most lamps still flickering*, he clears out the eastern one and leaves the western one flickering,

F. for from it did he kindle the candlestick at twilight.

G. *[If] he found that it had gone out, he cleaned it out and kindled it* from the altar of the whole-offering [M. 3:9E-F].

H. He took the oil-jar from the second step [M. 3:9I] and prostrated himself and went out.

M. 6:1

A. He who had won [the right to make use of] the firepan heaped up the cinders on the [inner] altar and tamped them down with the back of the firepan and prostrated himself and went out.

M. 6:2

A. He who had won [the right to prepare] the incense did take the dish from the middle of the ladle and gave it [the ladle] to his friend or his relative.

B. [If] it had spilled [from the firepan] into it [the ladle], he put it into his two hands.

C. And they instruct him: "Be careful not to begin in front of you lest you be burned."

D. He began to tamp down and come out.

E. The one who was to offer the incense did not offer the incense until the superintendent said to him, "Offer the incense."

F. If he was a high priest, the superintendent says, "My lord, high priest, offer the incense."

G. The people departed, and he offered the incense and prostrated himself and went out.

M. 6:3

The narrative superficially appears to be smooth, unadorned, and unglossed. But M. 6:1 goes over the ground of M. 3:9, nearly verbatim, as indicated by my italics, duplicating M. 3:9's account of the removal of ashes and kindling of the lamp. M. 3:9 then is understood to refer to the cleaning out of five lamps, M. 6:1, the two others (Albeck,

p. 429). What we have, however, is simply the effort to preserve two distinct, but closely parallel, versions of the same action. [15]

The point of M. 6:3C is that the priest should put the incense further at the back of the altar before putting incense near at hand, for otherwise he will have to put his hand over the smoke to reach the more distant cinders. These instructions are necessary, for the priest who does the rite may not do it again, so there always will be a novice at this particular part of the rite (M. 5:2).

7:1-4

A. When the high priest enters to prostrate himself, three [priests] support him: one by the right hand, one by the left, and one by the precious stones [on the shoulder-pieces of the ephod, Ex. 28:9].

B. And as soon as the superintendent heard the sound of the feet of the high priest, that he goes out [of the *heikhal*], he raised the curtain for him.

C. He went in and prostrated himself and went out.

D. And his brethren the priests went in and prostrated themselves and went out.

M. 7:1

A. They [the priests who had participated] came and stood on the steps of the porch.

B. They who were first [the one who removed the ashes of the inner altar, and the one who cleaned up the candlestick, the one who carried the shovel and the one who offered the incense and his associate] took up a position at the south of their brethren, the priests.

C. And five utensils were in their hand: (1) the ash-bin in the hand of one, and (2) the oil-jar in the hand of one, and (3) the fire-

---

15 "While the patterning of the language at M. 6:1 is very similar to that at M. 3:9 (hardly surprising), a comparison of the differences will show that we have a smooth, continuous narrative. The details of 3:9 are presupposed at 6:1, while the actions left unfinished there are here completed. In particular, the basket and oil-jar left there are now removed. The procedure for removing the ashes of the candlestick differs in each pericope, as Neusner notes. It is impossible to prove either that we have preserved 'two distinct, but closely parallel versions of the same action,' or that we have two distinct, sequential actions (as the narrative suggests). The interpretation of these data necessarily will flow from one's larger theory of the tractate's layout and construction. I am inclined to view Tamid as a continuous narrative (with interpolations). Admittedly, there are a lot of ashes that get cleaned out during the course of the narrative, but we deal with two altars—the outer one (M. 1:2-2:5) and the inner one (M. 3:6-9 and 6:1). We deal also with the incense rite, which involves activity at both altars (the outer one at M. 5:4-5, the inner one at M. 6:2-3). There are, consequently, *two* altar fires, one for animals and one for incense, both inside and outside (cf. M. 2:4-5), or *four* in all. Each of these four fires is cleaned out during the course of the morning ritual, and that is how a unitary narrative can give us so many ashes."—R.S.S.

shovel in the hand of one, and (4) the [incense] dish in the hand of one, and (5) the ladle and its cover [M. 5:4] in the hand of one.

D. They said one [priestly] blessing for the people [Num. 6:24-26].

E. *But: In the provinces they say it as three blessings, and in the sanctuary, as one blessing.*

F. *In the sanctuary they would pronounce the [divine] name as it is written, and in the provinces, by an epithet.*

G. *In the provinces the priests raise up the palms of their hands as high as their shoulders, and in the sanctuary, over their heads,*

H. *except for the high priest, who does not raise his hands higher than the frontlet.*

I. *R. Judah says, "Even the high priest raises his hands above the frontlet,*

J. *"since it is said, And Aaron lifted up his hands towards the people and blessed them* (Lev. 9:22)" [M. Sot. 7:6].[16]

M. 7:2

A. When the high priest wants to burn the offerings, he would go up on the ramp, with the prefect at his right.

B. [When] he reached the half way point of the ramp, the prefect took him by the right hand and led him up.

C. The first [of the nine priests, M. 4:3] handed him the head and the hind-leg, and he laid his hands on them and tossed them [into the altar-fire].

D. The second handed over to the first the two fore-legs. He gives them to the high priest. And he laid his hands on them and tossed them [into the altar-fire].

E. The second departed, going on his way.

F. And so did they hand over to him all the rest of the limbs, and he lays his hands on them, and tosses them [into the altar-fires].

G. And when he wants, he lays on his hands, but others throw [the pieces into the fire].

H. He comes then to walk around the altar [toward the right, to the southwestern corner].

I. *From what point does he begin?*

J. *From the southeastern corner, then northeastern one, northwestern, and southwestern* [see M. Zeb. 5:3].

K. They gave him wine to pour out.

L. The prefect stands at the corner, with a flag in his hand, and two priests stand at the table of the fat pieces, with two silver trumpets in their hands.

M. They sounded a prolonged sound (TQ^{c}), a wavering sound, and a prolonged sound.

---

[16] Ginzberg, *Tamid*, pp. 41f. maintains that the passage is inserted here from M. Sotah 7:6: "First, only the anonymous view given in Sotah was added as representing the standard Halakah, later the individual opinion of R. Judah was inserted to make Tamid 7:2 agree entirely with Sotah 7:6."

N. They came and stood near Ben Arza, one on his right, one on his left.

O. He stopped down to pour out the wine, and the prefect waved the flag, and Ben Arza dashed the cymbal, and the Levites broke out in song.

P. [When] they reached a break [in the singing], they sounded a prolonged sound, and the people prostrated themselves.

Q. At every break [in the singing] was a prolonged blast, and at every prolonged blast, a prostration.

R. This is the order of the daily whole-offering in the liturgy of the house of our God. May it be [his] will that it be rebuilt, soon, in our own days. Amen.

M. 7:3

A. The singing which the Levites did sing in the sanctuary:

B. On the first day they did sing, *The earth is the Lord's and the fulness thereof, the world and they who live therein* (Ps. 24).

C. On the second day they did sing, *Great is the Lord and highly to be praised in the city of our God, even upon his holy hill* (Ps. 48).

D. On the third day they did sing, *God stands in the congregation of God, he is a judge among the gods* (Ps. 82).

E. On the fourth day they did sing, *O Lord God to whom vengeance belongs, thou God to whom vengeance belongs, show yourself* (Ps. 94).

F. On the fifth day they did sing, *Sing we happily to God our strength, make a joyful noise to the God of Jacob* (Ps. 81).

G. On the sixth day they did sing, *The Lord is king and has put on glorious apparel* (Ps. 93).

H. On the Sabbath-day they did sing, *A Psalm, A song for the Sabbath-day* (Ps. 92)—

I. A psalm, a song for the world that is to come, for the day which is wholly Sabbath-rest for eternity.

M. 7:4

Chapter Seven is separate from Chapter Six only in the printed editions. All manuscripts treat the two chapters as one. M. 7:4 is a tacked-on pericope. M. 7:3R explicitly marks the conclusion of the narrative. M. 7:2E-J clearly interrupts the narrative; the several units are carefully formulated.

MIDDOT

CHAPTER SIXTEEN

INTRODUCTION TO MIDDOT
MIDDOT CHAPTERS ONE THROUGH FIVE

Middot presents the measurements of the Mishnah's Temple, which, it is generally assumed (Albeck, p. 313), bears some relationship to the Temple of Herod, destroyed in 70. "Those who built the Second Temple in the days of Ezra," Maimonides says (*The Temple* 1:4), "followed the pattern of Solomon's Temple and adapted some of the particulars described in Ezekiel." Maimonides further specifies the areas under discusson (*ibid.* 1:5):

> These are the things that were essential in the construction of the Temple: A Holy Place and a Holy of Holies were to be made. In front of the Holy Place there was to be a specific place called the Porch. Together, these three structures were called the Temple. Around the Temple, at a distance, another wall was erected, corresponding to the hangings of the court (of the tabernacle) in the wilderness. Everything comprised within this partition, which corresponded to the court of the Tent of meeting, was called the Court. All the aforementioned together was referred to as the Sanctuary.

Let us now turn to the topics treated by our tractate and how they are arranged. In order to indicate those pericopae which interrupt the fundamental sequence of units on the dimensions of the Temple, I place in brackets the references to the former set of units.

I. *Watch posts and gates.* 1:1-9

1:1 In three places do the priests keep watch in the sanctuary. And the Levites in twenty-one.
[1:2 The man in charge of the Temple mount would go around to every watch.]
1:3 Five *gates* were in the Temple mount.
1:4 Seven gates were in the courtyard.
1:5 Continuation of M. 1:4.
1:6 Four offices were in the room of the hearth.
1:7 Two gates were in the room of the hearth.
[1:8 The room of the hearth was vaulted.]
[1:9 And there was a place there, in which was a slab of marble.]

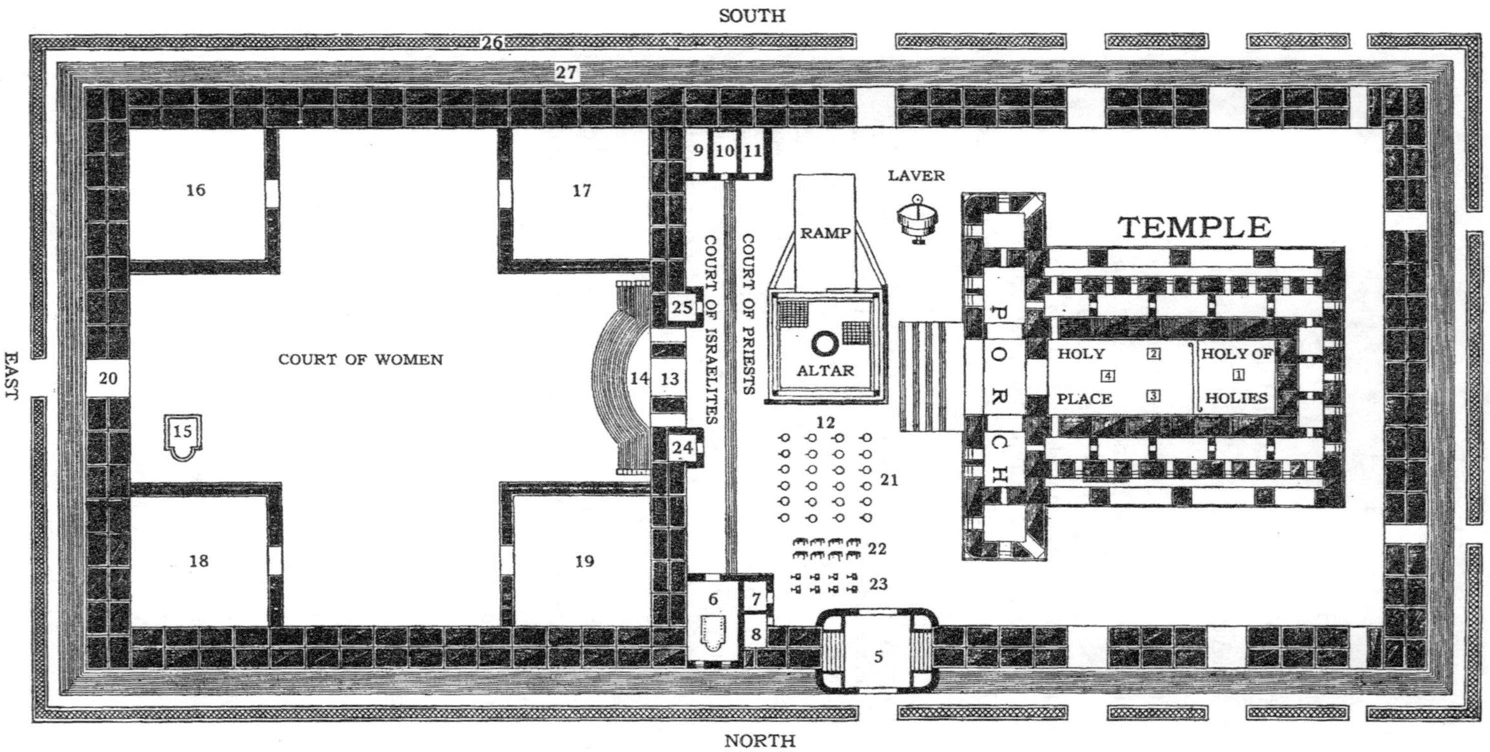

SOUTH

EAST

WEST

NORTH

Fig. 1. Ground plan of the Sanctuary (Temple and Courts), according to Maimonides. Adapted from a drawing in *Tiferet Israel,* a commentary to Mishnah Middot, Vilna, ROM Press, 1937.

1. Ark
2. Candlestick
3. Table
4. Altar of Incense
5. House of the Hearth
6. Chamber of Hewn Stone
7. Chamber of the Bowl
8. Wood Chamber
10. Parwa Chamber
11. Rinsing Chamber
12. "North side"
13. Gate of Nicanor
14. Fifteen Steps to the Temple Court
15. Chamber of the Law Court (not mentioned in the next)
16. Chamber of the Nazirites
17. Chamber of the House of Oil
19. Chamber of the Lepers
20. East Gate to the Court of Women
21. Rings of the Slaughtering Place
22. Tables of the Slaughtering Place
23. Place of Flaying
24. Chamber of Vestments
25. Chamber of Baked Cakes
26. Latticed Railing

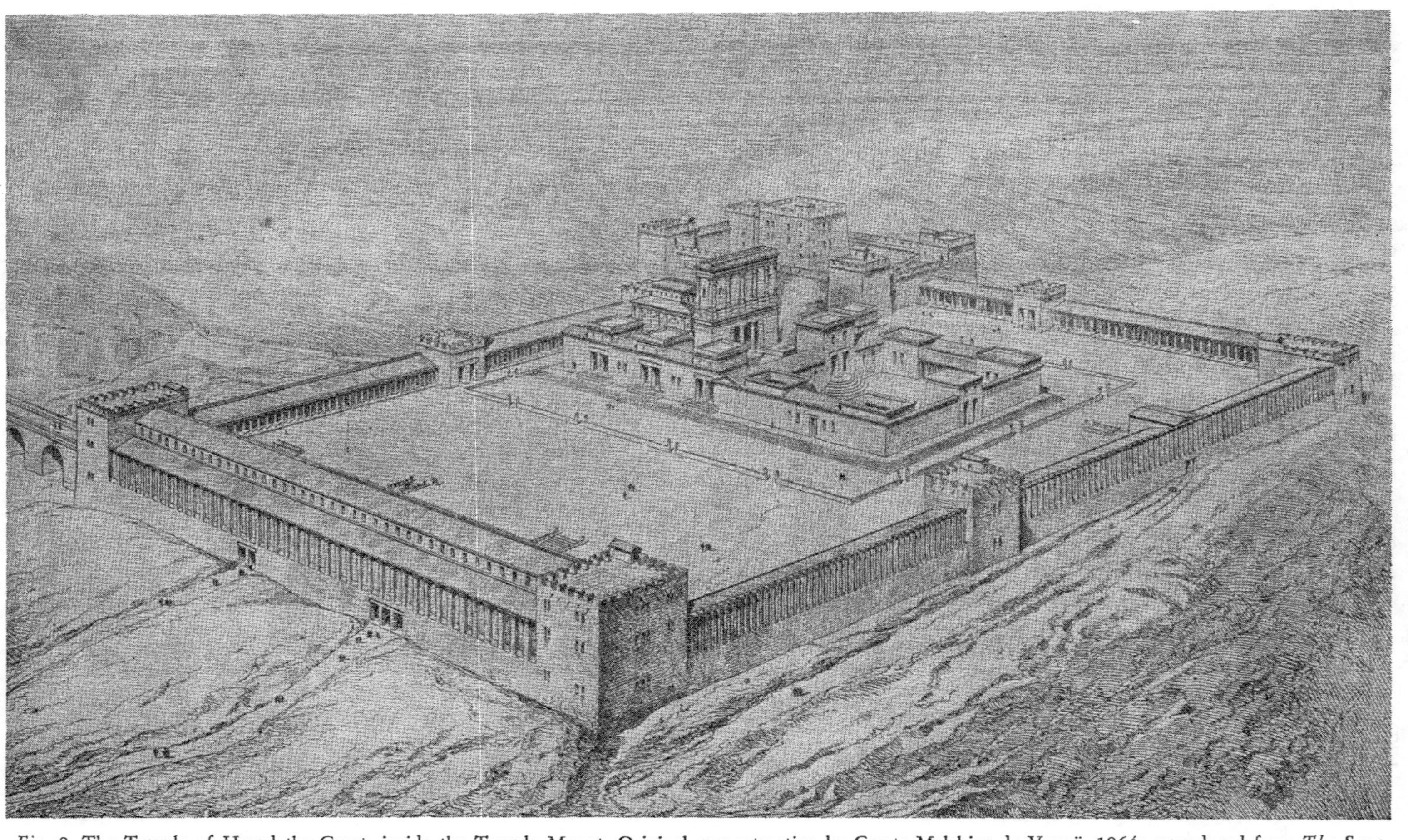

Fig. 2. The Temple of Herod the Great, inside the Temple Mount. Original reconstruction by Comte Melchior de Vogüë, 1864; reproduced from *The Saga of Jerusalem*, Universitas Press, 1954.

II. *The layout of the Temple mount.* 2:1-6

2:1 *The Temple mount* was five hundred cubits by five hundred.
[2:2 All those who enter the Temple mount enter at the right and leave at the left, except for...]
2:3 Inside it is a latticed railing.
[2:4 Continuation of M. 2:3's secondary construction.]
2:5 *The women's courtyard* was one hundred thirty-five cubits in length by one hundred thirty-five cubits in breadth.
2:6 And offices were located beneath the *Israelite courtyard.* [Continuation of M. 2:5's secondary construction.]

III. *The altar and porch.* 3:1-8

3:1 *The altar* was thirty-two by thirty-two cubits.
3:2 The southwestern corner of the altar.
3:3 Below, on the pavement.
3:4 All the same are the stones of the ramp and the stones of the altar.
3:5 Rings were on the north side of the altar.
3:6 The laver was between the porch and the altar.
3:7 *The entrance to the porch* was forty cubits high.
3:8 Cross-bars of cedar were set between the wall of the sanctuary and the wall of the porch.

IV. *The sanctuary and courtyard.* 4:1-7, 5:1-4

4:1 *The entrance of the sanctuary* is twenty cubits in height and ten in breadth.
4:2 Two little doors were in the great gate.
4:3 There were thirty-eight cells there.
4:4 The lower story of cells was five cubits wide.
4:5 There was a passage from the northeastern corner to the northwestern corner.
4:6 *And the sanctuary* was a hundred cubits by a hundred cubits, with a height of a hundred cubits.
4:7 From east to west was one hundred cubits.
5:1 *The courtyard of the Temple* was one hundred eighty-seven cubits in length by one hundred thirty-five in breadth.
5:2 From north to south.
5:3 Six offices were in the courtyard.
5:4 Those in the south.

The units are orderly. Unit I, which borrows much material from Tamid, is a suitable introduction, since it deals with the watchposts and gates to the Temple mount. The sequence leads us through the gates, onto the Mount, II, then directly to the altar and porch, III, and finally, outward again toward the sanctuary and courtyard, IV. [1]

Once again I have set in italics passages which clearly constitute major interpolations of extraneous materials.

The purpose of this commentary is not to bring Middot into relationship either with the account of Josephus or with the results of modern and contemporary archaeology. The former work has been done by Oscar Holtzmann, *Middot* (Giessen, 1913), pp. 15-43, and the latter, with even greater success, by F. J. Hollis, *The Archaeology of Herod's Temple. With a Commentary on the Tractate 'Middoth'* (London, 1934), pp. 233-349. These excellent works have now to be supplemented with the results of more recent archaeology as well. But that is not my task. The purpose of the present commentary is to give a brief account of the tractate, so that, when we turn to the formation of Rabbinic Judaism and the earliest evidences of its ideas, we may have some clear notion of its character. For the purpose of the history of ideas, a detailed comparison of the facts supplied by Josephus, Middot, and achaeology sheds remarkably little light. So far as the picture given in our tractate relates to the real Temple of Herod, we may be contented to give Hollis (p. 354) the last word and to rely upon his judgment when we turn to the interpretation of the place and meaning of Middot in the formative century of Judaism:

> The more the bald and precise statements of Middoth are studied, especially when full weight is given to the accounts of Josephus and to the explorations of the present day on the very site, the more it seems clear that Middoth is an honest attempt to relate facts, from a certain point of view, it is true, but that point of view was Jewish, not purely Rabbinic. The use made of Holy Scripture in the tractate is not such

---

[1] "Beginning at M. 2:1, the tractate's thematic units are articulated through a recurring formal pattern which gives the measurements of the particular area to be discussed in that unit. The leading phrases, given in italics, are as follows:

M. 2:1A: *The Temple mount* was five hundred cubits by five hundred cubits...
M. 2:5A: *The women's courtyard* was one hundred thirty-five cubits in length by one hundred thirty-five cubits in breadth...
M. 2:6D: *The Israelite courtyard* was one hundred thirty-five cubits in length by eleven cubits in breadth...
M. 2:6E: And so too was *the courtyard of the priests*...
M. 3:1A: *The altar* was thirty-two by thirty-two cubits...
M. 3:7A: *The entrance to the porch* was forty cubits high...
M. 4:1A: *The entrance to the sanctuary* is twenty cubits in height and ten in breadth...
M. 4:6A: And *the sanctuary* was one hundred cubits by one hundred cubits...
M. 5:1A: *The courtyard of the Temple* was one hundred eighty-seven cubits in length by one hundred thirty-five in breadth..."—R.S.S.

as to give the impression that somehow or other the words of Scripture are being followed, and violence done to fact, but rather that there was a fairly clear recollection of the Temple as it had been, with Holy Scripture appealed to illuminate the fact, not as authority to prove it.

We have no need, to accomplish our purpose in this sizable project, to dwell upon matters of detail of how the Herodian Temple actually was, or of how the rabbis of the late first and second centuries imagined it to have been. The translation and brief comments on the literary traits of the tractate suffice.

1:1-9

A. In three places do the priests keep watch in the sanctuary: (1) in the room of Abtinas, (2) in the room of the flame, and (3) in the room of the hearth.

B. And the Levites [keep watch] in twenty-one places [I Chron. 26:17-18]:[2]

C. five at the five gates of the Temple mount;

D. four at the four corners on the inside [of the Temple-wall];

E. five at the five gates of the courtyard;

F. four at the four corners on the outside [the wall of the courtyard];

G. and one at the office of the offering [M. 1:6],

H. and one at the office of the veil,

I. and one behind the Mercy Seat [outside of the western wall of the holy of holies, M. 5:1].

M. 1:1 [A = M. Tam. 1:1A]

A. *The man in charge of the Temple mount would go around to every watch, and lighted torches were [flaring] before him.*

B. *And to any watch which was not standing did the man in charge of the Temple mount say, "Peace be with you."*

C. [*If*] *it was obvious that he was sleeping, he beats him with his staff.*

D. *And he had the right to burn his garment.*

E. *And they say, "What is the noise in the courtyard?"*

F. *"It is the noise of a Levite being smitten, and his clothing being burned, for he went to sleep at his post."*

G. *R. Eliezer b. Jacob says, "One time they found my mother's brother sleeping and burned his garment."*

M. 1:2

A. Five gates were in the [wall of the] Temple mount:

B. two Hulda-gates at the south, serving for entry and exit;

C. Qiponos-gate on the west, serving for entry and exit;

[2] "I Chron. 26:17-18 is not entirely apposite here. It knows twenty-four Levitical watches, distributed in a different fashion from that of M. What we learn from this comparison is that, in this instance, M.'s account is not derived from scriptural exegesis."—R.S.S.

D. Tadi-gate on the north, serving no purpose at all;
E. the Eastern Gate—
F. *on it is a picture of the Walled City of Shushan—*
G. *through which the (high) priest who burns the red cow, and the cow, and all who assist in its rite, go forth to the Mount of Olives* [M. Par. 4:1].

M. 1:3

A. Seven gates were in the courtyard:
B. three at the north, three at the south, and one at the east.
C. That on the south was the gate for kindling, next to it, the gate for the firstlings, next to that, the gate for water.
D. And that on the east is the gate of Niqanor.
E. And it had two offices, one at the right, one at the left.
F. One was the office of Pinḥas, the keeper of the vestments, and one was the office of those who make the baked cakes [M. Tam. 1:3].

M. 1:4

A. And that on the north is the gate of the flame.
B. And it was like a portico, with an upper room built on it,
C. through which the priests keep watch from above, and the Levites from below.
D. And it had a door opening out to the rampart.
E. Next to it was the gate of the offering, and next to that, the [gate of] the room of the hearth.

M. 1:5 [B: M. Tam. 1:1]

A. Four offices were in the room of the hearth,
B. like cells opening into a hall,
C. two in the sanctuary, two in unconsecrated ground,
D. and flagstones' ends made a border between what was consecrated [in the area of the courtyard] and what was unconsecrated [north of the room of the hearth].
E. And what were their purposes?
F. That on the southwestern side was the office for the lamb-offerings.
G. That on the southeastern side was the office for those who make the show-bread.
H. In that on the northeastern side did the Hasmoneans put away the stones of the altar which had been rendered abominations by the kings of Greece.
I. Through that on the northwestern side do they go down to the room for immersion [M. Tam. 1:1: the office of the room of the hearth].

M. 1:6

A. Two gates were in the room of the hearth, one open to the rampart, and one open toward the courtyard.
B. Said R. Judah, "This one which was open toward the courtyard had a small door, through which they enter to inspect the courtyard."

M. 1:7

A. The room of the hearth is vaulted. And it was a large room, surrounded by a raised pavement of stone.

B. *And the mature members of the [priestly] household [of the day] sleep there [on the raised pavement], with the keys to the courtyard in their hands.*

C. *And the fledging priests [sleep], each with his mattress on the ground.*

M. 1:8 [M. Tam. 1:1D-H]

A. And there was a place there [in the room of the hearth], one cubit square, in which was a slab of marble, with a chain attached.

B. And the key-chain was suspended from it.

C. When the time came for locking up, one lifted up the slab by the ring and took the keys from the chain.

D. And the priest locked from the inside, and the Levite went to sleep on the outside.

E. [When] he finished locking, he returned the keys to the chain and the slab to its place.

F. *He put his bedding on it.*

G. *He went to sleep.*

H. *[If] one of them should have a nocturnal emission of semen, he goes out, proceeding along the passage that leads below the building—*

I. *and lamps flicker on this side and on that—*

J. *until he reaches the immersion-room.*

K. *R. Eliezer b. Jacob says, "He goes out by the passage which leads below the rampart, and so he came to the Tadi gate."*

M. 1:9 [H-J: M. Tam. 1:1K-M]

M. 1:2 breaks the flow begun at M. 1:1 and continued at M. 1:3ff. We certainly have nothing like the sustained narrative of Tamid, shown by the contrast between M. 1:2 and M. 1:1, 3-8. M. 1:9 returns us to the narrative style of Tamid and also focuses attention on a rite, rather than on the location of rooms. There were twenty-one guard posts (*vs.* I Chron. 26:17-18), M. 1:1, supervised as indicated, M. 1:2. M. 1:3-7 [+ M. 1:8 = M. Tam. 1:1D-H] seem to me a single and unitary pericope, even though there is no effort to replicate the same simple and tight sentence-structure throughout. M. 1:9 is tacked on. [3]

---

[3] "M. 1:9 is not tacked on. The detail about the key-chain (A-B) follows directly from M. 1:8A. The materials extraneous to Midd. are those which are integral to Tam., viz., M. 1:8B-C [= M. Tam. 1:1F-H], M. 1:9F-G [not in M. Tam., but links M. Midd. 1:9C-E with H-K], M. 1:9H-J+K [= M. Tam. 1:1K-M; Eliezer b. Jacob's gloss is more apposite to Tam., where it is not found, than to Midd., where it is]." —R.S.S.

2:1-6

A. The Temple mount was five hundred cubits by five hundred cubits [Ez. 42:20].

B. Its largest [open space] was at the south, second largest, at the east, third largest, at the north, and least, at the west.

C. The part which was the most extensive [of its open space] was [also] the part which was most used [by those entering the area].

M. 2:1

A. *All those who enter the Temple mount enter at the right, go around, and leave at the left,*

B. *except for him to whom something happened, who goes around to the left.*

C. *"What ails you, that you go around to the left?"*

D. *"For I am a mourner."*

E. *"May he who dwells in this house comfort you."*

F. *"That I am excommunicated."*

G. *" 'May he who dwells in this house put it into their heart that they draw you nigh again,' " the words of R. Meir.*

H. *Said to him R. Yosé, "You have treated the matter as if they have transgressed the law on his account.*

I. *"But: 'May he who dwells in this house put it into your heart that you listen to the opinion of your fellows, and they draw you nigh again.' "*

M. 2:2

A. Inside it [the Temple mount, surrounding the inner area which contained the women's court and the Temple court] is a latticed railing [SWRG], ten handbreadths high.

B. There were thirteen breaches it,

C. *which the kings of Greece opened up.*

D. *They went and closed them up again and decreed on their account thirteen prostrations.*

E. Inside it is the rampart, ten cubits [wide].

F. And there were twelve steps there [leading up from the rampart to the women's courtyard].

G. The height of each step is a half-cubit, and its tread, a half cubit.

I H. *All the steps which were three [within the Temple mount] were a half a cubit in height and a half-cubit in tread, except for those of the porch [which had a tread of a cubit].*

II I. *All of the entrances and gates which were there were twenty cubits high and ten cubits wide, except for that of the porch.*

III J. *All the entrances which were there had doors, except for that of the porch [M. 3:7].*

IV K. *All the gates which were there had intels, except for the Tadi-gate, which had two stones leaning against one another [as a pointed arch].*

V L. *All the gates which were there were changed [and covered] with gold, except for Niqanor's gate, because a miracle was done with them* [M. Yoma 3:10].

M. *And there are those who say, "Because their bronze shone like gold."*

M. 2:3

VI A. *All the walls which were there were high, except the eastern wall [of the Temple mount]* [Ez. 40:5].

B. *For the priest who burns the red cow stands at the top of the Mount of Olives and takes his direction, looking directly at the door of the heikhal, at the time of the tossing of blood.*

M. 2:4

A. The women's courtyard was one hundred thirty-five cubits in length by one hundred thirty-five cubits in breadth.

B. And there were four offices at each of its four corners, each forty cubits square.

C. They had no roofs.

D. *And so are they destined to be [in the future],*

E. *since it is written, Then he brought me forth into the outer court and caused me to pass by the four corners of the court; and behold, in every corner of the court there was a court. In the four corners of the court there were courts enclosed* [Ezek. 46:21-22]—

F. *and 'enclosed' means only, without roofs.*

G. And what was their purpose?

H. That in the southeastern corner was the office of the Nazirites,

in which the Nazirites cook their peace-offerings, shave off their hair, which they throw under the pot [Num. 6:18, M. Naz. 6:8].

I. That in the northeastern corner was the office in charge of the wood supply,

in which the priests who are blemished examine the wood [for worms].

J. *And any piece of wood in which a worm is found is invalid for use on the altar.*

K. That on the northwestern corner was the office of the lepers.

L. That in the southwestern corner—

M. *said R. Eliezer b. Jacob, "I forget what its purpose was."*

N. *Abba Saul says, "There did they keep the wine and oil."*

O. *It was called* the office of the oil-room.

P. *And it [the women's court] at first was empty [of buildings]. They surrounded it with a gallery, so that the women look on from above, with the men below, so that they should not mingle.*

Q. And fifteen steps go up from it to the Israelite courtyard,

R. *one each for the fifteen Songs of Ascents in Psalms [Ps. 120-134],*

S. on which the Levites say their song.

T. They were not four-square, but rounded like half of a round threshing floor.

M. 2:5

A. And offices were [located] underneath the Israelite courtyard,
B. opening out onto the women's courtyard,
C. in which the Levites keep their harps, lyres, cymbals, and other musical instruments.
D. The Israelite courtyard was one hundred thirty-five cubits in length by eleven cubits in breadth.
E. And so too was the courtyard of priests a hundred thirty-five cubits in length by eleven cubits in breadth.
F. And the tops of flagstones form a border between the Israelite courtyard and the priests' courtyard.
G. *R. Eliezer b. Jacob says, "There was a step, a cubit high, and the platform [for the Levites] was set on it, and on it were three [more] steps, each a half cubit high.*
H. *"It comes out that the priests' courtyard was two and a half cubits higher than the Israelite courtyard."*
I. All the courtyard was a hundred eighty-seven cubits long by a hundred and thirty-five cubits wide.
J. And there were thirteen places where prostrations were to take place there [M. 2:3D].
K. *Abba Yosé b. Ḥanan says, "Opposite thirteen gates [vs.* M. 1:4-5]."
L. The southern gates, [counting] from the west: (1) the upper gate, (2) the kindling gate, (3) the gate for the firstlings, (4) the gate for water.
M. *And why was it called the gate for water?*
N. *For through it do they bring in the glass of water for the water-libation on the Festival [Sukkot].*
O. *R. Eliezer b. Jacob says, "And through it the waters trickled forth [Ez. 47:2] and in the future will issue out from under the threshold of the house [Ez. 47:1]."*
P. And opposite them at the north [counting] from the west: (5) the gate of Jeconiah, (6) the gate for the offering, (7) the gate for women, (8) the gate for song.
Q. *And why was it called the gate of Jeconiah?*
R. *For through it did Jeconiah go forth when he went out into exile.*
S. And that in the east:
T. (9) Niqanor's gate.
T. And it had two doors, one on the right, and one on the left.
V. And (10, 11) the two [gates] on the west had no name.

M. 2:6

M. 2:2C-I clearly intervene in the unfolding of the picture of the Temple, but M. 2:2A-B may be deemed integral to the account, since they carry forward M. 2:1C. M. 2:3H-M+M. 2:4 are a six-part, carefully balanced construction, inserted whole after M. 2:3G for obvious reasons. The narrative resumes only at M. 2:5. The interpolations, M. 2:5D-F, are clear. I am inclined to see M. 2:5K as the primitive model for the whole, on which basis I designated the italicized passages of H, I, J, M-O, as glosses of the primary account. P likewise appears extraneous, though this is by no means so certain as in the foregoing. Interesting at M. 2:6 is Abba Yosé's view, K, that there were thirteen gates in the courtyard. [4] M. 1:4-5 know only seven.

3:1-8

A. The altar was thirty-two by thirty-two [cubits] [at the base].
B. It rose by one cubit and drew in by one cubit [on every side].
C. This is the foundation.
D. Thus was left [an area] thirty cubits by thirty.
E. It rose by five cubits and drew in by one cubit.
F. This is the circuit.
G. Thus was left [an area] twenty-eight by twenty-eight.
H. The area of the horns is a cubit on this side and a cubit on that side.
I. Thus was left [an area] twenty-six by twenty-six.
J. The place for the passage of the priests is a cubit on this side and a cubit on that side.
K. Thus was left [an area] twenty-four by twenty-four [as] the place for the [altar] fire.
L. *Said R. Yosé, "At the outset it was only twenty-eight by twenty-eight. It draws in and rises in this same measure, so that the area for the altar-fire turns out to be twenty by twenty* [II Chron. 4:1].
M. *"But when the men of the Exile came up, they added four cubits at the south and four cubits at the west, in the shape of a gamma,*
N. *"since it is said, And the altar hearth shall be twelve cubits long by twelve broad, square* (Ez. 43:16).
O. *"Is it possible that it should be only twelve by by twelve?*
P. *"But when it also says, In the four quarters thereof, it teaches that from the middle one measures twelve cubits in all directions"* [*so that the area for the altar-fire must be twenty-four by twenty-four*].
Q. And a red line goes around it at the middle, to effect a separation between the drops of blood which are tossed on the top and the drops of blood which are tossed on the bottom.
R. And the foundation extended all the length of the north side and all the length of the west side,
S. and projects one cubit to the south and one cubit to the east.
M. 3:1

A. And at the southwestern corner [of the foundation] were two holes,
B. like two narrow nostrils,

---

[4] "Although the sequel at L-V counts only eleven. Both Abba Yosé's statement at M. 2:6K and the anonymous narrative at M. 2:3B-D appear to be attempted aetiologies of the practice of thirteen prostrations in the Temple courtyard."—R.S.S.

C. through which the drops of blood which are tossed on the western foundation and on the southern foundation descend and mix together in the channel and go forth to Qidron brook [M. Tam. 4:1].

M. 3:2

A. Below, on the pavement, at that corner was a place a cubit by a cubit, on which was a slab of marble;

B. and a ring was fixed to it, on which they go down to the pit [M. Me. 3:3] and clean it.

C. And a ramp was at the south of the altar, thirty-two by a breadth of sixteen.

D. And on its western side was a hole,

E. into which they put those sin-offering of fowl which were invalid.

M. 3:3

A. All the same are the stones of the ramp and the stones of the altar:

B. [they come] from the valley of Bet Kerem.

C. *And they dig beneath virgin soil and bring whole stones from there, on which iron has not been lifted up [Deut. 27:5-6].*

D. *For iron invalidates [stone] by touching it.*

E. *And a blemish invalidates it in every regard.*

F. *[If] one of them is blemished, it is invalid, but all the rest of them are valid.*

G. And they clean them twice a year, once at Passover, and once at the Festival.

H. And as to the sanctuary, once a year, at Passover.

I. *Rabbi says, "Every Friday do they clean it with a cloth, because of the blood."*

J. *They did not plaster them with an iron trowl, lest it touch and invalidate [them].*

K. *For iron is created to shorten man's days, and the altar is created to lengthen man's days.*

L. *It is not fitting that that which shortens man's days should be waved over that which lengthens man's days.*

M. 3:4

A. Rings were on the north side of the altar, six rows of four [rings]—

B. *and some say, "Four rows of six each"*—

C. at which they slaughter the Holy Things.

D. The shambles [M. Tam. 3:5] was north of the altar.

E. And on it were eight short pillars, and square blocks of cedarwood were on top of them, and iron hooks were set into them.

F. And three rows were on each one,

G. on which they would suspend [the slaughtered beasts].

H. They flay them on marble tables between the pillars.

M. 3:5 [D-H = M. Tam. 3:5B-E]

A. The laver was between the porch and the altar, towards the south.

B. Between the porch and the altar [was a space of] twenty-two cubits.

C. There were twelve steps there.

D. The height of a step was a half-cubit, and its tread a cubit, [then another of] a cubit, [and another of] a cubit, [then] a terrace of three cubits, then two steps of one cubit's tread each, then a terrace of three cubits. At the two top were two steps, each of one cubit's tread, and a terrace of four cubits.

E. *R. Judah says, "At the top were two steps, each of one cubit's tread, and a terrace of five cubits."*

M. 3:6

A. The entrance to the porch was forty cubits high and its breadth was twenty cubits.

B. And five carved oak beams were on top of it.

C. The lowest one overhangs the entrance by a cubit on either side [= twenty-two wide]. The one above it overhangs it by a cubit on either side [= twenty-four]. The one on top [the fifth] turns out to be thirty cubits long.

D. And a course of stones was between every two beams.

M. 3:7

A. Cross-bars of cedar were set between the wall of the sanctuary and the wall of the porch,

B. so that it not budge.

C. And golden chains were fixed to the roof beam of the porch,

D. on which novice-priests climb up and see the crowns,

E. *since it is written, And the crowns shall be to Helem and to Tobijah and to Jedaiah and to Hen the son of Zephaniah for a memorial in the Temple of the Lord* (Zech. 6:14).

F. A golden vine was standing at the entrance of the sanctuary, trained over the posts.

G. Whoever gave a leaf or a berry or a cluster brings it and hangs it on it.

H. *Said R. Eleazar bar Ṣadoq, "There was an incident, and three hundred priests were appointed [to clear it since it was too heavy]."*

M. 3:8

M. 3:1L-P clearly gloss the foregoing. M. 3:4's homilies also are to be treated as extraneous to the narrative. The rest seems to me integral.

4:1-7

A. The entrance of the sanctuary is twenty cubits in height and ten cubits in breadth.

B. It had four doors, two inside, and two outside,

C. *since it is said, The temple and the sanctuary had two doors* (Ez. 41:23).

D. The outside ones open into the inside of the entrance to cover the thickness of the wall, and the inside ones open into the house, to cover the space behind the doors.

E. For the entire house is overlaid with gold [I Kings 6:20-22, 32, 35], except for the backside of the doors.

F. *R. Judah says, "Inside the entrance did they stand.*

G. *"And they were in the form of folding doors, which doubled back upon themselves."*

H. These were two cubits and a half, and those, two cubits and a half.

I. And the doorpost was a half cubit thick on one side, and the doorpost was a half cubit thick on the other,

J. *since it is said, And the doors had two leaves apiece, two Turning leaves, two leaves for the one door, and two leaves for the other* (Ez. 41:24).

M. 4:1

A. Two little doors did the great gate have, one at the north, and one at the south.

B. Through that at the south no man ever entered.

C. *And it is expressly stated by Ezekiel,*

D. *as it is said, And the Lord said unto me, "This gate shall be shut, it shall not be opened, neither shall any man enter in by it, for the Lord, the God Israel, has entered in by it, therefore it shall be shut"* (Ez. 44:2).

E. *He took the key and opened the gate and went into the cell, and from the cell to the sanctuary* [M. Tam. 3:7].

F. *R. Judah says, "He went along the thickness of the wall until he found himself standing between the two gates.*

G. *"And he opened the outer ones from the inside and the inner ones from the outside."*

M. 4:2

A. And thirty-eight cells were there, fifteen at the north, fifteen at the south, and eight at the west.

B. Those at the north and at the south were five on top of five, with five on top of them. And those at the west were three on top of three, with two more on top of them.

C. And each one had three entrances, one to the cell on the right, one to the cell on the left, and one to the cell on top.

D. And at the northeastern corner were five entrances, one into the cell at the right, one into the cell on top of it, one into the passage-way, one into the little door, and one into the sanctuary.

M. 4:3

A. The lower [story of cells] was five [cubits wide], and the floor above it was six, and the one in the middle, six, and the floor above it, seven.

B. The one on top was seven,

C. *as it is said, The nethermost story was five cubits broad, and the middle was six cubits broad, and the third was seven cubits broad* (I Kings 6:6).

M. 4:4

A. And a passage went up from the northeastern corner to the northwestern corner,

B. through which they would go up to the roofs of the cells.

C. One would go up the passageway facing westward, and walked across the entire northern side until he reached the west.

D. [When] he reached the west, he turned southward and walked across the entire western side until he reached the south.

E. [When] he reached the south, he turned eastward and walked across the southern side until he reached the entrance to the upper chamber.

F. For the entrance to the upper chamber was open toward the south.

G. And in the entrance to the upper chamber were two cedar posts,

H. by which they went up to the roof of the upper room.

I. And in the upper chamber the tops of flagstones mark the division between the sanctuary and the Holy of Holies.

J. And in the upper room were openings into the house of the holy of holies, through which they would lower down craftsmen in boxes [closed on three sides].

K. so that they should not feast their eyes on the house of the Holy of Holies.

M. 4:5

A. And the sanctuary [including the porch and the holy of holies] was a hundred cubits by a hundred cubits, with a height of a hundred cubits.

B. The substructure [solid basement] was six cubits, and the height [of the wall built on it] was forty cubits, the wall-frieze, a cubit, the place of drippings, two cubits, the roof-beams, one cubit, the plaster, one cubit [= 51].

C. And the height of the upper room was forty cubits, the wall-frieze, one cubit, the place of drippings, two cubits, the roof-beams, one cubit, and the plaster, one cubit.

D. And the parapet was three cubits.

E. And the scarecrow was one cubit [= 49].

F. *R. Judah says, "The scarecrow was not included in the measure; rather: the parapet was four cubits."*

M. 4:6

A. From east to west was one hundred cubits:

B. The wall of the porch was five [cubits thick], and the porch, eleven; the wall of the sanctuary, six, and its inside, forty cubits. The dividing space was one cubit, and the Holy of Holies, twenty; the wall of the sanctuary, six; the cell, six; and the wall of the cell, five.

C. From north to south was [an area of] seventy cubits:

D. the wall of the passageway was five, the passageway, three, the wall of the cell, five, and the cell, six, the wall of the sanctuary, six, and its inner area, twenty cubits, the wall of the sanctuary, six, and the cell, six, the wall of the cell, five, and the space for draining off water, three cubits, and the wall, five cubits.

E. The porch projected fifteen cubits at the north, and fifteen cubits at the south.

F. It was called the place of the room of the slaughter-knives, for there did they put away the knives.

G. The sanctuary was narrow behind and wide in front, *and like a lion—*

H. *since it is said, Ho, Ariel, Ariel, the city where David encamped* (Is. 29:1)—

I. *just as the lion is narrow behind and broad in front, so the sanctuary is narrow behind and broad in front.*

M. 4:7

Judah's saying, M. 4:1F-G, appears to be a gloss or an interpolation, but it can stand as the continuation of the descriptive narrative in place of D. [5] The proof-texts, M. 4:1J, M. 4:2C-D, clearly are extraneous. [6] M. 4:2E is curious. It seems to want to continue a narrative of how a priest went through the building. But, of course, our chapter has no such narrative. [7] M. Tam 3:7 would have welcomed this unit into its pericope. M. 4:3D accords with M. 4:2E, that is, there is a direct access from the cell into the sanctuary. Judah, M. 4:2F, has a door open not directly into the sanctuary but into the great gate. [8] We observe a further break at M. 4:5B, C; the former uses the plural, the latter, the singular. [9] There is a nice triplet at M. 4:6, M. 4:7A-B, C-D, concluded by E.

5:1-4

A. The courtyard [of the Temple, from the Israelite courtyard onward] in all was one hundred eighty-seven cubits in length by one hundred thirty-five in breadth.

[5] "Judah disputes with D's version."—R.S.S.

[6] "Substantively, the proof-texts hardly are extraneous. They lead us directly into the imagination of our 'authors', particularly to the extent to which they actually generate the conceptions they are supposed to 'prove'."—R.S.S.

[7] "But M. Tam. 3:7 does, and this detail of course is integral and primary there (at M. Tam, 3:7D-E)."—R.S.S.

[8] "M. Midd. 4:2F-G belongs at M. Tam. 3:7, but, curiously, is not given there. Similarly, Eliezer b. Jacob's lemma at M. Midd. 1:9K belongs at M. Tam. 1:1, but is not given there. The shaping of the same material into two different tractates, Tamid and Middot, is hard to follow precisely. The Tamid context appears to be primary." —R.S.S.

[9] "M. 4:5Cff. substantively is a secondary expansion of the foregoing."—R.S.S.

B. From east to west [the length] was one hundred eighty-seven:

C. The area trodden by Israelites, eleven cubits, the area trodden by priests, eleven cubits, the altar, thirty-two, the area between the porch and the altar, twenty-two cubits, the sanctuary, a hundred cubits, and eleven cubits behind the place of the Mercy Seat.

M. 5:1

A. From north to south was one hundred thirty-five:

B. the ramp and the altar, sixty-two, from the altar to the rings, eight cubits, the area of the rings, twenty-four, from the rings to the tables, four, from the tables to the small pillars, four, from the small pillars to the wall of the courtyard, eight cubits, and the remainder [twenty-five cubits] was between the ramp and the wall and [in] the place of the pillars.

M. 5:2

A. Six offices were in the courtyard, three in the north and three in the south.

B. Those in the north: the office in charge of salt, the *Parwah*-office, the office for rinsing.

C. The office in charge of salt:
there did they put salt on the offering.

D. The *Parwah*-office:
there did they salt the hides of Holy Things,

E. and on its roof was the room for immersion for the high priest on the Day of Atonement.

F. The office for rinsing:
for there did they rinse the innards of the Holy Things,

G. and from there did a passageway go up to the roof of the *Parwah*-office.

M. 5:3

A. Those in the south: the office made of wood, [10] the office for the Exile, the office made of hewn stone.

B. The office made of wood—

C. *said R. Eliezer b. Jacob, "I forgot what purpose it served"*—

D. *Abba Saul says, "It is the office of the high priest, and it was behind the other two [A], and the roof of all three of them was on the same level."*

E. The office for the exile:
there was a permanent cistern, and a wheel was placed on it, and from there did they draw water for the whole courtyard.

F. The office made of hewn stone:
there the great Sanhedrin of Israel was in session,

---

10 "In light of C-D, better to read 'the office *made of* wood' at A and B. This apparently is not the same 'office in charge of wood' as at M. 2:5I-J."—R.S.S.

G. *And it judged the priesthood.* [11] *And a priest in whom was found a cause of invalidation dresses himself in black clothing and cloaks himself in a black cloak and departs and goes his way.*

H. *And he in whom no cause of invalidation was found dresses himself in white clothing and cloaks himself in a white cloak and goes in and serves with his brethren, the priests.*

I. *And a festival day did they declare, for a cause of invalidation had not been found in the seed of Aaron the priest.* [12]

J. *And thus did they say, "Blessed is the Omnipresent, blessed be he, that a cause of invalidation has not been found in the seed of Aaron.*

K. *"Blessed is he who chose Aaron and his sons to stand to serve before the Lord in the house of the Holy of Holies."*

M. 5:4

M. 5:1A is systematically spelled out in the tightly-formulated catalogues, M. 5:1B-C, M. 5:2. [13] M. 5:3A then announces its topic, and the remainder systematically spell out the requisite data. The italicized parts do not advance the discussion and are distinct. In another tractate, one less cogent in style, we should have deemed M. 5:4G-K to be simply another pericope. But given the stylistic unity of this one, we must regard the whole as an interpolation.

---

[11] "A noteworthy detail, since the rabbis project themselves back into the Sanhedrin and view themselves as judging the priests (cf. also M.-T. Yoma, Parah, Negaim)." —R.S.S.

[12] "More likely, read as follows: 'And they declared that day a festival when no cause of invalidation could be found in the seed of Aaron the priest...' That is, there is here an implicit criticism of the priesthood (cf., for example, M. Yoma 1:5)." —R.S.S.

[13] "M. 5:1-2 formally are constructed along lines similar to M. 4:6-7, and follow nicely upon the latter set."—R.S.S.

QINNIM

CHAPTER SEVENTEEN

INTRODUCTION TO QINNIM

QINNIM CHAPTERS ONE THROUGH THREE

The present tractate, generally regarded as the most difficult in the whole of Mishnah, presents a series of conundrums, carefully arranged to lead from simple facts to complicated problems, which come at the end.

The subject-matter by itself hardly calls for spending so much intellectual energy. One may *vow* an offering of a pair of sacrificial birds (*qinnim*). In addition one may be *required* to offer a pair of birds in certain circumstances, specifically, transgressions arising out of an oath of testimony, contact with carrion or dead creeping things (Lev. 5:1-10), persons cured of being *Zab* (Lev. 15:14-15) or of *ṣaraᶜat* (Lev. 14:22), women after childbirth (Lev. 12:8), Nazirites who do not complete their vows incleanness (Num. 6:10). One of the birds of this required pair was a sin-offering, the other a burnt-offering. And, as I said, in addition, one could *vow* an offering of fowl (Lev. 1:14), both of which are offered only as burnt-offerings. These two birds might be turtledoves or young pigeons.

The issue of the tractate, however, is not rules on how these birds are offered, but a quite separate matter. Since these birds may be brought for different purposes by different people, we ask about how we settle affairs if the birds of two or more people become confused with one another. The problem is generated by the fact that the blood of the sin-offering of fowl is sprinkled below the red line and that of the burnt-offering above. If a person vows a freewill-offering of fowl, they are, moreover, offered as burnt-offerings only, as I said. Now if we confuse sin-offerings and burnt-offerings, or if we confuse different pairs of birds brought for diverse purposes, or if we confuse different kinds of birds, we have to reckon with some difficult dilemmas. The layout of the problems of the tractate will be given in a moment.

While the exegetical literature on our tractate is brilliant, commensurate with the difficulty of its problems, I have chosen to lay matters out in as simple a way as possible, congruent to the limited purpose for which the text here is translated and explained. That purpose is to provide an account of the history and the structure of the law as a whole. So far as we explain the present set of problems in one or another of the logically possible, and equally acceptable, ways, for historical purposes we shall not materially affect the net result. For the tractate is unitary, the work of a single hand, and, in its exceptional brilliance, it represents no more than an exercise in logic. What it tells us about the growth of the law, down to 200, will not differ however we explain the results of the exercise. For the fundamental principles of the law, which underlie the exercises at hand (M. 1:1), do not change at all. It is these data of the tractate which, in the end, constitute its point of interest for the present purpose. In order to follow a single and consistent approach to the exegesis of the tractate, I have appended, at the end of each pericope of Mishnah, the relevant account of the law supplied by Maimonides (*Offerings Rendered Unfit*, Chapters Seven through Ten, Lewittes, pp. 331-341). Given the range of logically possible exegeses, we shall in this way have the advantage of a completely consistent approach to the whole. Let us now turn to the sequence of units and how they are laid out.

1:1 The blood of the sin-offering of fowl is sprinkled below, that of beast, above the red line. The blood of burnt-offering of fowl is sprinkled above, of beast, below.
The proper rite of a pair of birds: a pair brought in fulfillment of an obligation is deemed to include one as a sin-offering and one as a burnt-offering; a pair brought as a vow or freewill-offering is deemed to be only burnt-offerings.

1:2 A sin-offering which was confused with a burnt-offering, or a burnt-offering with a sin-offering.
A bird designated as a sin-offering confused with birds which were not designated but brought in fulfillment of an obligation.

1:3 Under what circumstances? In the case of confusion of an offering brought in fulfillment of an obligation with one designated as a freewill-offering.

1:4 Continuation of 1:3.

2:1 An unassigned pair of birds from which one flew off into the air—let the owner purchase a mate for the second.

2:2 Continuation of 2:1

2:3 Continuation of 2:1

2:4 A pair of birds which had not been designated and a pair of birds which had been designated—a bird flew from one to the other. Continuation of 2:1.

2:5 A pair of birds for a sin-offering at one side, and a pair for a burnt-offering at the other, and an unassigned pair in the middle—if one of the unassigned ones flew from the middle to the sides, it has caused no loss. Completion of M. 2:4.

3:1-2 Under what circumstances [do the rules of M. 1:2-3 apply]?

In the case of a priest who makes an inquiry. But if he does not, so that a *post facto* decision is required—M. 1:3 now cited and spelled out.

3:3-5 M. 1:2 cited and spelled out, once more for a *post facto* decision.

3:6 A woman who said, "Lo, I pledge myself to bring a pair of birds if I bear a male child," if she has a boy, brings two pairs, one for the vow, one for the obligation. Reconsideration of the problem of M. 2:5J-N.

We see a remarkably tight and orderly sequence of units, all flowing from a single hand. Once we have our basic rule, M. 1:1, it is then used as the foundation for a set of problems, M. 1:2-4, which serve to illustrate the given rule and then generate M. 3:1-5. M. 2:1 complicates matters by raising the issue of filling out a pair with a new mate, once more continued by the remainder of its chapter. M. 3:1-5 treat M. 1:2-3's problems and solutions as sufficient under the circumstance of a *de jure* decision, but ask about how one would decide *post facto.* M. 3:6, finally, reverts to M. 2:5. So the whole of Chapter Three is a tertiary development of the secondary expansions of Chapter One (M. 1:1) and Chapter Two. As I have indicated, the commentary which follows in no way pretends to do justice to the exegetical potentialities of this complicated tractate, but claims only to provide a responsible and consistent account, serviceable for the quite distinct purpose for which the work to begin with is undertaken.

1:1

A. [The blood of] a sin-offering of fowl is sprinkled below, and [the blood] of a sin-offering of a beast, above [the red line around the altar].

B. [The blood of] a burnt-offering of fowl is sprinkled above, and [the blood of] a burnt-offering of a beast, below.

C. If one did otherwise in this or in that case, it is invalid.

D. The proper rite for [offering] a pair of birds is as follows:

E. [as to a pair of birds brought in fulfillment of] an obligation, one [bird] is deemed a sin-offering and one a burnt-offering.

F. In the case of [birds brought in fulfillment of] vows and as freewill-offerings, all are deemed to be burnt-offerings.

G. What is deemed [to be a pair of birds brought in fulfillment of] a vow?

H. He who says, "Lo, I pledge myself to bring a burnt-offering."

I. And what is deemed [to be a pair of birds brought] as a freewill-offering?

J. He who says, "Lo, this is a burnt-offering."

K. What is the difference between vows and freewill-offerings?

L. (ʾLʾ Š) In the case of vows, [if] they [the birds] died or were stolen, he is answerable for them [and must replace them (as he said at H)].

M. In the case of freewill-offerings, [if] they died or were stolen, they are not answerable for them [and need not replace them (J)].

M. 1:1

The opening pericope, handsomely articulated in balanced and disciplined stichs, lays out the ground-rules on which the tractate will be built. The facts of A-C are essential. Because the blood of a sin-offering of fowl is sprinkled below and that of a burnt-offering of fowl above, confusion of the two sorts of bird-offerings will have to be worked out, just as C insists. If the blood of both were sprinkled in the same area, confusion would not matter (and there would be no tractate). D joins the foregoing to what follows, but the whole is unitary (exclusive of the amplification at G-M). The rule introduced by D is E-F. When one *must* bring a pair of birds, one is a sin-offering and one a burnt-offering. But in the case of birds brought voluntarily and not in fulfillment of an obligation, both are burnt-offerings. So where there is confusion, it must be as A-C have specified. G-M then complete the discussion, which could not be stated more clearly.

1:2-4

A. A sin-offering which was confused with a burnt-offering,

B. or a burnt-offering with a sin-offering—

C. even one in ten thousand [of the other]—

D. all of them are left to die.

E. [A bird which was designated as] a sin-offering which was confused with [birds which were not designated at all but brought in fulfillment of] an obligation—

F. valid is only the number corresponding to the sin-offerings among [the offerings brought in fulfillment of] an obligation.

G. And so a burnt-offering which was confused with [unassigned bird which were brought in fulfillment of] an obligation,

H. valid is only the number corresponding to the burnt-offerings among [the offerings brought in fulfillment of] an obligation—

I. whether the birds designated in fulfillment of an obligation are many, and those as freewill-offerings are few,

J. whether the freewill-offerings are many, and those brought in fulfillment of an obligation are few,

K. whether both are of equal number.

M. 1:2

A. Under what circumstances?

B. In the case of [confusion of] an offering brought in fulfillment of an obligation [confused] with one designated as a freewill-offering.

C. But in the case of bird-offerings brought in fulfillment of an obligation which were confused with one another—

D. one pair belonging to this one and one to that, or two to this woman and two to that, or three to this woman and three to that—

E. half are valid, and half are invalid.

F. [If] one belongs to this one, two to that, three to this woman ten to that, and a hundred to that—

G. the smallest number is valid—

H. whether they are of a single class or two classes,

I. whether they belong to one woman or to two women.

M. 1:3

A. How [is a case involving] a single class [M. 1:3H]?

B. [If one pair of birds was brought by a woman on account of] having given birth, and [the other pair brought by the same woman was because of another] birth,

C. [or one pair of birds brought by a woman was on account of having been unclean by reason of] *zibah*, and [another pair of birds was brought by the same woman because of another] *zibah*—

D. [this is deemed a case involving birds of] a single class.

E. [What is a case involving] two classes?

F. [Birds brought by one woman because of] having given birth and [birds brought by the same woman] because of having been unclean by reason of *zibah*.

G. How [is a case involving] two women [M. 1:3I]?

H. [If the two pairs were brought by] this woman on account of having given birth, and by that for having given birth—

by this one on account of having been unclean by reason of *zibah* and by that one for having been unclean by reason of *zibah*—

I. this is a case involving birds of a single class [of two different women].

J. Two classes?

K. [If the two pairs of birds were brought] by one woman because of birth; and by the other because of having been unclean by reason of *zibah*.

L. R. Yosé says, "Two women who purchased their pairs of birds in partnership,

M. "or who paid over the money for their pairs of birds to a priest—

N. "for whichever one the priest wants should he offer one as a sin-offering, and for whichever one he wants he offers one as a burnt-offering—

O. "whether [the birds had to be brought because of] one class or two classes."

M. 1:4

M. 1:2, spelled out by M. 1:3, which itself then is augmented by M. 1:4, presents the first rule of the tractate. In fact, it goes over the ground of M. 1:1A-C, but more topically. If a bird brought as a sin-offering is confused with one brought as a burnt-offering, both are left to die. The blood cannot be tossed, for the reason specified at M. 1:1A-C: The sin-offering of fowl is done below the line, and the burnt-offering, above. They cannot be left to suffer a blemish, since fowl are not subject to redemption (M. Men. 12-1). E-F and G-H then raise a related question. What if birds brought as sin-offerings are mixed up with birds brought in fulfillment of an obligation, but not yet designated as either the burnt offering or the sin-offering which fulfillment of the obligation is going to require? Now the confusion is between birds which are sin-offerings, on the one side, and birds, some of which are going to be sin-offerings and some of which are not, on the other. The solution is stated at F. If I have a dozen pair of birds brought in fulfillment of an obligation, then twelve birds are going to be sin-offerings, and those twelve birds are going to be valid.

If, then, I have a sin-offering of fowl mixed with a single pair—three birds in all—then one sin-offering may be offered under all circumstances. Why? That is either the sin-offering which was confused with the pair, or it is the sin-offering of the pair itself. But one cannot offer two sin-offerings. Both of them may derive from the pair, and one offers only a single sin-offering for a given pair. The burnt-offering cannot be offered at all, for the reason stated at M. 1:2A-D. G-H make the same point for the burnt-offering.

I-K augment G-H. To understand why it is important to add the set, we recall, M. 1:1H, that all birds brought in fulfillment of vows and freewill offerings are burnt-offerings. Now at G we refer to a burnt-offering confused with unassigned birds brought in fulfillment of an obligation. I refers, for instance, to two pairs of birds brought as burnt-offerings, mixed with three pairs of birds brought in fulfillment of an obligation. We go by the number of burnt-offerings in the pairs of birds brought in fulfillment of an obligation. (This obviously will apply in the case of the sin-offering as well.) K then says that if we have two burnt-offerings confused with one pair of birds brought in fulfillment of an obligation, valid is only one burnt-offering—despite the fact that of the four birds, three are burnt-offerings.

M. 1:3 carries this point further. It asks about the circumstances in which one person's burnt-offerings or sin-offerings which have been designated as such have been mixed up with another person's pairs of birds brought in fulfillment of an obligation which have not been designated as burnt-offering and sin-offering, respectively. When is it so that those valid correspond to the number of sin-offerings or burnt-offerings among the pairs of birds brought in fulfillment of an obligation? This is specifically when we have a confusion of an offering brought in fulfillment of an obligation with one designated as a free-will-offering. In that case—for instance, with one bird designated as a sin-offering and a pair of birds brought in fulfillment of an obligation and yet undesignated—one of the three may be offered as a sin-offering.

But what if I have a pair, or two, or three, belonging to one woman, mixed together with a pair, or two, or three, belonging to another? Then half are valid, and half not. That is, the priest offers half of them as a sin-offering and one burnt-offering, but not *two* sin-offerings or *two* burnt-offerings. Why not? Both of them may belong to one woman alone. She has to bring *only one* sin-offering and *one* burnt-offering. So if both of them belong to one woman, one will be invalid. F-G restate the same matter, now in much different terms. If only one pair of birds belongs to one woman, and a hundred to some other, and the one hundred and one were confused, only one pair will be validly offered. The priest offers one sin-offering and one burnt-offering. But he must not risk offering more birds than that number, since they may belong to the woman who owes only the smallest number.

The explication at M. 1:4A-K of M. 1:3H, I, is clear as given. One woman owes two pairs of birds for the same reason, B, C, or she owes two pairs of birds for two different reasons, F; two women owe birds for the same reason, H, or for two different reasons, K. In all of these cases, we invoke the rule of M. 1:3.

Yosé adds, L-O, that if women enter a partnership or if the funds brought by the two are commingled, then the priest offers for whichever woman he wants a bird as a sin-offering and one as a burnt-offering. He chooses and then designates the birds for their respective purposes. The saying is included because of the case of two women, mentioned just now. If the two women bring their birds together, then we do not invoke the rule of M. 1:3 + M. 1:4G-K but allow all the birds to be offered for the necessary purposes, as the priest shall decide. This is the final limitation on M. 1:3.

Maimonides (*Offerings Rendered Unfit* 8:1-6) states matters as follows:

> 1. If a bird sin-offering had become confused with a bird burnt-offering, or if a bird burnt-offering had become confused with a bird sin-offering, even if one (of one kind) was confused with ten thousand

(of the other kind), all were left to die. This law applied only if, at the time of its purchase by the owner, it had been designated as a sin-offering or as a burnt-offering. But if a man had brought birds for his obligation, some of them for a sin-offering and some for a burnt-offering, and did not designate them but left them all unspecified, and a sin-offering or a burnt-offering became confused with the birds of this unspecified obligation, other rules applied to them.

2. What were these rules? If a bird sin-offering had become confused with birds of this unspecified obligation, only the number of sin-offerings contained in the obligation remained valid. But the number of burnt-offerings in the obligation and the sin-offering confused with them were deemed invalid, since this was a case of a sin-offering being confused with burnt-offerings.

3. Therefore if the obligation now confused with the sin-offering consisted of two pairs of birds, half of the obligation was valid and half was invalid. It appears to me, however, that all of them were to be offered below, in the manner of a sin-offering.

4. Similarly, if a bird burnt-offering had become confused with the birds of this unspecified obligation, only the number of burnt-offerings contained in the obligation were valid. But the number of sin-offerings in the obligation and the burnt-offering confused with them were invalid; since in this case a burnt-offering was confused with sin-offerings. This was so whether the (number of birds in the) unspecified obligation was greater than the number of burnt-offerings confused with it, or whether the number of burnt-offerings was greater than those in the obligation, or whether both were equal in number; in each instance only the number of burnt-offerings in the obligation were valid. Therefore, if the obligation confused with the burnt-offerings consisted of two pairs of birds, half of the obligation was valid and half was invalid. It appears to me, however, that all of them were to be offered above, in the manner of a burnt-offering.

5. If birds of one unspecified obligation became confused with birds of another unspecified obligation—whether both groups were being brought because of the same obligation, as when pairs of a man with flux were confused with pairs of another man with flux; or whether they were brought because of two different obligations, as when pairs of a man with flux were confused with pairs of a woman after childbirth; or whether both belonged to one person or both belonged to different persons—if the number of birds in each obligation was equal, half of them were valid and half invalid. It mattered not whether all were offered above or all below, or half above and half below; in any event half were deemed valid and half invalid. For in all events, half of the birds were burnt-offerings and half were sin-offerings, and sin-offerings were to be offered below and burnt-offerings were to be offered above. Now if all were offered above, half of them were valid as burnt-offerings; if all were offered below, half of them were valid as sin-offerings; again, if half were offered below and half above, only half of the half offered above were valid as burnt-offerings, because of

the confusion; and half of the half offered below were valid as sin-offerings.

6. If (the number of birds in) one of the two unspecified obligations was greater than in the other—for example, if one was comprised of four birds and the other of six—then if all were offered above or all were offered below, half were deemed invalid and half valid, for the reason mentioned above. If half were offered below and half above, then the smaller number was valid if the priest had offered them thus after having made inquiry. But if he had offered them of his own volition, the larger number was valid.

2:1-3

A. An unassigned pair of birds from which one pigeon flew off into the air—

B. or one of which flew among birds which had been left to die—

C. or one of which died—

D. let [the owner] purchase a mate for the second.

E. [If] it flew among those which are to be offered, it is invalid and invalidates the one which is its match [in the pair].

F. For: The pigeon which flies away is invalid and invalidates the one which is its match [in the pair].

M. 2:1

A. How so?

B. Two women—

C. this one has two pairs of [unassigned] birds, and that one has two pairs of [unassigned] birds—

D. it [a bird] flew from this one to that one—

[Danby: "the one that belonged to the first woman flew among them that belonged to the second"]

E. it invalidates by its flying away one [of the birds from which it flew off].

F. [If] one [of the second woman's birds] returned, it invalidates by its flying back one [from the group to which it flew and from which it now flies away].

G. [If] it flew away and flew back, flew away and flew back,

H. it [nonetheless] has caused no [further] loss at all,

I. for even if they are confused, there are no less than two [pairs which may be offered].

M. 2:2

A. This one has one [pair of birds], this one two [pairs], this one three, this one four, this one five, this one six, this one seven—

B. one [bird] flew from the first to the second, then one [flew from the second] to the third, [then one flew from the third] to the fourth, [then one flew from the fourth] to the fifth, [then one flew from the fifth] to the sixth, [then one flew from the sixth] to the seventh—

C. [and] it returned [one from each returned, in the same order]—
D. it invalidates one by flying away and one by flying back.
E. The first and second [women] have none [which may be offered], the third has one [pair], the fourth has two, the fifth has three, the sixth has four, the seventh has six.
F. [Again] one flew away and flew back [in the same order as above]—
G. it invalidates one by flying away and one by flying back.
H. The third and the fourth have none, the fifth has one [pair], the sixth has two, the seventh has five.
I. [Again] one flew away and flew back [in the same order]—
J. it invalidates one by flying away and one by flying back.
K. The fifth and the sixth have none, the seventh has four.
L. And some say, "The seventh has lost nothing."
M. And if one from among the birds which had been left to die flew among any of them, lo, all of them are left to die.

M. 2:3

M. 2:1 is extensively instantiated, as in the first chapter. Let us take up the rule, then its exemplifications. The rule, A-D, is stated in mild apocopation, A, B, or C+D. E then carries forward the opening set, and F repeats E, rather than explaining it, let alone generalizing on the difference between A-D and E. [1] The whole, as we see, sets the stage for what is to follow. At A we have a pair of birds which have not been designated for their respective offerings, so we do not know which bird is for a sin-offering and which is for a burnt-offering. One of the birds flies off. Jumping to D, we learn that that owner may purchase a mate for the second. Why? Because the remaining bird is undesignated. If it had been designated for one or the other purpose, then we should have to know which bird has flown off, the sin-offering or the burnt-offering. Otherwise we shall not be able to designate the newly purchased bird for its proper purpose. But now we can. We return then to B. One of the birds flew among birds left to die. It too must be left to die (M. 1:2), since we cannot determine which among the group of birds is the one which has flown off from our pair at A. Or, C, one of the two died. In these cases, B and C, we have no reason to refrain from purchasing a mate for the remaining bird. In point of fact A+D would have sufficed, and the excessive instantiation may be deemed gloss of A, augmenting what requires no augmentation.

At E, we have a new case. The bird of A has flown into a group

[1] "F appears to be a citation of a previously-formulated rule, thus accounting for the disjuncture of E and F."—R.S.S.

of birds which are going to be offered, half as sin-offerings, half as burnt-offerings. F would have helped us, had it explained E, rather than merely repeating it. To interpret E, we recall M. 1:2: if we have a sin-offering confused with birds which are brought in fulfillment of an obligation, then the number of sin-offerings contained in that group of birds brought in fulfillment of an obligation remains valid. But what is the status of our bird? A has made it clear that our bird is undesignated. In the group to which it has flown, it invalidates only one bird, that is, one equivalent to itself. Why? Because if it is prepared with its blood sprinkled above, we have to take account of the possibility that it is a sin-offering, and if its blood is sprinkled below, we have to take account of the chance that it is a burnt-offering. And the same applies to the mate left behind. We simply do not know the status of either one, since that of the other is unclear. The important side, however, is that, spoiled in this larger group (E) is only a single bird, and not the number indicated by M. 1:2.

The illustration, M. 2:2, phrases in severe apocopation the case of two women, each with two pairs of birds. A bird from those of one flies over to the collection of the other. E-F require explanation. In line with M. 2:1, by flying away, the bird has invalidated one of the birds left behind. The woman whose bird has flown the nest has lost that bird and one other, as follows: She has three birds left. One of these may be offered as a sin-offering, one as a burnt-offering. The third cannot be offered at all, in line with M. 2:1E-F. The other woman has five birds. Two of these may be offered as sin-offerings, as we know from M. 1:2. Two are burnt-offerings.

We return now to the lady who has lost the bird and has only three. What if she were to offer the third as a sin-offering? Then its mate, which is now among the group of five, cannot be offered as a sin-offering. But we do not know which bird is that mate. Hence we cannot permit the third bird of the first lady to be designated and offered at all, lest it turn out to be a duplicate sin-offering (or: to cause the duplication of a sin-offering). And for the same reason, only four of the five birds the other woman has are deemed valid. The bird which escapes disqualifies itself and a bird from the group from which it has flown. So the woman who lost the bird offers two of her three remaining ones, and the woman who has gained a bird and has five offers only four of them. So much for E, a clear illustration of M. 2:1E.

F simply carries the process one step further. A bird of the five in the possession of the second woman now goes and flies back to the collection of the first lady, who has three birds. The second woman has lost that bird, and now, in line with M. 2:1E, one more in her collection is invalid. The first woman, who now has four birds in hand, finds one of these invalidated. The second woman, who has four birds, may offer only two of them, one as a burnt-offering and the other as a sin-offering. Why? Because the one which returned may not be the one which flew off in the first place, and a bird which flies off invalidates itself and the one which is its match (M. 2:1E). If, however, this process repeats itself yet a third time (or more than that), it does not matter. There still will be no fewer than two sin-offerings and two burnt-offerings, in line with M. 1:3C-E.

This brings us to M. 2:3, which takes the case of M. 2:2—two women—and complicates it by supplying us with a sequence of seven women. The first woman has one pair of birds, the second, two, and so on. One of the first woman's two birds flies over to the second woman's four; one of the second woman's four birds flies over to the third woman's six birds; and so on, down the line. Then the process reverses itself. A bird of the seven pairs—fourteen—belonging to the seventh woman flies back to the six pairs of birds belonging to the sixth, then a bird of the twelve birds belonging to the sixth flies over to the five pairs—ten birds—belonging to the fifth, and so on down the line. D simply invokes M. 2:1E, F. E requires explanation, and this, of course, is in line with M. 2:2. The first woman had two birds. She now has none. The second had four. In the process, she has lost all four—just as at M. 2:2E-F. There is no further loss for the third; she had three pairs, now she has one, just as M. 2:2G-I say. The fourth had four, now has two; the fifth has three, and the sixth has four. The seventh only loses one pair, since, when the bird flew off, she lost only one pair at the time that the bird flew from her to the sixth woman.

E continues this sad tale. After the citation of M. 2:1E, F, at G, the expected results are before us at H. The only interesting question remaining is at the third go-around, I-K. Obviously the fifth and sixth will have none left. The seventh has four, instead of five. L proposes that the seventh loses nothing in the third go-around. Why? Because all the rest of the pairs of birds are now invalid. There is no reason to invalidate any birds—as potential duplicate sin-offerings— in the hands of the seventh lady. M reminds us of the rule of M. 2:1B. Maimonides (*Offerings Rendered Unfit* 9:1-5) states:

> 1. If one of an unspecified pair of bird offerings flew off into the air, or if it flew among birds that were all required to be left to die,

or if one of the pair died, the rule was that a partner was to be supplied for the other bird.

2. If it flew among pairs of birds about to be offered, it thereby became invalid itself and rendered invalid another bird in its wake; for the rule was that a bird that flew from an unspecified pair to pairs of birds about to be offered became itself invalid and rendered invalid another bird in its wake. For example: Assume that a bird from an unspecified pair flew among ten unspecified birds; if the priest then offered five below and six above, only five burnt offerings would have been valid from among the six offered above and only four sin offerings from among the five offered below, for the assumption prevailed that perchance the flying bird was one of the five offered below.[2] Similarly, if the priest offered six below and five above, only five sin offerings and four burnt offerings would have been valid, for the presumption prevailed, again, that perhaps the flying bird was one of the five offered above. Thus of the ten birds only nine remained valid, and thus (following the rule) the flying bird had rendered one invalid (in its wake).

3. If there were four unspecified birds in one group of offerings and four other unspecified birds in another group, and one of the first group flew among the other group, it rendered invalid one of the second group. If after they had thus become confused, one of the second group flew back among the first group, it in turn rendered invalid one of the first group, thus leaving only two of the first group valid.

4. If, then, one of the first group again flew back among the second group, even if it kept flying back and forth all day, it did not continue to render invalid more than this; for even if all of one group became confused with all of the other group, half the number of birds remained valid and half invalid, as we have explained above.

5. If one group had only two birds, a second group four birds, a third six, a fourth eight, a fifth ten, a sixth twelve, and a seventh fourteen, and a bird flew from the first group to the second, then a bird from the second group to the third, then (one) from the third to the fourth, then (one) from the fourth to the fifth, then (one) from the fifth to the sixth, then (one) from the sixth to the seventh, and then one flew back from group to group until it reached the group from which a bird and flown first—(following the above rule) each bird rendered another invalid upon arriving at another group and upon returning; (with the result that) the first and second groups now had none valid, the third had two (valid) birds, the fourth had four, the fifth had six, the sixth had eight, and the seventh had twelve.

If, after this, a bird flew a second time from one group to another and then a bird flew from the last group to the group before the last and so on until one flew back to the first group—again (following

---

[2] "Note that Maimonides has a different theory of the case, namely, the bird renders invalid one in the group *to* which it flies, rather than *from* which it flies." —R.S.S.

the above rule) each flying bird rendered another bird invalid upon arriving and upon returning; (with the result that) the third and fourth groups now had none valid, the fifth had two valid birds, the sixth had four, and the seventh ten.

If a third time a bird flew from one group to another and a fourth time a bird flew back from one to another, they again rendered invalid one upon arriving and one upon returning; thus the birds in the fifth and sixth groups were now all invalid and only eight birds remained valid in the seventh group. Therefore, if of the fourteen birds (of the seventh group) seven were offered above and seven below, only eight of them were valid, while six were invalid because of the intermingling of the birds that flew to and fro.

2:4

A. A pair of birds which had not been designated and a pair of birds which had been designated—

B. [one bird] flew from the birds which had not been designated to the birds which had been designated—

C. let him purchase a mate for the second.

D. [If] it flew back,

E. or [if] at first one which had been designated flew [to the undesignated pair],

F. lo, all of them are left to die.

M. 2:4

The matter begun at M. 2:1 is now fully worked out. We have one pair of birds which have not been designated for their respective purposes, and another pair of birds which have. If one bird which has not been designated either as a sin-offering or as a guilt-offering flew over to the pair which have been designated, then, in line with M. 2:1A-D, we purchase a mate for the remaining bird. Why? Because the three birds of that second (designated) set are now going to be left to die in any case. D is what is interesting. A bird of those three then flies back and joins the bird which remains of that first, undesignated set. We have no idea which bird is which. All four now are left to die. And if, to begin with, one of the two designated birds joins the undesignated pair, since we do not know which is which among the three, nor do we know which bird remains, then, in line with M. 1:2, all four birds are left to die. There are no problems in this set, which essentially links M. 2:1 to M. 1:2 and states what already is quite clear. Maimonides (*ibid.*, 9:6) renders as follows:

> If there were an unspecified pair of birds and a specified pair, and one bird flew from the unspecified to the specified birds, a partner had to be taken for the other unspecified bird. If a bird flew back (from the

specified to the unspecified), or if one of the specified flew to the unspecified birds, and it was not known whether it was a burnt offering or a sin offering, all the birds found in the unspecified group had to be left to die; for if it was a burnt offering that had become confused with them, all the sin offerings therein had become invalid; and if it was a sin offering that had become confused with them, all the burnt offerings therein had become invalid. Therefore all had to be left to die.

2:5

A. [A pair of birds for] a sin-offering at this side, and [a pair of birds for] a burnt-offering at this side, and an unassigned pair in the middle—

B. [if] one [of the unassigned birds] flew from the middle to the sides, one in this direction, one in that,

C. it has caused no loss at all.

D. But let him [now designate the birds and] say, "This one which has gone to the sin-offerings is a sin-offering, and this which has gone to the burnt-offerings is a burnt-offering."

E. [If] one went back to the middle [from each side], the ones in the middle [then] are to be left to die.

F. These [to one side] are offered as sin-offerings, and these [to the other side] are offered as burnt-offerings.

G. [If] it [again] went

H. and [alt: or if] flew from the middle to the sides,

I. lo, all of them are left to die.

J. They do not bring turtledoves to make up pairs for young pigeons, or young pigeons to make up pairs for turtledoves.

K. How so?

L. The woman who brought her sin-offering as a turtledove and her burnt-offering as a young pigeon should double up and bring a turtledove as her burnt-offering.

M. [If she brought] a turtledove for her burnt-offering and a young pigeon for her sin-offering, let her double up and bring a young pigeon as her burnt-offering.

N. Ben ᶜAzzai says, "They follow the status of the first [to be offered]."

O. The woman who brought her sin-offering, and died—

P. let the heirs bring her burnt-offering.

Q. [If she brought] her burnt-offering and died, the heirs do not bring her sin-offering.

M. 2:5

M. 2:5A-I complete the foregoing and pose no problems. Then we have two further units, J-N, and O-Q, tacked on to J-N. The final instantiation is entirely clear. If we have sin-offering-birds on one side and burnt-offering-birds on the other, and in the middle are an unassigned pair, then, B-D, there is no reason in the world not to designate the bird from the middle which has flown to one side for the purpose for which the other birds on that side are meant to be offered (M. 1:4). Obviously, if then birds from the side fly back to the middle, the ones in the middle are left to die, since we do not know what they are, so they cannot be offered. But the ones on the side are valid as before. Finally, we have a bird from the middle flying off to the sides again. There is no remedy; all are left to die.

The point of J is clear at K-M. Ben ᶜAzzai's position accords with J, but, qualifying the matter, he holds that we follow the status of the first bird to be offered. If the woman brought a turtledove as a burnt-offering and then a young pigeon as a sin-offering, she should double up and bring a turtledove as a sin-offering. O-Q supplement the foregoing, but only in a farfetched way. The point is that if a sin-offering is lacking but the burnt-offering is already given, the former must be supplied. But if the burnt-offering is given, and the woman died, then we have a case in which the owner has effected atonement through death, so there is no need for the sin-offering (M. Tem. 2:2). Why locate the matter here? I assume because it runs parallel to L, M, that is, the notion of having the burnt-offering and sin-offering conform to a single law is here given an exception. Maimonides (*ibid.*, 9:7) gives:

> If on one side there were bird sin-offerings and on another side bird burnt-offerings and an unspecified pair of birds in the middle, and from the middle one bird flew to one side and another bird to the other side, nothing was lost. Rather, the one that flew to the sin-offering was designated as a sin-offering and the one that flew to the burnt-offering was designated as a burnt-offering. If after they were thus intermingled one bird flew back from one side and another bird from the other side to the middle, the two middle ones had to be left to die, since this was now a case of a sin-offering and a burnt-offering confused with each other. As for the birds on the sides, one group was to be offered as sin-offerings and the other group as burnt-offerings, as they had been designated. If, then, one from the middle flew to either side, all (on that side) had to be left to die, for fear that a burnt-offering should become confused with sin-offerings, or a sin-offering with burnt-offerings.

3:1-2

A. Under what circumstances [do the rules of M. 1:2-3 apply]?

B. In the case of a priest who makes inquiry.

C. But in the case of a priest who does not make inquiry—

D. *one belongs to this and one to that woman, two to this and two to that woman, three to this and three to that woman* [M. 1:3D]—

E. [if] he prepared all of them above [the red line],

F. *half is valid, and half is invalid* [= M. 1:3E].

G. [If he prepared] all of them below [the red line], *half is valid, and half is invalid.*

H. [If he prepared] half of them above and half of them below,

I. of that prepared above,

J. half is valid, and half is invalid,

K. and of that prepared below, half is valid and half is invalid.

M. 3:1

A. [*If*] *one belongs to this woman, and two to that, and three to that, and ten to that, and a hundred to that* [M. 1:3F]—

B. [If] he prepared all of them above [the red line], half is valid, and half is invalid.

C. [If he prepared] all of them below [the red line], half is valid, and half invalid.

D. [If he prepared] half of them above and half of them below,

E. the majority is valid. [The number of pairs deemed valid is equivalent to the largest number brought by a single woman.]

F. This is the general principle:

G. In any situation in which you can divide the pairs of bird-offerings [into two equal groups] so that those belonging to one woman do not [have their blood sprinkled] both above and below the line, half is valid and half invalid.

H. In any situation in which you cannot divide the pairs of bird-offerings [into two equal groups] so that those belonging to one woman do not [have their blood] sprinkled both above and below the line, the majority is valid.

M. 3:2

Maimonides (*ibid.*, 8:7) gives M. 3:2F-H as follows:

> This was the rule: whenever the priest offered half above and half below of his own volition, so that it was inevitable that from one (the larger) obligation some had been offered above and some below, the larger obligation was valid. For whenever it would become certain that part of a person's offerings had been offered above and part offered below, it was assumed that all his offerings were valid.

M. 3:1A refers us back to M. 1:2-3. There we are told that, in the case of the confusion of birds set aside as burnt-offerings with those set aside as sin-offerings, all are left to die. If we have birds designated as sin-offerings confused with those brought in fulfillment of an obligation, valid is only the number of birds corresponding to the sin-offerings among the offerings brought in fulfillment of an obligation. Further, at M. 1:3, we restrict that rule to the case of confusion of offerings brought in fulfillment of an obligation with those brought as freewill-offerings. But if we have bird offerings brought in fulfillment of an obligation confused with one another, then, if we have one pair belonging to one woman and one to another, or two and two, or three and three, then half are valid and half are invalid. This brings us to the present case. These rules, B says, apply in the case of a priest who makes inquiry. This is understood to mean that the priest seeks a decision as to how to proceed. But what if he acts on his own initiative? Then how do we adjudicate the results of his action? In other words, we remove from consideration cases which are subject to a *de jure*-procedure and ask about a *de facto*-decision.

At M. 3:1D we have two or four or six pairs of birds, divided among two women. The priest prepares all of them, sprinkling the blood below the red line. Or he does the same, above the red line. Or he sprinkles the blood of half below, and half above the red line. In all cases, we impose, as the *post facto*-decision, the judgment that half of what has been done is valid. Why? Since the birds have not been designated for a particular purpose, half are brought as sin-offerings and half as burnt-offerings. If the blood of all is sprinkled above, that of half has been properly sprinkled. The operative consideration of H-K, which rule that we do not validate all of the birds, is that they may have belonged to only one of the two women, and only half of those will have to have been offered above, and half below.

M. 3:2 completes the reexposition of M. 1:3, going now to its second case, the one in which the number of birds belonging to the several women is not the same. At M. 1:3, in a *de jure* decision, we are told that the smallest number only is valid. But here, C, *de facto*, we rule that half are valid. We assume, as at M. 3:1, that half of the birds have been treated properly when the blood of all of them is sprinkled in the same area, above or below. If then half the blood of half of the birds is sprinkled above, and that of half, below, we rule that the majority is valid. This is spelled out by Lehrman (p. 15, n. 3) as follows:

> If the one pair belonging to A gets confused with the two pairs belonging to B, all together six birds, and the priest offered three above and three below, then four birds are valid. For if we are to assume that all the three birds that were offered above belonged to B, then two of them are valid; and if on the other hand we are to assume that two of the three offered above belonged to A, then these two birds are also valid, and the same applies to the three birds offered below, so that we have four birds, corresponding to the number belonging to B, valid. And the same applies to the case where the

confusion arose among the pairs belonging to a larger number of women. If the one pair belonging to A gets confused with the two pairs belonging to B, and then with three other pairs or ten pairs or a hundred other pairs belonging to others—a hundred and sixteen pairs altogether—and the priest offered up half of these birds above and half below the red line, then a hundred pairs are valid and sixteen pairs invalid. Why? If the one hundred and sixteen birds offered above belong to her who brought a hundred pairs, then a hundred birds are valid above, and sixteen invalid; but even if thirty-two of these hundred and sixteen belong to the other women, who brought these between them (one plus two plus three plus ten pairs), eighty-four birds are still valid since they belong to her who brought a hundred pairs, and of the thirty-two birds belonging to the others, sixteen would be valid above and sixteen below, thus still leaving a hundred birds valid, whether offered above or below.

G-H generalize on M. 3:1-2. If we can divide the pairs of birds so that those belonging to one woman need not have part offered above and part below, then half will be assumed valid and half invalid [= M. 3:1]. The priest thus offers half of the birds above and half below. But if one cannot so divide the pairs of birds without some of those belonging to one woman being offered above and some below [= M. 3:2], then the number contained by the larger part (e.g., the hundred of M. 3:2A) is valid.

3:3-5

A. Sin-offerings belonging to this woman, and burnt-offerings to that one—

B. [if] he prepared all of them above [the red line],

C. half is valid, and half invalid.

D. [If he prepared] all of them below the red line, half of them is valid, and half invalid.

E. [If he prepared] half of them above, and half of them below, both of them are invalid.

F. For I maintain, "The sin-offering was offered above, and the burnt-offering below [the red line]."

M. 3:3

A. Sin-offerings and burnt-offerings, and one pair of birds which were not designated, and one which were designated [for their particular purposes]—

B. [if] he prepared all of them above the red line, half is valid, and half is invalid.

C. [If he prepared] all of them below the red line, half of them is valid and half invalid.

D. [If he prepared] half of them above and half below,

E. valid is only the undesignated pair.
F. And it is divided between them.

M. 3:4

A. [*A pair of birds designated as*] *a sin-offering which was confused with* [*a pair designated*] *in fulfillment of an obligation—*

B. *valid is only the number corresponding to the sin-offerings among the birds designated in fulfillment of an obligation* [= M. 1:2E-F].

[Danby: "There remain valid only as many as the number of the sin-offering among the offerings of obligation."]

C. [If] the number of birds brought in fulfillment of an obligation is twice as many as the number of birds brought as sin-offerings,

D. half is valid and half is invalid.

E. And [if] the number of birds brought as a sin-offering is twice the number of birds brought in fulfillment of an obligation, only the number of birds brought in fulfillment of an obligation is valid.

[Danby: "There remain valid as many as the number of the (unassigned) offerings of obligation."]

F. *And so birds brought as a burnt-offering which were confused with birds brought in fulfillment of an obligation—*

G. *valid is only the number corresponding to the birds brought as burnt-offerings among the birds brought in fulfillment of an obligation* [M. 1:2G-H].

H. [If] the number of birds brought in fulfillment of an obligation is twice that of the number of birds brought as a burnt-offering, half is valid, and half invalid.

I. [If] the number of birds brought as a burnt-offering is twice the number of birds brought in fulfillment of an obligation,

J. the number of birds brought in fulfillment of an obligation is valid.

M. 3:5

The elucidation of *post-facto* decisions continues in this elegant pericope. M. 3:3 corresponds to M. 1:2A-C. If we have a sin-offering mixed with a burnt-offering, even one in ten thousand—all are left to die. But *de facto*, there is a different decision.

M. 3:4 adds its somewhat more complex problem. The point at D-E+F is that the sin-offerings and burnt-offerings which have been designated among the birds, half of which have been offered above and half below, are invalid, in line with M. 3:3. The only valid birds are the undesignated pairs, for these can be offered above as a burnt-offering, or below as a sin-offering, as the priest may prefer. The birds are divided among the women, who then form a partnership to complete their obligation.

M. 3:5A-B cite M. 1:2E-F. Then an interesting point is added. If we have a confusion of two pairs of birds brought in fulfillment of an obligation with one pair of birds brought as sin-offerings, half are deemed valid and half invalid. That is, there are two valid sin-offerings and one valid burnt-offering. Three birds have been offered below. Two are valid, for in the two assigned pairs and the two unassigned pairs of birds, there are two sin-offerings. Of the three offered above, one is valid as a burnt-offering. Even if two were sin-offerings, the third must be a burnt-offering. At E we have two pairs of birds brought as a sin-offering, and one pair in fulfillment of an obligation. Then two birds—brought in fulfillment of an obligation—are valid. Maimonides (*ibid.*, 8:9) gives:

> If a priest had before him a group of bird sin-offerings and a group of bird burnt-offerings and he offered both groups above or both below, half were valid and half were invalid. If he had offered half above and half below but did not know whether he had offered the sin-offerings or the burnt-offerings below, they were all deemed invalid; for it was presumed that perchance he had offered the burnt-offerings below and the sin-offerings above.

3:6

A. The woman who said, "Lo, I pledge myself to bring a pair of birds if I bear a male child"—

B. [if] she bore a male child,

C. she brings two pairs of birds, one for her vow and one in fulfillment of her obligation.

D. [If before she had assigned them, designating two as burnt-offerings in fulfillment of her vow, and one as a sin-offering and one as a burnt-offering in fulfillment of her obligation], she gave them to the priest,

E. so that the priest has to prepare three birds above [the red line] and one below.

F. [but] he did not do so,

G. [and], rather, he prepared two above and two below—

H. and he did not first make inquiry [= M. 3:1A]—

I. she has to bring another bird.

J. And he then offers it above the red line.

I K. [The foregoing rule applies if she had originally brought birds of] the same kind.

L. [If, however, she had brought] two kinds, then she must bring two birds of each kind.

II M. [If] she had expressly vowed [which kind she would bring], then she must bring three birds.

N. [This rule applies if she had originally brought birds] of the same kind.

O. [If she had brought them] of two different kinds, she must bring four more.

III P. [If] she had determined in her vow [to bring her offering of obligation and her offering as a vow at the same kind and at the same time], she must bring five more birds.

Q. [This rule applies if she had originally brought birds] of a single kind.

R. If she had brought them of two different kinds, she must bring six.

S. [If] she gave them to the priest, and it is not known what [in fact] she gave,

T. [if] the priest went and prepared them, and it is not known what he has done by way of preparation—

U. she must bring another four birds in fulfillment of her vow, and two in fulfillment of her obligation, and one sin-offering.

V. Ben ᶜAzzai says, "Two sin-offerings."

W. Said R. Joshua, "This illustrates that which they have said, 'When it [the animal] is alive, its voice is one. When it is dead, its voice is seven.' "

X. How is its voice seven?

Y. Its two horns become two trumpets, its two leg-bones, two flutes, its hide is made into a drum, its innards are used for lyres, and its intestines, for harps.

Z. Some say, Also its wool is made into blue [for the high priest's blue pomegranates] [Ex. 28:33].

AA. R. Simeon b. ᶜAqashyaᵓ says, "As the elders of the *ᶜam haᵓareṣ*, grow old, their understanding is loosened from them, as it is said, *He removes the speech of the trusty and takes away the understanding of the elders* (Job 12:20).

BB. "But sages of Torah are not that way. But while they are growing old, their understanding is strengthened for them, as it is said *With aged men is wisdom and in length of days understanding* (Job 12:12)."

M. 3:6

A-J set the stage for the triplet of problems, K-L, M-O, P-R. S-V form a related entry, with Joshua's comment thereon, U. This is glossed by a wildly irrelevant passage, X-Z. The order draws to an appropriate conclusion with its tacked-on homiletical appendix. The whole recalls the concerns of Menahot Chapter Thirteen.

The case laid out at A-C is clear. The woman now owes a pair of birds to fulfill her obligation in consequence of childbirth, one, a burnt-offering, the other, a sin-offering. She also owes two birds as a freewill-offering, both of which will be burnt-offerings. She brings them to the priest. He is not told which is which. He has to sprinkle the blood of three of the birds above the red line—they are burnt-offerings—and one of the bird's blood is to be tossed below, as a sin-offering (M. 1:1). But the priest does not do it that way. He sprinkles the blood of two above, the blood of two below. This is a *de facto*-case. The woman has to bring another bird, completing the three to be offered above as burnt-offerings, I-J. All of this is preliminary to the triplet of cases, which expand M. 2:5J-N: *They do not bring turtledoves to make up pairs for young pigeons or vice versa.*

K specifies that the rule just now given applies if the woman originally brought her birds from a single species, e.g., all were turtledoves or young pigeons. But what if she brought the two pairs from two different, but acceptable species—one, turtledoves, the other, young pigeons? The priest then has offered one turtledove above and one below, one pigeon above and one below, treating them as birds brought in fulfillment of an obligation. The woman now has to bring two turtledoves or two young pigeons. And we do not know which bird was invalidated below, the turtledove or the pigeon. So the woman has to bring another of each kind, in line with M. 2:5.

At M-O, we have a somewhat more complicated case. When the woman vowed, she specified which kind of bird she would bring, turtledoves or pigeons. She forgot she brought one pair for the vow and one pair for the obligation. The priest has done his thing. She must now provide three birds for burnt-offerings. We recall that she does not know which kind she has made explicit. At the outset she had to bring for her vow two pairs of the two kinds, one pair of turtledoves and one pair of pigeons, since she is not sure which she owes. And she also had to bring a pair for her obligatory offering. One bird is invalidated. She has to bring a bird of that kind to complete the invalid pair. She has to bring another pair of the other kind. If, however, she brought her offerings of two kinds of birds—two pairs, one of each kind—then she has to bring four birds for the burnt-offering. The first was prepared below, as a sin-offering. It was valid. Her obligation is complete. But the second was invalid. It was a burnt-offering and was to be prepared above. We do not know whether that invalid one was a pigeon or a turtledove. We also do not know which she has vowed to begin with—turtledoves or pigeons. Therefore she brings two pairs of birds in fulfillment of her vow, one of turtledoves and one of pigeons.

The final case, P-R, has yet one more complication. At P-R, the woman has at the time of vowing specified what kind of birds she would bring in fulfillment of her vow, and she has forgotten what kind she specified. She has brought two pair of birds of the same kind, specifying that one is in fulfillment of her vow. The second pair is for her obligation. The priest has prepared two birds above the line and two below. She now has to bring five birds: two of the kind other than that which she brought, since she had been obligated to bring in fulfillment of her vow two pairs, one of each kind. She also brings three birds of the kind which she has *already* brought, two as burnt-offerings, and one as a sin-offering. If, however, she *had* brought two different kinds, we then do not know whether these were for her vow (for we do not know whether she vowed pigeons or turtledoves) or whether one pair was for her vow and one for her obligation. The priest, for his part, has prepared the two turtledoves, one above and one below, and so the two pigeons. She must now bring six birds. Why? Because the first four birds may have been burnt-offerings for her vow. Two have been invalidated, being prepared below—that is, one turtledove and one pigeon. She has to bring two birds for her obligatory offering. There is, moreover, the possibility that one pair was for her obligatory offering, which has been carried out. But one bird of the burnt-offering prepared below was invalid. We do not know which kind it was. For this and related doubts, she has to go and bring two pairs for her vow, one of turtledoves and one of pigeons, and one pair for her obligatory offering.

S-U+V set up yet another case. The woman has given birds to the priest. We do not know what she has handed over. But she does know that her vow had included the specification of a particular kind of bird, and she has forgotten what it was. Then the priest offered the birds. But we do not know what he has done. The woman has now to bring four birds in fulfillment of her vow—two of each sort—and two birds in fulfillment of her obligation, and, U adds, a sin-offering. Except for the sin-offering, we are where we were at R. Why four birds for the vow? She brings two turtledoves and two pigeons as a matter of doubt. We do not know which kind she already has brought, therefore which kind she must now add. She brings a sin-offering, since the sin-offering she already brought may have been invalidated. The pair brought in fulfillment of an obligation may, after all, have been offered above, but one should have been done below. But it also is possible that the obligatory pair was prepared below, and the sin-offering was valid. She has then to bring a burnt-offering of the same kind of bird as the kind of which the sin-offering had been offered. But we do not know what this was. She then has to bring two birds, a pigeon and a turtledove, for the burnt-offering which is part of her obligatory offering, thus completing the sin-offering.

Ben ᶜAzzai wants two sin-offerings, one pigeon, one turtledove. In line with his view at M. 2:5N, Ben ᶜAzzai reasons as follows: The burnt-offering in the pair brought as obligatory offerings may have been prepared above and thus have been valid. The woman has to bring a sin-offering of the same kind of bird as was the burnt-offering, just as at M. 2:5N. Since we do not know what kind that was, she brings two sin-offerings, one of each kind. S then has seven, and Ben ᶜAzzai, V, eight. The relevance of the numbers seven and eight [3] accounts for the curious attachment at W-Z. Maimonides (*ibid.*, 10:1-5) states:

> If a woman had said, "I pledge myself to bring a pair of birds if I bear a son," she was required to bring four birds if she bore a son: two for her vow—and they were offered as burnt-offerings, as has been explained—and two for her obligation because of childbirth, of which one was a burnt-offering and the other a sin-offering. You thus learn that the priest had to offer three of the birds above and one bird below. If he erred and offered two above and two below without having inquired, the woman was required to bring another bird to be offered above. This rule applied only when the four birds the woman had brought were all of the same kind; for example, when they were all turtledoves or all young pigeons. But if they were two turtledoves and two young pigeons and two were offered above and two below, she was required to bring another turtledove and another young pigeon, both of which were offered above, in order to fulfill her obligation. For if in the beginning the two turtledoves had been offered below, she now needed another turtledove to be offered above in order to complete her obligation; and if the two young pigeons had been offered below, she now needed a young pigeon to be offered above in order to complete her obligation. For a person might not bring for his obligation a pair of birds of which one was a turtledove and the other a young pigeon; he might bring only two turtledoves or two young pigeons.
>
> 2. If she had specified (the birds for) her vow and said to the priest, "These birds are for my vow and these are for my obligation," and the priest had offered them two above and two below but he no longer knew which of them he had offered above and which below, she was required to bring three birds, two for her vow and one to complete her obligation. Two of them were then offered above, since she had specified the birds for her vow and it was possible that they had been offered below and thus had become invalid. This law applied only if the four birds, of which the two for her vow had been specified,

[3] "I see seven, not eight. W refers back to U."—R.S.S.

were of one kind. But if they were of two kinds, she was required to bring four other birds; two of the kind that she had specified for her vow—and they were now offered for her vow—and two of any kind she wished for her obligation, which were offered one above and one below.

3. If she had specified the kind for her vow and she had said, "If I bear a son I pledge myself to bring two turtledoves," and she bore (a son) and brought four birds, two for her vow and two for her obligation, but the priest offered two above and two below and no longer knew which had been offered above and which below, and she herself no longer remembered which kind she had specified for her vow, whether turtledoves or young pigeons—the rule was that the woman was required to bring two turtledoves with two young pigeons for her vow and all four were then offered above. In addition, she had to bring one bird to complete her obligation, which was offered above [for two had already been offered below and they were sin-offerings].

This law applied only if the four birds which she had brought in the beginning were of one kind. But if they were of two kinds, she was now to bring six birds; two turtledoves with two young pigeons for her vow, and two turtledoves or two young pigeons for her obligation, one of which was offered above and the other below. Similarly, if she had given the birds to the priest but forgot which kind she had given him, and the priest went and offered them but no longer knew where he had offered them, whether all above or all below or half above or half below—in such a case she was also required to bring two turtledoves with two young pigeons for her vow and two turtledoves or two young pigeons for her obligation.

4. If she had specified the kind for her obligation and the kind for her vow but she forgot which kind she had specified, and it was possible that her obligation consisted of a lamb for a burnt-offering and a bird—either a turtledove or a young pigeon—for a sin-offering, she was accordingly obliged to bring six birds, four for her vow and two for her obligation, and also another sin-offering, either a young pigeon or a turtledove, together with a lamb. Thus we find that she was required to bring seven birds [and a lamb].

At the end, we may humbly remind ourselves of the judgment of the great master, Louis Ginzberg (*Tamid*, pp. 294-5):

> Kinnim has more commentaries than any other tractate of the Mishnah, but is nevertheless the most obscure, and this is only partly due to the poor disposition of the matter treated. A great deal of the obscurities we meet in Kinnin is to be ascribed to the effort made by the author to exhaust all possible—or impossible!—complications of a given Halakah and also herein does the rest of our Mishnah differ essentially from this tractate.

INDEX TO BIBLICAL AND TALMUDIC REFERENCES

The index was prepared by Mr. Arthur Woodman, Canaan, New Hampshire.

BIBLE

I Chronicles
26:17-18 174, 176

II Chronicles
4:1 180

Deuteronomy
6:4-9 159
11:13-21 160
12:6 120
12:17 80
27:5-6 181

Exodus
6:26 75
12:19 8
28:9 163
28:33 212
31:14 8

Ezekiel
40:5 178
41:23 183
41:24 183
42:20 177
44:2 155 183
46:16 180
46:21-22 178
47:1 179
47:2 179

Genesis
2:4 74
17:14 8

Isaiah
5:2 111
29:1 185

Job
12:12 212
12:20 212

II Kings
6:20-22 183
6:32 183
6:35 183

Leviticus
1:14 191
4:23 41, 46-47
4:28 71
4:32 74
5:1 23
5:2 9
5:2-3 23
5:4 23
5:6-7 8
5:11 8
5:15 67, 80
5:15-16 51
5:16 80
5:17 8
5:17-18 46
5:17-19 3
6:3 151
6:13-14 151
7:25 8
7:26-27 50
11:29-30 121
12:1-6 7, 13
12:5-6 14
12:6 12, 74
12:6-8 23
12:8 191
14:10ff 23
14:22 191
15:1-10 191
15:14-15 191
17:9 8
17:14 50
18:6ff 8
18:17 34
18:21 8
19:3 74-75
19:7-8 8
19:20 22
19:20-21 23
20:6 8
22:3 8

23:18 101
23:29-30 8
26:42 75

Numbers
5:15ff 23
6:9-12 20
6:10 191
6:14 20, 106
6:18 178
6:19 106-107
6:24-26 164
9:13 8-9
15:20 120
15:29 8
15:30 8
15:31 8
15:37-41 160
19:20 8

28:3-4 147
28:7 111
32:12 75

Psalms
24 165
48 165
81 165
82 165
92 165
93 165
120-34 178

Song of Songs
7:14 160

Zechariah
6:14 182

MISHNAH

ᶜErubin
8:2 123

Ḥullin
8:6 110
9:7-8 38

Kelim
27:1-2 123
27:3 123

Keritot
1:1 7-11, 35
1:1-2 3, 5, 7-11, 50
1:2 8-10, 22, 25, 49, 52, 66
1:3 3, 11-13
1:3-5 3, 7, 11-13
1:4 7, 12-13, 17, 53, 57
1:5 12-13
1:6 3, 7, 13-16, 23
1:7 3, 7, 16-19
2:1 19-21
2:1-2 4, 19-21
2:2 19-20, 23
2:3 19-27
2:3-6 4, 21-27
2:4 19, 22-27, 72
2:5 19, 22-23, 26-27
2:6 19, 22-23, 25, 27
3:1 4, 28-30
3:2 4, 30, 32, 37-40
3:2-3 4, 28, 30-32
3:3 30-32
3:4 33
3:4-6 4, 28, 32-35, 37
3:4-10 28
3:5 33-34
3:5-6 34
3:6 33-35
3:6-9 28
3:7 35, 37
3:7-9 28, 37
3:7-10 4-5, 28, 35-38
3:8 35, 37
3:9 36-38, 133
3:10 37-38
4:1 39-41, 43, 45
4:2 39, 41-43, 45-48
4:2-3 4-5, 39-48, 61-63, 71
4:3 39, 41-42, 46-47
5:1 49-51
5:1-3 5
5:2 42-54, 57
5:2-3 49, 51-55, 57
5:3 52-54, 142
5:4 55-58, 60-61
5:4-8 5, 49, 55-61, 66
5:5 55-57, 61
5:6 56-57
5:7 56-57
5:8 56-57
6:1 62-64, 71
6:1-2 5, 62-65, 67
6:1-6 62

6:2 54, 62, 65-65
6:3 5, 62-63, 65-67
6:3-5 62
6:4 65-67
6:4-5 5, 62, 66-67
6:5 53, 62, 67
6:6 5, 62-63, 67-70
6:6-7 5, 62
6:7 62-63, 70-72
6:7-8 68
6:8 5, 62-63, 72-74
6:9 5, 63, 74-75

Me^cilah
1:1 80, 85-89, 94, 98
1:1-3 97
1:2 85, 89-91, 94
1:1-2 80, 88-97
1:3 85, 89-91, 94
1:4 80, 85, 90, 93, 97-98, 107, 110, 143
2:1 99
2:1-5 81
2:1-9 80-81, 99-103
2:2 100, 102
2:3 99-100, 102-103
2:4 100, 102
2:5 100, 102, 105
2:6 99, 102
2:6-9 81, 102
2:7 101-102
2:8 101
2:9 101-102
3:1 104-107
3:1-2 81, 104
3:2 104-10
3:3 81, 104, 110-11, 181
3:4 111-12
3:4-5 81, 104
3:5 112-16
3:6 81, 104-105, 112-16, 119
3:7 105, 116-18
3:7-8 81
3:8 105, 118
4:1 81, 119-20
4:1-2 121
4:2 81, 120-21
4:3 121-22, 124
4:3-6 81
4:4 81, 122
4:5 122-24
4:6 82, 123-24
5:1 126-29
5:1-2 82, 125-28
5:2 126-27
5:3 82, 125, 128-31
5:4 82, 121, 125, 129-32
5:5 82, 125, 130, 132-33
6:1 82, 127, 134-37, 139-40
6:2 82, 134, 136-37
6:3 83, 134, 138-39
6:4 83, 134, 140-41
6:5 83, 134, 141
6:6 83, 135, 142-43

Menaḥot
3:3 95
3:4 97
4:5 151
12:1 73, 196

Middot
1:1 169, 174, 176
1:1-9 169, 174-76
1:2 169, 174, 176
1:3 169, 175-76
1:4 169, 175
1:4-5 179-80
1:5 169, 175
1:6 169, 174-75
1:7 169, 175
1:8 169, 176
1:9 169, 176
2:1 172, 177, 179
2:1-6 172, 177-80
2:2 172, 177, 179
2:3 172, 178-79
2:4 172, 178-79
2:5 172, 178-80
2:6 172, 179
3:1 172, 180
3:1-8 172, 180-82
3:2 172, 181
3:3 172, 181
3:4 172, 181-82
3:5 172, 181
3:6 172, 182
3:7 172, 177, 182
3:8 172, 182
4:1 172, 183, 185
4:1-7 172, 182-85
4:2 172, 183, 185
4:3 172, 183, 185
4:4 172, 184
4:5 172, 184
4:6 172, 184-85

4:7 172, 185
5:1 172, 174, 186-87
5:1-4 172, 185-87
5:2 172, 186-87
5:3 172, 186-87
5:4 172, 187

Nazir
6:8 178

Nega^cim
14:11 23

Niddah
3:2-4 13
3:5 12
5:1 13
5:7 13

ᶜOrlah
2:1 123

Parah
4:1 175

Qinnim
1:1 20, 192-94, 196, 213
1:2 192, 194-96, 200-201, 204, 210-11
1:2-3 193, 206-207
1:2-4 193-99
1:3 192, 195-97, 202, 206-208
1:4 192, 195, 197, 206
2:1 192-93, 199-202, 204
2:1-3 199-204
2:2 192, 199, 202
2:3 192, 200, 202
2:4 192, 204-205
2:5 192-93, 205, 213, 215
3:1 207-209, 211
3:1-2 192, 206-209
3:1-5 193
3:2 207-209
3:3 209-10
3:3-5 193, 209-11
3:4 210
3:5 210
3:6 193, 211-16

Shabuᶜot
4:2-3 20
5:1-2 20
7:4 123

Soṭah
7:6 164

Tamid
1:1 147, 150-51, 174-76
1:1-4 149
1:1-4-2:1-5 147
1:2 147, 150-51
1:3 147, 151, 175
1:4 147, 151
2:1 147, 152
2:1-5 152-53
2:2 147, 152-53
2:3 147, 152-53
2:4 147, 152
2:4-5 153
2:5 147, 153
3:1 148, 153, 156
3:1-5 148
3:1-9 153
3:2 148, 153, 156
3:3 148, 154
3:4 126, 148, 154, 156
3:5 148, 154, 181
3:6 154, 156, 162
3:6-8 148
3:7 155-57, 181, 185
3:8 155-56
3:9 149, 156-57, 162
4:1 148, 157, 181
4:1-3 148, 157-59
4:2 148, 158
4:3 148, 153, 159, 164
5:1 148, 160-61
5:1-4 148
5:1-6 159-61
5:2 148, 160-61, 163
5:3 148, 160-61
5:4 148, 160-61, 164
5:5 148, 161
5:6 148, 155, 161
6:1 148-49, 162
6:1-3 162-63
6:2 148, 162
6:3 148, 162-63
7:1 148, 163
7:1-4 163-65
7:2 148, 164-65
7:3 149, 165
7:4 149, 165

Temurah
2:2 206

3:3 64, 68
4:1 70, 104
4:3 90
7:3 126
7:4 65

Tohorot
1:5 123

Yoma
3:10 151, 178

5:6 110
8:2 123

Zebaḥim
Ch. 2 83
2:4 94
4:3 101-102
5:1-5 86
5:3 169
5:6 106-107
6:4 102

TOSEFTA

Keritot
1:1 10-11
1:2 10-11
1:3 10-11
1:4 10-11
1:5 10
1:5-6 11
1:6 11
1:7 13
1:8 13
1:9 16
1:10 17-18
1:11 20-21
1:12 20-21
1:13 21, 24, 27
1:14 24
1:15 25, 27
1:16 26-27
1:17 26-27
1:18 26-27
1:19 27
1:20 31-32
1:21 35
1:22 38
2:1 30
2:2 32
2:3 32, 43, 45
2:3-12 43
2:4 43, 45
2:4-9 45
2:5 43
2:5-6 45
2:6 44
2:7 44
2:7-8 45
2:8 44
2:9 44-45
2:10 45
2:10-11 45
2:11 45
2:12 46-47
2:12-15 47
2:13 46, 48
2:14 47-48
2:15 47-48
2:16 47-48
2:17 50
2:18 51
2:19 51
2:20 54
2:21 54
2:22 54
3:1 58, 60
3:2 58, 61
3:3 58, 61
3:4 59, 61
3:5 59, 61
3:6 59
3:6-8 61
3:7 59
3:8 60
4:1 60-61, 74
4:2 61, 65
4:3 65
4:4 66
4:5 69-70
4:5-6 70
4:6 69-70
4:7 69-70
4:7-10 70
4:8 70
4:9 70
4:10 70
4:11 71
4:12 71
4:13 73
4:14 73
4:15 75

Me^c^ilah
1:1 87
1:2 87
1:3 88
1:4 90, 94
1:5 91
1:6 91
1:7 102
1:8 106
1:9 107, 110
1:10 108, 110
1:11 108, 110
1:12 109-10
1:13 109
1:13-15 110
1:14 109
1:15 109
1:16 111
1:17 114, 116
1:18 115-6
1:19 115-16
1:20 115-16
1:21 115-16
1:22 115
1:22-23 116
1:23 116
1:24 117
1:25 118
1:26 131-32
1:26-27 121, 132
1:27 132
1:28 121
1:29 124
1:30 124
2:1 127-28
2:2 130-31
2:2-4 131
2:3 130
2:4 130
2:5 130
2:6 128, 136
2:7 138
2:8 138
2:9 139
2:10 141
2:11 141
3:1 142-43
3:2 143

Menaḥot
4:9 95
4:9-15 97
4:10 95
4:11 95
4:12 96
4:13 96
4:14 96
4:15 97
8:30 132

Nazir
3:16 107, 109
4:8 24

Nega^c^im
9:7 24

Pesaḥim
1:12 32

Terumot
7:3 32

Yoma
5(4):3 32

Zebaḥim
4:1ff 94
4:4 92-93
4:4-8 97
4:4-9 97
4:5 92, 94
4:6 92
4:7 93
4:8 93
12:17 10-11

BABYLONIAN TALMUD

Keritot
15b 36
19a 41
26b 54

Me^c^ilah
9b 143
11a 110
12b 113
13e 113
18a 127

MAIMONIDES

Offerings Rendered Unfit
Ch. 7-10 192
8:1-6 197-99
8:7 207
8:9 211
9:1-5 202-204
9:6 204
9:7 206
10:1-5 215-16

The Temple
1:4 169

Trespass
1:1-3 79
4:7 143
5:6 117
6:4 131
7:2 136

GENERAL INDEX

Abba Saul, temple at Jerusalem, measurements, 178
Abba Yosé b. Ḥanan, temple at Jerusalem, measurements, 179-80
Albeck, Ḥanokh, burnt offering: clearing ashes, 162; temple property, sacrilege of, 124
ᶜAqiba, sacrifices, sacrilege of, 85, 88-96; single sin-offering and multiple sins, 22, 26, 35-36, 38; sin offering: 9, 17-18; suspense guilt-offering, 47; temple property, sacrilege of, 125, 127, 133, 135, 142

Baba b. Buti, suspense guilt-offering, 66
Ben ᶜAzzai, birds, offerings of, 205
Birds, offerings of, 191-216
Burnt offering: 147-65; birds as, 191-216; blessing congregation, 148, 159-60; clearing ashes, 147-57, 160-63; selecting and slaughtering, 148, 153-54, 157-59

Caleb, suspense guilt-offering, 75
Cashdan, Eli, single sin-offering and multiple sins, 35

Danby, Herbert, birds, offerings of, 210; single sin-offering and multiple sins, 30

Eleazar, single sin-offering and multiple sins, 30
Eleazar b. ᶜAzariah, single sin-offering and multiple sins, 22, 26
Eleazar b. Diglai, burnt offering: clearing ashes, 155
Eleazar bar Ṣadoq, sacrifices, sacrilege of, 111, 116; temple at Jerusalem, measurements, 182
Eleazar b. R. Simeon, sacrifices, sacrilege of, 97, 115
Eliezer, sacrifices, sacrilege of, 85, 88-96; single sin-offering and multiple sins, 24, 27-28, 31, 36; suspense guilt-offering, 39-41, 45-47
Eliezer b. Jacob, burnt offering: blessing congregation, 160-61; sin offering: 19-20; temple at Jerusalem, measurements, 174, 176, 178-79, 186
Eliezer bar Simeon, suspense guilt-offering, 60

Gamaliel, single sin-offering and multiple sins, 28, 35
Ginzberg, Louis, birds, offerings of, 216

Hillel, sin offering: 14-16
Hollis, F. J., 173
Holtzmann, Oscar, 173

Ishmael, single sin-offering and multiple sins, 22, 26-27; suspense guilt-offering, 47

Josephus, 173
Joshua, birds, offerings of, 212; sacrifices, sacrilege of, 86-89, 94; single sin-offering and multiple sins, 28, 35-36, 38; suspense guilt-offering, 39-42, 45-48; temple property, sacrilege of, 121, 124
Judah, burnt offering: 164; single sin-offering and multiple sins, 21, 23, 25, 28, 30-31; sin offering: 9, 11; suspense guilt-offering, 41-42, 46; temple at Jerusalem, measurements, 175, 182-85; temple property, sacrilege of, 134, 140-41

Lehrman, S. M., birds, offering of, 208
Lieberman, Saul, sacrifices, sacrilege of, 106; single sin-offering and multiple sins, 24; sin offering: 13, 15; suspense guilt-offering, 48

Maimonides, sacrifices, sacrilege of, 110, 113; suspense guilt-offering, 42; temple property, sacrilege of, 129
Meir, sacrifices, sacrilege of, 111; single sin-offering and multiple sins, 25, 27, 29, 33-34; sin offering: 8-11; suspense guilt-offering, 63
Matya b. Samuel, burnt offering: clearing ashes, 153, 156; burnt offering: selecting and slaughtering, 153

Neḥemiah, temple property, sacrilege of, 128

Offerings, birds as, 191-216

Papa, sacrifices, sacrilege of, 113

Sacrifices, sacrilege of, 80, 85-118
Sacrilege: sacrifices, 80, 85-118; temple property, 81-83, 119-43
Sarason, Richard S., birds, offerings of, 200n, 203n, 215n; burnt offering: 149n, 150n, 153n, 154n, 155n, 156n, 157n, 159n, 160n, 161n, 163n, 164n; sacrifices, sacrilege of, 86, 93n, 118n; single sin-offering and multiple sins, 24n, 25n, 27n, 31n, 32n, 38n; sin offering: 4n, 9, 11n, 12n, 20n, 21n; suspense guilt-offering, 40n, 43n, 49n, 50n, 64n, 67n; temple at Jerusalem, measurements, 173n, 174n, 176n, 180n, 185n; temple property, sacrilege of, 120n, 127, 129n, 131n, 132n, 136n, 142n
Shammai, single sin-offering and multiple sins, 23; sin offering: 14-15
Simeon, sacrifices, sacrilege of, 90, 110-11, 113-14; single sin-offering and multiple sins, 24, 29-30, 36, 38; sin offering: 20; sin offering: 12-13, 21; suspense guilt-offering, 41-42, 46-48; temple property, sacrilege of, 123-24
Simeon b. ᶜAqashya, birds, offerings of, 212
Simeon b. Gamaliel, sin offering; 16, 18
Simeon Shezuri, suspense guilt-offering, 41-42, 47-48
Single sin-offering and multiple sins, 4, 21-38
Sin-offering: 3-21; birds as, 191-216
Suspense guilt-offering, 39-75

Ṭarfon, suspense guilt-offering, 49
Temple at Jerusalem: altar and porch, 171, 180-82; *illus.* 170-71; layout of Temple mount, 172, 177-80; measurements, 167-87; sanctuary and courtyard, 172, 182-87; watch posts and gates, 169, 174-76
Temple property, sacrilege of, 81-83, 119-43

Vows, offering birds, 191-216

Yoḥanan, suspense guilt-offering, 55
Yoḥanan b. Nuri, single sin-offering and multiple sins, 33-34; sin offering: 17
Yosé, birds, offerings of, 195; sacrifices, sacrilege of, 115-16; single sin-offering and multiple sins, 33; sin offering, 12; suspense guilt-offering, 40, 42, 44, 46-48; temple at Jerusalem, measurements, 177, 180
Yosé bar Judah, single sin-offering and multiple sins, 31; suspense guilt-offering, 60

www.ingramcontent.com/pod-product-compliance
Lightning Source LLC
LaVergne TN
LVHW012330100826
845148LV00017B/1698
* 9 7 8 1 5 5 6 3 5 3 5 3 6 *